T0316198

Reflections *on* American Progressivism

Reflections

on American

Progressivism

Sidney A. Pearson, Jr.

Routledge
Taylor & Francis Group

LONDON AND NEW YORK

First published 2014 by Transaction Publishers

2 Park Square, Milton Park, Abingdon, Oxfordshire OX14 4RN
711 Third Avenue, New York, NY 10017

Routledge is an imprint of the Taylor & Francis Group, an informa business

First issued in paperback 2017

Copyright © 2014 Taylor & Francis

Library of Congress Catalog Number: 2014010756

Library of Congress Cataloging-in-Publication Data

Pearson, Sidney A.
  Reflections on American progressivism / Sidney A. Pearson, Jr.
    pages cm
  Includes bibliographical references and index.
  ISBN 978-1-4128-5494-8
  1. Progressivism (United States politics) 2. United States—Politics and government. I. Title.
  JK275.P376 2014
  320.530973—dc23

                                                        2014010756

ISBN 13: 978-1-4128-5494-8 (hbk)
ISBN 13: 978-1-138-51401-0 (pbk)

Contents

Introduction: Reflections on American Progressivism

Yet there is no doubt that statesmen have written more successfully about politics than philosophers; for since experience has been their guide, they have taught nothing that could not be put into practice.
(*Spinoza*, A Treatise on Politics)

John Dewey observed that a lengthy introduction is a sure sign that the author has a feeling that he has not made himself clear in the text. This introduction is written with the nagging feeling that observation contains more than a gram of truth. The idea of progress in American political thought is a labyrinth. But reflections on American progressivism is a fascinating topic for anyone interested in the course of American political thought since the founding. Thinking out loud about American progressivism, therefore, requires no more justification than making the point that it is an interesting topic followed up with a modicum of curiosity about its nature. Progressivism is, I think, an interesting topic. At the same time it is a sufficiently complex subject of inquiry that a few preliminary remarks are in order, all made with due respect to Dewey.

So powerful is the term "progressive" in academic circles that grown people retreat from being labeled "anti-progressive" the way schools of fish retreat from the spreading ink of a squid. To be "unprogressive" in the modern academy is to be at minimum a "reactionary" and more likely branded as a closet fascist. For someone like myself, who is skeptical of the progressive mind, I would like to be able to say that I think the progressive era is drawing to a close—a victim of its own internal contradictions, both intellectual as well as practical; contradictions I have tried to discuss here. But I also quote Spinoza at the outset because I think he has put his finger on the fundamental problem of why the influence of the progressive intellectual on practical politics is likely to persist. I cannot help but note that Spinoza's dictum has been around for well over three hundred years and the problem he pointed out with such pithy precision is still with us; abstract academic speculation seems to be one of the constants in politics that is immune to any contrary reality. Further, it has been argued, accurately I think, that while there are no permanent majorities in American politics there are permanent factions.[1] Even temporary majorities, if they are sufficiently united, can enact long-lasting changes in public policy. Progressivism seems to be one of those factions. Whether such temporary majorities can permanently change the nature of the regime is an open question. Who knows when Fate is waiting just around the corner with another surprise for both the wary and the unwary alike?

The hold the progressive mind has on the modern academy seems impervious to any counterarguments or narratives. It is most often presented as the opposite of "conservative," but this is only partly true. Progressivism is a cathedral of thought, but it is a structure built on a foundation that may not fully support its spires. Thomas Kuhn was no doubt correct, I think, that paradigms persist even in the face of their inability to explain reality until a better paradigm comes along. He might have added that, at least for political science, ideologies persist independent of a superior paradigm. There is much that is wrong with the progressive paradigm, in my opinion, but it is not obvious what would take its place or that counterarguments alone will carry the day. Marxism is a case in point. There was some speculation initially that the demise of Marxism in the old Soviet Union would be the death knell for the ideology of progress; Marxism would henceforth be a subject for historical study and not a living idea. But the idea of progress in the Marxist sense has taken hold in some academic quarters even stronger than during the Cold War; this even as the principles of the American regime were helping to defeat it abroad. The modern idea of historical progress appears to be as strong as ever, albeit in ever changing forms of expression. This has led me to conclude that much of the persistence of the progressive model is rooted in the foundations of American progressivism, which are, of course, in turn rooted in certain strands of European progressivism that came out of the Enlightenment. It is not clear that the idea of progress is in fact rooted in a superior model of political explanation. If it cannot be explained entirely in rational terms, it can at lest be studied in rational terms. Such at least is the interpretation I try to develop here.

What is the character of the progressive challenge to the founding principles of the American regime? One might begin with a number of points, but natural law seems to stand out as the core issue in any discussion of progressives. Natural law, much like divine law, is by definition a law outside of the reach of human law and progressives could no more easily tolerate a power outside of their own control than they could tolerate any restraints on their own exercise of power. Progressives have tended to think of themselves as pragmatists in politics, but the foundations of progressivism tell a different story. Progressives introduced a foundational skepticism into the study of the founding principles of the American regime that is, in practice, very much indistinguishable from nihilism, John Dewey's well-known defense of pragmatism to the contrary notwithstanding. As an exercise in pragmatism, American progressivism does not seem to me to correspond to what we ordinarily think of as pragmatism; a matter-of-fact treatment of things that treats things in terms of their immediate practical consequences. This makes the study of the origins of American progressivism a subject that speaks to its own importance and there seems to me no need to belabor this point. At the level of theoretical analysis, the issue is who has the intellectual and moral authority to interpret the nature of the American regime, the founders or the progressives? It may be possible to imagine some sort of practical accommodation between the two, but at the theoretical level I seriously doubt that such an accommodation is possible. To the extent that theory drives practice, the opposition between the two appears to be a permanent source of fundamental conflict in American politics because it is a conflict rooted in regime principles and not in particular policies. The progressive critique of the American regime is a critique of the founding principles of the regime.

In a broad sense the foundations of the regime would begin with the Declaration of Independence and the strands of political thought that informed it. It would then include the various arguments, practical as well as philosophical, that led to the call for a Constitutional Convention in 1787. And it would surely include the debates over the ratification of the Constitution, beginning perhaps with the internal debates during the Convention recorded by James Madison and a few others who attended the Convention. In this context, Herbert Storing has taught students of the founding period to regard the Anti-Federalist critics of the Constitution as entitled to be considered as part of the worthy company we rightly regard as the founders of the American regime. And finally a relatively easy case can be made to consider the work of the first Congress as integral to the founding project. I consider all of these examples to constitute the founding of the regime. Nevertheless, when progressives launched their critique of the founding they generally had in mind a critique of natural law and the organization of the government under the Constitution. This meant a critique of the Declaration of Independence and the defense of the Constitution in the eighty-five essays that comprise *The Federalist*, authored by James Madison, Alexander Hamilton, and John Jay. For the sake of both brevity and in an effort to keep the focus on the progressives, I also use the term "founders" in the more limited sense that was used by most progressives, at least during its formative period in American history.

The purpose of this inquiry into progressivism is not to provide a definitive account of its origins. Nor is it intended to be an historical account, although historical context cannot be ignored. I will leave it to others to comb through the literally hundreds of authors who might provide a more complete and comprehensive account of the historical origins of progressivism. My immediate concern is one of interpretation of what I take to be the main outlines of the founding arguments in progressivism. This work is presented as an interpretative essay more than a scholarly account rightly understood. I have tried to take the progressives at their own word as to the proper foundations for a science of politics. By their own account, a proper science of politics is at once both secular and scientific. There is more than a passing measure of truth in this assumption for any science of politics. But much of progressive political science often looks very much like a Manichean morality tale; what initially began as a serious inquiry into the nature of politics has become instead the reigning academic ideology of the late twentieth and early twenty-first centuries.

I further take progressives at their word when they use these terms of secularism and science and that the terms do have meaning. Secularism may be understood to mean banishing any reference to God or a transcendent order from political discourse. References to God, especially in American political thought, suggest a religious ground of argument. Further, the natural law foundations of the Declaration of Independence have complicated the religious argument over the proper foundations or a just moral order. Natural law arguments can be separated from religious arguments, although both progressives and their critics, such as myself, are aware that one source does not necessarily exclude the other. The two foundations are not logically incompatible and are frequently used in tandem or synonymously. Unless otherwise indicated, I have tried to use these terms as they have been used in the progressive tradition. Progressives have uniformly used the term "secular" in the modern sense of an outlook that denies the possibility of transcendent moral knowledge. Indeed, moral knowledge derived from either religion or the natural law reasoning of the Declaration appears as an oxymoron in the progressive lexicon; the first axiom of progressive political science is that only science can provide anything approaching knowledge.

Further, there is surely a sense in which the progressive use of the term "secular society" tends to be a tautology because the idea of secularism is latent in the modern idea of society. I am prepared to accept most of the argument of Charles Taylor that a wholly secular society in the terms outlined earlier in the progressive tradition may be a metaphysical impossibility. Nevertheless, the continued use of the term and the meaning attached to it by progressives makes it imperative that we try to understand secular society in terms that make sense to its most ardent defenders who do not seem to think it is a metaphysical impossibility.[2]

Further, I must hasten to add this is not an inquiry into motives; I follow Alexander Hamilton's truism that motives are often hidden, even our own motives from ourselves, and cannot be judged impartially in any case. But political arguments, openly stated, are open to all and may be judged by all on the strengths and weaknesses of their presentation. I assume that people who write mean what they say even if they do not always say everything they mean. I am in no more position to judge the motives of either the founders or the progressives than was Hamilton. This approach has a number of implied assumptions that ought to be stated as clearly as possible at the outset.

Because science meant secularism in the progressive scheme of things it immediately leads us to what I take to be the core questions of progressive political science; what does a radically secular interpretation of American politics look like? What is the foundation of such an interpretation? Is such an interpretation valid? To this more limited end of interpretation, the authors' chosen for consideration are selected on whether or not and how well they have articulated the foundational assumptions of progressivism. There is some cherry picking involved in the selection of authors for discussion, but it is not, I hope, wholly arbitrary. Foundational assumptions, self-evident truths, are typically more explicit at the outset of any tradition of political science than they are as the tradition develops; hence the preponderance of early progressives as opposed to later authors. The selection of authors here does not aim to be a complete roster of even some significant progressive writers. Some, such as John Dewey, probably deserve a more complete treatment than is to be found here and his essay "The Influence of Darwin on Philosophy," which is discussed at length, is not as important in the corpus of his work as his *Reconstruction in Philosophy*, for example. But the Darwinian metaphor is so pervasive in the early literature of progressivism that I have singled it out for specific discussion. A great deal of Dewey's thought is implicit in this one essay and much of what needs to be said about Dewey's influence on progressivism can be gleaned from it.

Some writers are conspicuous by their absence and someone looking for a comprehensive discussion of progressive writers may be disappointed. Lester Ward, the father of American sociology, is case in point. Ward's *Dynamic Sociology or Applied Social Science* (1883) is one of the least explored works of the progressive tradition and is noted here only in passing. The formative influence of the nineteenth century French intellectual Auguste Comte on early American sociology in the work of a writer such as Ward is worthy of a distinct treatment in its own right. Some of Comte is evident in Herbert Croly, who is discussed at length here, and in terms of the first principles of progressivism Croly may serve as a substitute for Ward. Croly's influence seems to me to have been more explicit and hence more easily traced than that of Ward.

Charles Beard is another such example of a major progressive historian who is only mentioned in passing. Beard is probably the best-known American historian in the twentieth century. History majors applying to graduate school in history are routinely asked on the Graduate Record Exams in History something about the "Beard Thesis" on the Constitution. But it is not obvious at the outset of the twenty-first century how much influence the "Beard Thesis" continues to exert over how the founders are interpreted. The most recent study of the Constitutional Convention by Richard Beeman does not even mention Beard. And the best account of the ratification debates by Pauline Maier mentions Beard only briefly in the Introduction, ignores him completely in the text, and fails to even record Beard as an entry in her very extensive index. At any rate, I have nothing to new offer by way of an interpretation of Beard as an historian that has not already been made by others. And to the extent that much of the progressive argument insists that American politics can be reduced to an economic foundation, which is the essence of the "Beard Thesis," other progressives have made much the same case.

Nor have I spent a great deal of time discussing progressive policy proposals. Progressivism can appear to be a mosaic of conflicting arguments if the focus is on policy. This work is not an account of the various policy proposals that have been promoted by progressive politicians and intellectuals at different times and places. The study of foundational arguments is here intended to illuminate the assumed basis for whatever policy proposals may be advanced. Many of the progressive policies have been supported by a broad coalition of factions, some of which are decidedly not in the progressive camp. But this should only serve to remind us that a great deal of practical politics does not easily lend itself to interpretation in terms of formal categories and the messy business of actually governing a factious regime, such as the United States further complicates such analysis. The progressive mind, however, remains distinctive and can be separated from some of the political coalitions with which it occasionally finds itself allied.

And finally, I have not spent any time discussing the role of the Supreme Court either as it has advanced the progressive thesis or blocked some part of it in one of its rulings. I do this for two reasons. First, I think Supreme Court rulings on religion and the First Amendment over the past century collectively border on the incoherent. Beginning with *Pierce v. Society of Sisters* (1925) the Court has been increasingly involved in various religious issues in a way that seems to defy categorization. Perhaps the incoherence is itself a consequence of progressive influence. Any particular decision might be defensible at one level, but collectively court opinions are all over the map and it is difficult to find a common thread. Second, and perhaps under the influence progressive thought, the general trend of American jurisprudence seems to be one of substituting law and legal procedure for the classical conception of justice. Classical political science focused on justice, but the American regime increasingly focuses on law; the two are not the same. Collectively we seem more inclined to ask if something is constitutional rather than is it just. Only the great questions of slavery and civil rights for minorities, abortion, and perhaps a few other issues, invoke a resort to first principles rather than law. I am mindful of the role the Supreme Court has played in the quarrel between the founders and the progressives on a host of issues, but I also think the nature of the progressive challenge to the founders requires first and foremost a discussion of first principles. It is on the question of first principles, very often articulated by sources outside of the judiciary, that Court decisions may be interpreted.

The progressive quarrel with the founders is distinctively of a different order than progressive quarrels with this or that individual or policy or judicial ruling; it is here that we must focus our attention. Progressives do not accept the self-evident truths of the Declaration and as a consequence is often difficult to understand exactly what is the basis of their objections to the Constitution unless we also understand their quarrel with the natural law. The Declaration is the foundation of the founders' science of politics; it answers the question of what is the *purpose* of government. The Constitution answers the other two foundational questions of politics; *who* should govern and *how* should they govern. Neither the Declaration of Independence nor the Constitution separately can provide a complete understanding of the founders' science of politics; a proper understanding of the Constitution presupposes a proper understanding of the Declaration. If the two documents are separated for purposes of regime interpretation the result is bound to be confusion.

This conflict between the founders and the liberal-progressive science of politics is not merely one of abstract conflict; one of those seemingly interminable arguments between college professors that can bring tears to the eyes of even the most stoic individuals. There is more involved here than a quarrel between dueling academics. One of the fundamental reasons for any science of politics is to diagnose political problems and to prescribe appropriate improvements for a particular regime, or replacement of that regime by a better form of government if circumstances warrant. Practical politics and theory are connected, hopefully, but the more theories are unconnected from experience the more likely they are to follow Spinoza's dictum. The value of any science of politics is not necessarily whether its prescriptions are followed, but the degree to which any prescriptions are valid if they were followed.[3] That is why we so frequently find ourselves wishing we had earlier followed a different course of political action. No prescription for curing whatever ails a particular regime can be advanced until a reasonably accurate diagnosis of its problems is made in the first instance. And every diagnosis involves some set of assumptions about the nature of the regime and principles of justice; what is commonly referred to as a science of politics. Spinoza's observation could not be more timely. The consequences of a faulty diagnosis will be faulty prescriptions in the form of policies that risk not merely modest or occasional failures, which are an inevitable part of all politics, but certain types of what may be termed "structural" failures that are rooted in failures that can destroy the regime itself. The conflict between the founders and the liberal-progressive science of politics cannot avoid raising these issues.

Some contemporary scholars, who refer to themselves as "anti-foundationalists," have argued that all political science is just ideology anyway because there is no foundational basis for accepting one theory over another. The result is a series of seemingly endless academic quarrels over what do we know and how do we know it? But this seems to me to be one of the many offshoots of the value relativism introduced by progressive methodology in the human sciences. The original progressives had a strong sense of the scientific foundations of their work that has remained an essential part of the progressive tradition. The latent nihilism of the later anti-foundationalists was perhaps present at the beginning, but the early progressive writers thought a new foundation of politics in science would either overcome, or at least compensate, for the value relativism that some darkly foresaw in their new science but seldom explored systematically.

The significance and the potential consequences of liberal-progressive critique of the founders may be illustrated by reference to an observation made by Leo Strauss shortly after the end of World War II. Strauss thought that the abandonment by American academics of the founders' natural law political science, an idea inseparable from the Declaration of Independence and the Constitution, gave to American academics an uncomfortable affinity with certain aspects of nineteenth century German thought that had culminated in the German catastrophe of the twentieth century.[4] Strauss attributed the German catastrophe to the science of politics that made value relativism its foundational principle, a principle that he took to be the essence of what he called "historicism"; a historicism that Strauss in turn thought to be one of the legacies of the liberal-progressive science of politics. This new historicism he noted, but without exploring it precisely in its American context, was the antithesis of the founding principles of the American regime; principles that had made America unique among the nations of the modern world.

No one should suggest a precise analogy of cause and effect between two political cultures as vastly different as the United States and Germany, even if they both adopt a similar approach to foundational arguments in politics, and Strauss did not do so. But culture is mutable and is affected by changes in how we think about our culture and the new progressives sought to change the culture as much as the constitutional system. History may not exactly repeat itself, as Marx thought, but there are patterns of human thought that have had demonstrably analogous results across time and it is one of the tasks of political science to probe these connections. At any event, such a sober judgment from a major Jewish scholar who was a refugee from Nazi Germany in the 1930s, with all of its inescapable implications, should be enough to alert us all to the importance of the subject.

How the liberal-progressive science of politics came to dominate the academic interpretation of American politics and the consequences of that interpretation is a subject that cannot be studied too closely by students of contemporary American politics. Progressive ideas drove much of the policy debates in the New Deal and its subsequent interpretation. Almost as soon as the liberal-progressive science of politics was articulated in the rarified atmosphere of universities it presumed to set the terms of the debate over the nature of the American regime and the interpretation of ordinary politics. Eventually it overshadowed, at least in academic circles, the republican political science of *The Federalist*, for example, which increasingly became less of a reference point for serious analysis and much more often as an after thought or an opportunity for an occasional rhetorical flourish but was too often drained of all substance. The practical consequences of this shift in the study of American politics have continued to play out in ordinary regime politics.

But such a study as this has its own perils that are shaped by the very influence that the liberal-progressive science of politics has exerted in regime analysis. The problem does not begin with methodology but it is reflected in methodology. The academic study of politics that emerged in the Progressive Era made both historical analysis and science the lynchpin for the study of politics. This marriage of science and history was not as farfetched as it may seem; the two reinforced each other. This in turn has tended to make a study of the liberal-progressive science a politics a matter of getting the historical chronology right and searching for the first glimmer of scientism in the mind of a particular writer. Academic wars have been fought in countless footnotes over whether this or that author ought or ought not to be considered a "progressive." It should be acknowledged at the outset that dating the origins of the liberal-progressive tradition in American politics imprecise at best. And it needs to be noted that any search for precision on this point is likely to begin with some sort of Original Sin and risks becoming a history of everything beginning with an always somewhat arbitrary starting point. Some scholars, for example, have traced its origins to a particular thinker or writer that predates the Civil War by decades.[5] This approach has its merits if what we seek is a history of the movement as well as its antecedents, but by itself it does not address the heart of the matter and may beg the question of why the liberal-progressive tradition is so important in the first place. In this particular account, interpretation takes precedence over chronology even with a full awareness of the importance of chronology.

If historical dating of origins becomes the primary methodological concern, combined with a chronological listing of the appropriate authors to be included, such an approach further risks becoming a historicized analysis of liberal-progressivism; its foundational principles tend to be understood primarily, if not solely, as a product of a particular time, place, and circumstance. And since times change, its influence can be reduced in a similar way to the historical period under study. The Progressive Movement thus makes its own methodology the basis for an inquiry into itself and in doing so implicitly passes judgment in favor of its own science over that of the founders at the outset. But it is precisely this assumption that needs to be challenged and reconsidered. The persistence of the progressive mind, despite repeated failures of progressive politics on the grand scale of Marxist regimes, points toward a problem that may only be emerging in American politics. American politics at the outset of the twenty-first century suggests that progressivism will only continue to grow in significance. The conflict between the American founders and the progressives seems to be never ending. Nevertheless, we may fairly ask whether who interprets of regime principles makes any practical difference. The progressive assumption that the latest idea deserves pride of place in any interpretation of politics is an assumption that cannot be challenged too often.

The founders' natural rights political science, as is the case with Plato, Machiavelli, Hobbes, and every other political philosopher of note, is also a product of time, place, and circumstance, but the founders did not consider republican principles to be bound simply to the eighteenth century American republic any more than progressives thought their foundations in science was time bound. With certain limitations, I tend to agree with both propositions. Facts never speak for themselves but are always filtered through some theory that is outside of the facts. We should expect that any diagnosis of regime issues would be different when viewed through the theoretical prism of the founders or the progressives. This sort of conflict over how to interpret events great and small goes to the very heart of all debates over American politics at all times, no less the founders than their later liberal-progressive critics.

There is no doubt some truth to an historical approach since all such arguments are found in particular persons and at particular times and places. Any analysis must start somewhere and chronology is one important element in establishing simple cause and effect in politics. But, James Madison's famous riposte that "if every Athenian citizen had been a Socrates, every Athenian assembly would still have been a mob" notwithstanding, the relevance of a Plato in political science is not entirely bound up with a study of fifth century B.C. Athens, however useful such context may be as a matter of interpretation; the greatest writers are never bound wholly by historical context. Context is a set of circumstances, it is not, or ought not to be, an intellectual prison. If we read the liberal-progressive writers, as they understood themselves we will have to conclude that they believed they were laying the proper scientific foundations for a study of politics that would endure beyond their own time; they may have been relativists in their own way, but they did not think of their science and methodology as relativistic. Further, since the liberal-progressive science of politics shifted the foundational study of American politics away from the founders and toward something else it is important to know what that something else is and the reasons behind this shift. Trying to understand the liberal-progressive science of politics both in its origins and its influence is therefore less a matter of chronology, although that is important, than a matter understanding these foundational assumptions.

Finally, I use the much overworked term "paradigm" in the sense popularized by Thomas Kuhn, although not as precisely as he may have intended, because it seems to be the best word to describe the liberal-progressive tradition.[6] Much of the importance of Kuhn's theory of how paradigms guide ordinary research is in how he calls our attention to foundational arguments that are typically taken for granted.[7] This seems to me to be true of political science as well as the hard sciences. Political science is not as strictly defined as the natural sciences, but it has, I think, its own autonomy as an inquiry into political things that should command respect if not always agreement. The liberal-progressive tradition, as with the founders, must be understood in its foundational arguments if it is to be seriously understood at all. Progressives also demand respect if not agreement. Any inquiry into the foundations of progressives should keep in its forefront "What are the arguments progressives think are 'self-evident' whenever they advance any particular political argument or proposal?" It is a question that requires an answer if progressivism is to be understood as progressives understand themselves as well as any critique of progressivism.

It must also be said at this point that the truth or accuracy of any paradigm may be defined as the congruence between thought and the objects of thought; a point that is sometimes unclear in Kuhn. In the study of various authors who helped to establish the liberal-progressive tradition in American politics it is fair to observe that the accuracy of their analysis is to be judged by the congruence between their writing and the system they are trying to describe. There can never be a one-to-one congruence by the very nature of object of study, but matters of degree are not trivial and can amount to a difference of kind. The dilemma the liberal-progressive model faces in this context is that the political reality they are trying to analyze is the American constitutional system; a system that was set in motion at the founding by a political science very much at odds with their own science of politics. What they both share is an attempt to provide a political science appropriate for a popular form of government. In both traditions "popular government," for example, is a common term, but the meaning attached to the term is not the same and the changed meaning cannot be reduced simply to changed historical circumstances. It is not merely words that are the object of study, but the meaning attached to common terms.

I start with the belief that the founders' science of politics, in the sense that I have used "the founders" in a somewhat generic sense here, to be superior to that of the political science that came out of the Progressive Era; it better explains what is happening in a way that ratifies Spinoza's dictum. But I am also aware of Alexis de Tocqueville's observation in *Democracy in America* that God does not need theories of human behavior because He sees into the heart of every individual: Men need theories because they cannot pretend to the degree of knowledge that would be required to dispense with theories. The founders would have to be like gods if they were always right. Precision, as Aristotle observed, is not to be expected in the science of politics, as it would be demanded in the science of mathematics. Properly understood, therefore, every theory of politics is a confession of ignorance in some sense; this is a truism for both the theories of the founders and the liberal-progressives.

I am therefore respectful of the liberal-progressive tradition even where I most profoundly disagree with it. Every science of politics is to be measured by its power to explain historical variances (How does A cause or affect B?), and by its power to guide those who must act in politics. Both the founders and the liberal-progressives have staked their political science on the power of their ideas to promote a popular form of government; there is no other form of government under consideration. Democratic government must therefore be the touchstone for any comparison between them. Which science of politics better defends and promotes a democratic government we all say we want? I take this to be the practical question that drives every argument over politics in the American regime. The answer is not to be decided by an *a priori* methodology that decides in favor or one or the other. It is rather to be decided by an inquiry into each as a science of politics that explains and promotes this particular goal of regime principles. Alexander Hamilton made the adoption of the Constitution a matter of "reflection and choice"; we would not do justice either to the original founders or to the liberal-progressive revolt against them if we allowed either science to prevail through ignorance or a failure to rightly choose following a serious reflection.

Notes

1. Sean Trende, *The Lost Majority: Why the Future of Government Is Up for Grabs and Who Will Take It* (New York: Palgrave Macmillan, 2012).
2. Charles Taylor, *A Secular Age* (Cambridge, MA: The Belknap Press of Harvard University Press, 2007).
3. My personal guide on this point is James W. Ceaser, *Liberal Democracy and Political Science* (Baltimore: Johns Hopkins University Press, 1990).
4. Leo Strauss, *Natural Right in History* (Chicago: The University of Chicago Press, 1953), 1.
5. Eldon J. Eisenach, for example, has made the case for the prototype of the progressive intellectual in the person of David Francis Bacon (1813–1866). See his Introduction to his edited collection of excerpts from the progressive tradition *The Social and Political Thought of American Progressivism* (Indianapolis, IN: Hackett Publishing Company, Inc., 2006).
6. Thomas S. Kuhn, *The Structure of Scientific Revolutions* (Chicago: The University of Chicago Press, 1962). This is not the place to discuss all of the controversies surrounding Kuhn's thesis. I take it that the central problem posed by Kuhn may broadly stated as asking whether or not scientific laws articulate the interests and even extrascientific beliefs of scientists, or are they simply descriptions of reality based on a scientifically defined series of facts? Do facts speak for themselves? Many of the criticisms of Kuhn center on the implicit scientific relativism in his idea of how paradigms operate. When the notion of a scientific paradigm shows up in the social sciences, I assume that it cannot operate just as it might in the natural sciences. My assumption is that facts in both natural and human sciences do not speak for themselves: They need to be interpreted by theories that are not necessarily

self-evident. Modern Liberalism, Conservatism, Rationalism, Marxism, and various other "isms" of the modern world may each be interpreted as a sort of paradigm that attempts to make sense of the world as a whole. I hold to the notion that the truth or the accuracy of any particular paradigm, scientific or social, may be defined as the congruence between thought and the objects of thought.

7. The best recent study of foundational concepts in political science is James W. Ceaser, *Nature and History in American Political Development: A Debate* (Cambridge, MA: Harvard University Press, 2006). Ceaser observes, "Science, even in the looser sense in which that term applies to the study of politics, must begin with shared concepts, so that each researcher does not, like Sisyphus, need to begin the task anew," 171.

I

The Progressive Project: Darwinian Foundations and Political Science

At the outset of the twenty-first century the term "progressive" has become one of the most potent symbols in American politics. In a generic sense the term "progress" is perhaps most commonly used as a synonym for "improvement." At a minimum progress in this sense means movement in a desired direction and away from something that is less desired. But the identification of a certain type of politics as progressive in America dates to the late nineteenth and early twentieth centuries in what is typically referred to by historians as the Progressive Movement. The term itself seems innocuous enough. Properly understood, we are all in favor of progress as movement in a desired direction. Just as clearly we all agree that movement in an undesired direction does not seem like progress. But this, of course, merely begs the question of what is desirable and what is undesirable and why; central questions in any study of politics. The problematic character of progress may be somewhat clearer when we recall that the idea of progress has a mixed heritage in the lexicon of American politics, beginning with the founders themselves.

Both the original American founders, the authors of the Declaration of Independence and the Constitution, and the modern progressives were nourished by ideas about progress that came out of the broad movement we refer to as the Enlightenment of the seventeenth and eighteenth centuries. In this context it should be noted that the American were much more influenced by the English Enlightenment, which stressed "moral virtue" over the French Enlightenment that stressed "rationality." The American regime is founded on the notion that republican government represented an improvement over the classical forms of government through the discovery and application of certain principles that were either not known or imperfectly known to the ancients. In this sense, the original founders accepted and embraced the idea that republican political science had progressed since the Greeks; the efficient means of this progress was the prudential application of natural rights principles to contemporary political conditions. The founders' natural rights arguments seemed unobjectionable in the context of the dominant Protestant political culture of the English colonies. The political science of *The Federalist* was secular, but the natural rights of the Declaration of Independence tethered it to a religious culture. This understanding of natural rights, while not explicitly religious by any means, was not hostile to religion broadly understood. Indeed, natural rights had been an integral part of the Christian political tradition at least since St. Thomas Aquinas in the thirteenth century and the classical tradition before that.

While the idea of progress was not foreign to the founders, it was different in important ways from the idea of progress that emerged from the Progressive Movement. The difference was the place of natural rights in each science of politics. Progressives attacked natural rights in the name of both science and history. In attitudes, what Alexis de Tocqueville called "habits of the heart," progressives were more attuned to the French version of the Enlightenment than the American version.[1] That is, they made scientific reason the organizing principle of politics rather than moral virtue. It is with this distinction that we can divide the progressive critique of the founders into the scientific critique and the historicist critique. Both are inseparably linked but it seems appropriate to begin with the scientific critique as a point of departure.

Darwinian Science and the Progressive Critique of Natural Law

Progressives made evolutionary progress, following in outline the arguments advanced by Charles Darwin, rather than progress in the application of natural rights, the basis for a science of politics; the efficient means of this new sense of progress was an evolutionary process that explicitly denied natural rights and was at least agnostic, and frequently hostile, toward any hint of Divine purpose. The authority of Darwin for progressives was like the pillar of fire that led the Israelites across the desert. Darwin helped to make autonomous moral progress the very definition of personal freedom. The natural rights of the Declaration had also made the pursuit of happiness an individual pursuit, but its ties to an older natural rights tradition and the religious culture of the American regime softened its harder edges. The founders' natural rights tradition assumed that we inherit certain duties and obligations that are natural to the human condition. Some superficial similarities aside, progress in the founders' sense of the term and the modern progressive sense of the term have been in conflict ever since. The former have retained an aura of American exceptionalism while the latter have increasingly come to resemble a more European sense of historicized progress. At its origins it is appropriate to regard the progressive tradition as a genuine, if truncated, effort to understand the nature of modern politics under the impact of revolutions in scientific thinking.

Progress in the progressive sense of the term carried with it particular corollaries that are not always explicit in later formulations. Secularism is the most conspicuous example. For American progressives, as was generally true for their European cousins, secularism, and progress were mutually supporting terms. This made the progressive identification of any idea of justice with a secular political-economic ideal almost inevitable as natural rights lost its status as a foundation for political debates. At the level of ordinary politics, progressives frequently quarreled with each other, and it is easy to lose sight of their common opposition to the political science of the American founding in all of its aspects. This foundational unity reflects the conscious knowledge that their challenge to the founders, whatever their intermural disagreements, required nothing less than a total refounding of the American regime on new, more scientific, political principles.

This fundamental quarrel goes to the heart of what is meant by a science of politics. That political science is a science of human nature no one doubts. And whether human nature somehow evolves is a serious question. Is the term "political science" the oxymoron that almost every college student thinks it is? Much will depend on the nature of what we mean by science and how it affects our understanding of human nature. The correct answer is, as is so often the case, "it depends." Precision, especially in the study of politics, must always be a matter of degree, but we must also keep in mind that the difference between freezing and boiling is also a matter of degree.

To begin with, the original founders understood political science to be a science that was fundamentally different from that of the natural sciences. This is, no doubt, the source of so much undergraduate confusion on the subject. Whatever the differences the founders had with the classical tradition, one aspect of their thought reached back to Aristotle's *Ethics*; that the human sciences had an autonomy that required a different definition of science than did the natural sciences—one that did not demand the same degree of precision. This was more in keeping with dominant features of the English Enlightenment. Progressives, on the other hand, explicitly rejected the classical argument that the natural and human sciences required a different approach. This is most obvious on the subject of natural law; whereas the founders made natural law the foundation for a republican form of government, the progressives made Darwinian science the foundation for progressive politics. Science defined in Darwinian terms at least suggested, when it did not require, a precision that natural law reasoning could never attain. This in turn led progressives to accept the corresponding idea that a of science politics not founded on the principles and methodology of the natural sciences could never aspire to be a science in the precise meaning of the term. It was a potent academic marriage, but it was a marriage that did considerable violence to any description of practical politics that was typically anything but precise. Intellectual consistency took precedence over the congruence between theory and practice.

At a practical level it has become commonplace to view the founders' science of republican government, the political science of *The Federalist*, as vulnerable on grounds derived from their own natural law principles. The Achilles heel of the founders' natural law republic, as every schoolchild knows, was the rift between political theory, in the Declaration of Independence, and political practice, in the Constitution, on the issue of slavery. Slavery, and its later offshoots as separate but equal, were and remain incompatible with the natural law purpose of government stated so eloquently in the Declaration of Independence. Slavery and racism were, however, elevated problems for a natural law science of politics precisely because they were incompatible with natural law, as most of the founders' fully recognized during their more candid moments. Absent natural law, it is not obvious why slavery is a problem. Natural law would seem to make the most sense in a crisis when a Lincoln was in charge.

The solution within the founders' science of politics, as Lincoln so eloquently understood, was to make political practice, the Constitution, conform to the natural rights political theory of the Declaration. Natural law in practice was not self-correcting, some assembly was required, but prudential and courageous actions pointed toward at least a potential solution within a republican form of government. The founders' republic did not always require statesmen committed to natural rights to be at the helm to make it work, but it was designed to make such statesmanship a realistic aspiration.

4

The Achilles heel of the progressive science of politics, on the other hand, was inherent in its foundations that aped the natural sciences. The modern view of a mechanistic science has little or no room for a high moral purpose and progressives were nothing if not a purpose-driven political class. At a practical level progressives also opposed slavery, but it is not as obvious that there is a purely scientific argument against slavery as there is a natural rights argument. If natural selection, following Darwin, is the truth of our evolution as a species, as Darwin certainly implied, perhaps slavery is merely an example of the strong weeding out the weak; this is certainly an argument that has had its defenders at different times and places. Could the case be made that slavery is economically efficient? No progressive ever made this argument and it is introduced here simply as an illustration of how foundational arguments might proceed for a science of politics built on purely scientific foundation. Evolution may be a perfectly valid explanation for biological development but it does not therefore follow that it explains politics. Darwin may be perfectly true as biology and remain perfectly false as a science of politics. How?

Evolution, as Darwin conceived it, was a process of "random selection" in nature. Evolution as a concept was not new and did not necessarily attract the opposition of religious leaders nor was it necessarily hostile to natural law. The sticking point with Darwin, however, was the notion of random selection. What caught the attention of progressives in Darwin's theory of evolution was how random selection eviscerated natural law and any notion of Divine purpose in the human condition. It meant that natural law, religion, and other superstitions were rapidly being replaced with true knowledge based on irrefutable science. Whatever was left of the idea of God, for example, it was the god-of-the-gaps; God was an idea that was used to explain those gaps in our knowledge that were not yet penetrated by science. As science expanded our knowledge of those gaps, it followed that the god-of-the-gaps explanations would gradually shrink. In this sense, a universe that could ultimately be rationally explained without reference to God may be said to be at least the implicit end of progressive knowledge. In politics this particular mindset pointed in the direction of social perfection because there was no longer any permanent quality about the human condition, such as sin, to limit perfection. This close relationship between secularism and evolutionary political perfection explains much of the Promethean quality to be found in the prototype progressive intellectual.

This progressive notion of science in turn rested on the argument, or more of an empirically unsupported idea really, that the natural sciences were, or soon would be, the source of all relevant knowledge about the human sciences. Faith in science was thus the bedrock of progressive scholarship and it shaped their methodology for the study of history in general and politics in particular. Progressives viewed science as a subject that was studied with a kind of Socratic detachment; scientists were conceived almost as a disembodied species whose methodology was untainted with any biases that were not self-correcting. Scientists, as scientists, did not suffer the strengths, weaknesses, foibles, vanities, and other characteristics that afflicted the human condition. This was certainly an idea with consequences. The origins of this attitude that came out of the Enlightenment are clear enough and has been studied intently.[2] What needs to be done here is to follow this secularization of historical–political interpretation through the course of American political science at the foundations.

A thoroughly secular understanding of the human condition of the sort promoted by the progressive tradition had an undoubted appeal at one level. The reason was superficially obvious. If God set the universe in motion as a first cause without a cause, it seemed to follow that science alone could never provide the certainty of historical interpretation progressives so ardently desired; every interpretation would have to loop back toward the supposition of a purposeful Creator. And a purposeful Creator was unlikely to utilize strictly random selection as a means of creation. Natural law set in motion by a creator puts limits on what we might expect from any polity. The more secular progressives certainly regarded purposeful creation, as imbedded in religion as well as natural law, as the enemy of science and this was reflected in their supposition that there was a natural hostility between the two forces. Again, the reasons are not difficult to discern. Modern science, especially in the wake of Newton and Darwin, emerged as focused almost exclusively on material and efficient causality. The study of first and/or final causality, the realm of the Divine, was relegated to an unscientific embarrassment. When Darwin came along he reinforced this mechanistic notion, perhaps begun by Newton, that the essence of science was method.

Whether the agnostic secularism or the science came first in terms of causality for progressives is perhaps impossible to say. It is certainly true that progressives thought science and secularism mutually supported each other. But, it must also be noted; this desire to know is not exclusively the province of the secular progressive tradition. It seems to be part of the DNA of the human condition. What marks the difference in this regard between the founders and progressives? The answer is the degree of knowledge we may expect from any science of politics.

What typically separates progressives from others is not the desire for greater knowledge, but the degree of belief in whether certainty is philosophically possible. Progressives made science the sole source of knowledge and, in effect, made science into an idol that was as jealous of any rivals as any monotheism. Philosophical certainty in this context may be seen by the degree of faith that progress in the natural sciences, in areas such as physics and biology can be replicated in the human sciences, particularly political science and historical interpretation. It is not surprising that faith in the certainty of absolute scientific knowledge would also lead to the corresponding faith that absolute political knowledge, based on science, would somehow produce results superior to the hodgepodge of previous regimes.

But Darwin as science poses particular problems for a science of politics that are not so obvious in other natural sciences because biology is both a natural and a human science. Biology cannot escape questions about human nature in the same way that mathematics, for example, can avoid them. This dual nature of biology makes it difficult to pin down precisely what is useful and what is not in any theory of evolution as a source of explanation in the uniquely human sciences such as political science. In this regard, Darwinian science consists of two distinct components that can be separated for analytic purposes. The first component is the purely physical mechanism whereby life is created and dispersed. The second component is more nebulous and consists of whatever philosophy may be attached to that mechanism by various scientists or philosophers of science. The former requires some precision, the latter less so. Obviously there is overlap between these two components, as there is in every aspect of science. But it is the implicitly secularized philosophy of Darwinian evolution that has captured the imagination of progressive intellectuals and it is this philosophical portion of the Darwinian paradigm that must command our attention here. Mechanism and philosophy converge to form a single foundation, albeit an uneasy linkage at times.

Evolutionary Progress and Perfection

As an interpretation of history, the Progressive Movement tended to alternate between the ideas that progress was something akin to a mechanical movement, what Darwin called "natural selection," and the idea, not part of Darwin's own argument, that progressive development was something that required purposeful human action in order to complete. The two parts did not always fit easily together but that scarcely mattered for most progressives.

We can get some sense of the progressive use of Darwin as a science to challenge the founders when we ask, "What was there about the founders' science of politics they found most immediately objectionable?" The answer is deceptively simple, but complex in elaboration. The problem is linked to the issue of teleological perfection; the founders accepted imperfection as a permanent part of the human condition whereas the progressives did not. This is what makes Darwin so important in the progressive science of politics. The founders' argument for human imperfection reflected their experience in politics; the progressive argument for political perfection reflected their imagination. The idealism of the Progressive tradition has consistently pointed in the direction of a perfected polity, not, as Plato had argued, perfection in speech, very likely for heuristic reasons, but as Marx had argued, perfection in historical time. This required a science of politics that treated the idea of progress itself as a form of knowledge. And because it required human perfection to make such a polity work, it was not a science of politics ultimately built on an ordinary understanding of human nature. But it was built on a concept of human nature shaped by what progressives took to be the clear implications of science defined in Darwinian terms. Human action would accomplish what nature intended but, for some unknown reason, failed to achieve. This tension at the level of a foundational assumption has bedeviled progressivism since its origins.

One of the most iconic writers who help to build the teleological foundations of American progressivism as a form of social perfection was Herbert Croly, who put it this way; "For better or worse, democracy cannot be distinguished from an aspiration toward human perfectibility, and hence from the adoption of measures looking in the direction of realizing such an aspiration."[3] More will be said of Croly later. But this statement of fundamentals raises the next question of what understanding of human knowledge lies behind a political science that requires human perfection to make it work? The most cursory survey of the major works in the liberal-progressive tradition suggests an unambiguous answer—the desire for fundamental knowledge regarding the world we live in. In the words of John Dewey (1859–1952), perhaps the foremost philosopher who embodied the ethos of the Progressive Movement, "the quest for certainty," above all else, was "an effort to transcend belief."[4] What he meant by this was a knowledge that would replace all previous religious, philosophical, and moral systems that littered the pages of history with a new form of knowledge based on science. All pretentions to knowledge not based on the empirical science born of the scientific revolution were mere opinions and not worthy of serious study.

Progressives demanded a level of certainty that was foreign to both the classical and religious understanding of what we may reasonably expect from any knowledge of the human condition. We might say at the outset that the passion for something approaching absolute certainty is what shaped the secular nature of the quest as distinct from a classical philosophic or religious quest that assumed uncertainty about ultimate questions. In particular, what progressives passionately desired was form of knowledge about politics that would place the objects required for the study of politics beyond dispute and beyond doubt. Modern science was not only the means of acquiring such knowledge it was the end as well. It was a demand that came with a steep price. And it is an attitude that has persisted in the face of repeated failure because inherent in the idea of secular progress is the corresponding notion that future success is just over the horizon or just around the corner; what the philosopher Eric Voegelin has insightfully described as "the immanentization of the eschaton"; an awkward but accurate description of a particular mindset that the end of progress is immanent.[5] It is also a mindset that tends to make the idea of progress impervious to counter arguments or even ordinary political experience.

The passion that began with a desire to understand the world scientifically has, in practice, been inseparable from an equally passionate desire to change the world scientifically. The idea of secular progress based on modern science satisfied a certain quality in the secular mind in much the way St. Thomas Aquinas satisfies a certain quality in the religious mind. It is difficult, perhaps impossible, to decide which comes first; a particular mindset or the ideas, which satisfy that mindset. To paraphrase Marx, the idea of a collective secular progress was the opium of the progressive intellectual class. Few progressives were outright Marxists, but most believed in some form of materialistic determinism and shared the notion that the study of politics could best be studied by the analysis of something other than politics. And they certainly shared his belief that secular intellectuals could rationally understand the world better than classical philosophers or theologians. There were, however, serious obstacles to the idea of secular progress in the American polity, such as natural law and the religious character of the American people, which have helped to shape its development. These obstacles also need to be understood because they help to highlight the progressive argument at its source.

Darwin, Science, and Progressive Political Science

Charles Darwin's epic account of biological evolution in his *On the Origin of the Species* (1859) must surely rank as among the most influential books ever written, and not only in the study of biology. Evolution was a subject of much debate before Darwin, but Darwin gave evolution an intellectual heft that was denied to his predecessors. It was Darwin who made evolution scientific rather than primarily philosophic, as it was for Rousseau and Hegel and early biologists. After Darwin, evolution was treated as a natural science, in much the same sense that Newton represented physical science. Darwin's argument for natural selection was simple and required no first or final cause to explain how it worked. What is most important to note here is that Darwin's influence extends beyond biology and into the study of subjects such as history and politics, as John Dewey made clear in *The Influence of Darwin on Philosophy* (1910). It is a remarkable achievement.

Yet *The Origin of the Species* just as surely must rank as among the least read of that handful of books that have had so much influence outside their own specific focus. Indeed, reading the original *Origin of the Species* is likely to be a mind numbing experience for all but the most dedicated historians of biology. This is perhaps especially true for twentieth century readers who are all at least dimly aware of discoveries in genetics, microbiology, and chemistry, all of which have altered what may be called "original Darwinism," developments that the first Darwinians and progressive scholars were largely, but not wholly, unaware. Nevertheless, its influence outside of biology suggests that one need not necessarily read Darwin in order to be a Darwinian. To accept Darwinian evolution is the mark of an educated person in the post-Darwinian world. The influence may be understandable for biologists since Darwin was, after all, a biologist, and the paradigmatic quality of science does not require that every scientist read everything written by their predecessors. But Darwin as a foundation for the study of politics or history represents something of a puzzle that requires explanation. Until Darwin came along, most people interested in the study of politics seldom made biology their starting point; when they did it was with the assumption that biology and nature had fixed the human condition in a more or less permanent state that did not change substantively over time. It was what one might describe as a "steady-state" theory of nature; we had no reason to believe that nature was anything other than what it now seemed to be. One could read Aristotle, for example, two thousand years after he wrote, and still learn the fundamentals of a science of politics in a way that was not true of biology.

Darwin's notion of "random selection" as the material and efficient causes of evolution does not suggest that evolution has anything to do with progress in the generally accepted usage of the word. Or perhaps it might be said that "progress" and "improvement" assumed a new, more limited meaning. As Darwin put it, "Improvement implies, I suppose, each form obtaining many parts, or organs, all excellently adapted for their functions."[6] The idea of better implies teleological purpose and a final cause set in motion presumably by a first cause. Random selection, on the other hand, excluded any notion of teleological progress; it could focus on material and efficient causality. Progress and evolution might therefore appear at first glance to be distinctly different ideas. The marriage of progress and evolution was consummated, however, by the combination of history with science. During the time Darwin first appeared American progressives were already thoroughly immersed in German historicism and the historical relativism that followed in its wake. Hegel taught that history was the eschatological unfolding of the World Spirit, which was progress of a sort, and even when the World Spirit was abandoned in favor of the proletariat, or some other utopian end, evolutionary progress was firmly in the DNA of the Progressive Movement.[7] But while history might aspire to be a science after the manner of Darwin, it clearly was not. What it lacked, according to some, was the right methodology that could emulate the natural sciences.

The Darwinian connection with how the system of American government ought to be interpreted has affected both the sorts of metaphors that are thought to be analogous to that study as well as the foundations of study. The former is perhaps best illustrated by the work of Woodrow Wilson and the latter by John Dewey. Both are connected by an umbilical cord supplied by Darwin that cannot easily be separated without doing violence to each. They each need to be studied as examples of what a Darwinian interpretation of American politics looks like while the new methodology of progressivism will be treated separately in Chapter IV.

Woodrow Wilson: Evolution and the Progressive Theory of Constitutional Government

The political thought of Woodrow Wilson is a case study in the influence of Darwin on political science. It is not clear if Wilson ever actually read Darwin, but it really does not matter; he was a Darwinian to the core. Even if Wilson had not been elected president in 1912, he would still remain as one of the primary proponents of the progressive science of politics. The fact that he was elected president only increases his importance in any interpretation of progressivism in general and the role of Darwin in particular. Wilson did not merely popularize the Darwinian metaphor; he showed how it could serve as the scientific foundation for a science of politics that replaced the founders. We can catch a glimpse of the easy movement between Darwin, historicism, and the critique of the American founding in his political thought.

In his own words, he described himself as a "literary politician" rather than a practicing politician. But by this term, Wilson did not mean a mere academic pundit. It was more akin to his idea of a philosopher, although he did not use the specific term; "A man who knows polities, and yet does not handle policies."[8] The literary politician was an academic intellectual; what passes for a philosopher in our time. Further, Wilson asserted, the role of the literary politician was superior to that of the ordinary politician. He described him as a man "born into the world whose mission it evidently is to clarify the thought of his generation, and to vivify it; to give it speed where it is slow, vision where it is blind, balance where it is most out of poise . . ."[9] Wilson was here referring to Walter Bagehot, who had taught young Wilson the superior virtues of the British parliamentary system, but he might just as well been describing his own projected influence on constitutional interpretation. At about the same time he wrote these comments about Bagehot on the superiority of the literary politician, he also wrote in his confidential journal, "why may not the present age write, through me, its political Autobiography?"[10] It is a good question. It deserves a good answer. And no one can say Wilson did not try to provide one, even as it strikes us as a bit narcissistic.

It was Wilson's explicit intention to replace the political science of the founders with one of his own and, in effect, to refound the American regime on principles he thought were more scientific. This necessarily meant a new understanding of constitutional government. This was the commonly accepted progressive view. The difference was not merely one that included the rejection of natural law foundations, although it did include that, but, unlike many academic progressives, Wilson also offered a blueprint of how to think about constitutional government in a more practical way; a way that did not require any mention of the natural law. The founders' saw the purpose of government as one that promoted freedom by means of controlling the effects of faction. Wilson saw the purpose of government as the enactment of policies willed by democratic majorities. Not freedom, but democratic equality was the ultimate purpose of progressivism. But the founders' purpose of government made the existing Constitution an obstacle to progressive policies. The founders' Constitution was the object of his discussion, but it was not the foundation of his new science of politics.

Wilson's views began to take shape, as has often been noted, with an undergraduate essay he wrote at Princeton entitled "Cabinet Government."[11] The ideas were borrowed from Walter Bagehot's influential *The English Constitution* (1867/1872), where the term "living constitution" appears as an organizing principle of English constitutional development.[12] What Wilson learned from Bagehot was the value of unified political power as the necessary prerequisite to enact any policy-driven agenda, especially one animated by assumptions contrary to those of the American founding. Parliamentary supremacy meant there was no law above human law; thus did natural law disappear in progressive democracy. It was this point that brought him most directly into conflict with the founders constitutional system with its separation of powers and weak party cohesion that divided responsibility for policy outcomes. The concentration of power did not seem to be possible under existing constitutional arrangements. It took Wilson some time to work his way through this conundrum.

In *Congressional Government* Wilson launched his analysis of the American regime with a matter-of-fact critique of the founders' constitutional system. In his "Introductory" to that famous work, he wrote, "We are the first Americans to hear our own countrymen ask whether the Constitution is still adapted to serve the purposes for which it was intended; the first to entertain any serious doubts about the superiority of our own institutions as compared with the systems of Europe; the first to think of remodeling the administrative machinery of the federal government, and forcing new forms of responsibility upon Congress."[13] He specifically charged that the founders' Constitution was inadequate to the task of modern government. Further, that it "is now our *form of government* rather in name than in reality." That is, the theory of republican government expounded in *The Federalist* no longer matched the practice of American government. His perception of legislative dominance as the actual practice of American government revealed the depths of that rift. And finally he argued that external forces were now shaping American politics more than the intentions of the founders.[14] Properly understood, American politics does not reflect the development of ideas embodied in the founding, but rather movement away from those ideas and principles. Whatever else the notion of a "living constitution" might mean, it inescapably meant the concentration of political power and treating the founding principles as the chief obstacle to that concentration.

What *Congressional Government* did not contain was a theoretical account of what caused the rift between the founders' theory and modern practice. He outlined what was wrong with the founders but not how to replace them with something better; in progressive terms, he lacked a "science" that could provide a foundation for a more complete political analysis. Wilson apparently decided, and rightly so, that what *Congressional Government* lacked was a broad theory of constitutionalism in general. This was not a problem for the founders who understood a constitution to be a written document that reflected the self-evident truths of every science of politics; procedures for how the many would rule. But academic historicism did not take these founding truths to be self-evident in the first place and any constitution built on natural law was built on an absurdity. The new methodology of the social sciences demanded a new definition of a constitution. Wilson provided such a definition and gave a thorough account of the practical implications of this new definition.

The foundation upon which Wilson builds his argument in *Constitutional Government* is his definition of the term "constitution." He seems to have been at least partly aware that this was one of the criticisms of *Congressional Government*.[15] At any rate, his critique of the founders in *Constitutional Government* was deeper and more focused on the foundations of their arguments than his earlier work. At one level, his argument was deceptively simple and in keeping with the progressive tradition in general. The founders, for all of their undisputed brilliance, had simply misunderstood the nature of government itself; they lacked the tools of scientific analysis. This meant that their science of politics, whatever utility it may have had at the time, was not up to the task of providing realistic guidance for a modern democracy. What set Wilson apart from his contemporaries was the way he drew the implications of this new definition of constitutional government in institutional terms. It is perhaps this quality more than any other that has given Wilson's constitutional interpretation its remarkable longevity as the idea of a "living constitution." It is an idea in which Darwin is inescapably linked.

Constitutional Government is carefully organized around three separate but mutually supporting arguments intended to plug the theoretical holes left in *Congressional Government*. First is the idea that constitutional government evolves historically from primitive beginnings of the state toward a universal and ideal form. It is an idea that conforms to the influence of German historical philosophy in general and Hegel in particular that was also reflected in influential works such as George Bancroft's *History of the Formation of the Constitution of the United States of America* (1882).[16] Second, this idea of historical evolution contains within it an analysis of how and where the founders' Constitution fits into this evolutionary process as a whole. It is in the context of this second point that Wilson provides his explicit criticism of the founders' science of politics. Third, the historical thesis of constitutional development provides a prescription for bringing American government, and with it the American Constitution, into accord with his ideal form of modern democracy that lies somewhere in the future. It is this last argument where he describes his new model presidency that brings together the literary politician with the practical statesman. In Wilson's hands, it was Darwinism that made history into the science so much of the historical profession at the time so ardently desired.

Constitutional Government begins with an arresting definition of "constitutional government" that is missing from his earlier works and is unique among the early progressives but became more or less the standard paradigm for the progressive tradition. He wrote, "A constitutional government is one whose powers have been adopted to the interests of the people and the maintenance of individual liberty."[17] His definition, however, raises questions of its own, questions Wilson sought to answer through his paradigm of historical evolution. What, for example, are the interests of the people? What are the proper criteria for deciding whether or not the Constitution has been adapted to the interests of the people? What tensions exist, if any, between the general interests of the people and the individual liberty that Wilson suggests is the proper end of government? Whatever the question, evolution as science was the methodology that supplied the answer.

At this point it becomes clear that Wilson is not talking about a legalistic definition of American constitutional government or a definition derived from any reference to the original intentions of the founders. Nor does it have any foundation in any recognizable historical experience. It is a definition of constitutional government in terms of where historical progress is taking us; the more perfectly developed future. What Wilson provides is a verbal picture of a broad historical development that culminates in what is, essentially, a romantic vision of a democratic community that is very Rousseauean in essence. Until that vision can be made real, there is no true constitutional government. The realization of this ideal is the only solution to the rift between the theory and practice of progressive constitutionalism. In effect, the United States cannot be said to have ever had a constitutional form of government in the true meaning of the term; only the ideal form is a true form of constitutionalism that comes at the culmination of evolutionary development.

In *Constitutional Government*, Wilson found his science in Darwin; it was science perfectly adapted to the Hegelian historicism that Leo Strauss found so troublesome a half century later. His comment on this point is one of the most oft quoted passages in Wilson's academic work. He wrote, "The government of the United States was constructed upon a Whig theory of political dynamics, which was a sort of unconscious copy of the Newtonian theory of the universe. In our own day, whenever we discuss the structure or development of anything, whether in nature of in society, we consciously or unconsciously follow Mr. Darwin; but before Mr. Darwin, they followed Newton."[18] Although the metaphor was a reference to Darwin, the reasoning behind it owed at least as much to Hegel. Wilson no doubt misrepresented *The Federalist* on this point, for example, but it helped to give his political science an explicit foundation in the natural sciences that was lacking in *Congressional Government*. It did not misrepresent Hegel. Wilson, by the use of this metaphor, announced that he was scientific whereas the founders were not.

The true evolution of constitutional government begins, according to Wilson with the English *Magna Carta* in 1215. This choice of English constitutional development as the model for the best form of democracy was foreshadowed in his undergraduate days by his reading of Bagehot and interest in "Cabinet Government." But although Wilson begins his discussion of constitutionalism with the *Magna Carta*, he is careful to point out that constitutionalism has no necessary connection with a written document.[19] The only true form of constitutional government is that type found in modern democracies that are a "harmonious community," and not the national community of diverse factions described by James Madison in *The Federalist*. Indeed, Wilson takes the existence of factional diversity as proof that a true democracy does not yet exist in historical time. Rousseau, of course, had located that harmony of equals at the beginning of the evolutionary progress, but placing it at the end, as did Wilson, was no more fanciful and had the added advantage of being a source of optimism and not merely source of lost innocence. And since factional diversity is built into the founders' Constitution, we can begin to see what is wrong with their science of politics; it is at once too primitive and too focused on the individual. Darwin taught that it was the collective that should be the focus of scientific analysis in the evolutionary movement of the species. In a similar way, Wilson shifted the focus of political analysis from preservation of individual political liberty to a focus on collective development of the community as a whole.

The question of whether the United States is a constitutional form of government in Wilson's meaning of the term turns on the nature of community. "A people not conscious of any unity, inorganic, unthoughtful, without concert of action, can manifestly neither form nor sustain a constitutional system . . . Nothing but a community can have a constitutional form of government, and if a nation has not become a community, it cannot have that sort of polity."[20] It was clear to Wilson that American politics lacked a singleness of purpose that the rational unfolding of history clearly revealed as the true course of things. He had said as much in *Congressional Government*. The chief obstacle to the achievement of a national community, as was now abundantly clear, was the Constitution itself.[21] True constitutional government could not be built on an assumption of imperfection that assumed the protection of individual liberty as a natural right; natural rights, as they were enunciated in the Declaration, did not evolve, they were discovered. If they existed independent of evolution they would put limits on political evolution. Limits on evolution, as Wilson instinctively understood, meant limits on political power.

According to Wilson, constitutional government evolves through four distinct stages along a historical continuum that is universal in its descriptive features. Each step in this process is progressively more harmonious than the preceding one. In the first stage, the government is described as "the master" and people are ruled by sheer force. In the second stage, the government continues to rule by force but force is now combined with the superior virtues of an aristocratic ruling class; the great majority of people are not yet sufficiently mature to rule for themselves. The third stage is more of a transitional process than a clearly defined stage, but it is the most crucial point in the entire evolutionary process. It is described by Wilson as a revolutionary stage that witnesses a breakdown of traditional aristocratic authority, the overthrow of ruling elites, and the first tentative signs that the people are ready to rule themselves. Once the right of the people to rule themselves is thus established, the pathway is open to the fourth and final stage of constitutional development in which "the leaders of the people themselves become the government, and the development is complete."[22] The argument had come full circle.

The first two stages are relatively unimportant because they deal with historical development before actual constitutions begin to make their appearance. Wilson wastes little time discussing politics in these types of regimes. It is the third and fourth stages that are the most important and he gave them most detailed discussion. In the third stage, communities stand on the threshold of harmony and true constitutional government begins to take shape. But only in the fourth stage can any polity experience true democracy and true constitutional government. It is at this final stage that constitutional government and democratic government are one and the same. It is this framework that provides the key to understanding Wilson's criticism of the founders' Constitution. For Wilson the fourth stage is the future, which is a transformed Hegelian *telos* that can be known in advance because such knowledge is scientific in the sense that Darwin's evolution is scientific.

In Wilson's definition of constitutional government, the United States has not yet become a constitutional polity because the people have not yet entered the fourth and final stage of development. Properly understood, the political science of popular government defended in *The Federalist* ought to be nothing more than a historical footnote in the third stage. It is perhaps interesting in an antiquarian sense, much like the works of Plato, Aristotle, Locke, and other philosophers of government, but not especially useful for understanding either the theory of constitutionalism in general or the actual practice of American government in particular. Furthermore, because the U.S. Constitution is a written document it has had the effect of permanently freezing the otherwise natural development of the American polity in the peculiar nature of the third stage. In Wilson's account, it is not necessarily the case that the founders were wrong in their time, but that they are necessarily wrong for later time; they did not really understand the logic of historical progress because they were too wedded to natural rights as a permanent reality of the human condition.

By way of contrast with the original founders' stunted science of politics, Wilson described the English constitutional and praised it precisely because it is "unwritten" in the American meaning of the term. The fact that the English constitution is whatever Parliament says it is at any particular time means that it permits the unimpeded movement of the organic English community through each of the successive stages of political development; there were no theoretical limits on the exercise of power by parliament. Wilson did not believe, nor did he mean to imply, that in his own day the United States had yet become a "single, homogeneous community" in the mold of the fourth and final stage—he was far too sensitive a political observer to make such a glaring mistake. But he did believe that the fourth stage was immanent and that the Constitution was an impediment to true constitutionalism as he had defined the term. He wrote, ". . . we have come within sight of the merely nationalizing process. Contrasts between region and region become every year less obvious, conflicts of interest less disturbing."[23]

In Wilson's view of constitutional government, factional diversity is found only in the first three stages. Which is to say that factional conflict is a more primitive aspect of the human condition than is the social harmony of the final stage. The mistake of *The Federalist* was that it mistook factional diversity, which was real enough at the time and in the past, for a permanent feature of the human condition. When that assumption was written into the Constitution, with its fragmentation of power into three separate branches of government, the result was that the government remained static while the community continued to grow in accord with its natural evolution.[24] And as the American community moves further away from the time of the founding, the rupture between the theory and practice of American constitutionalism becomes increasingly pronounced. The empirical reality of the continued existence of factions in the regime can be explained more as a defect of the founders' political science than to any intrinsic qualities of human nature. The sin of the founders may be said to lie in their institutionalization of a transitory diversity they mistook for a permanent part of the human condition.

19

Wilson's argument that the Constitution was fundamentally undemocratic was characteristic of the Progressive Movement as a whole. And like his contemporary progressives, Wilson's mindset was one that saw the Constitution as a problem to be overcome rather than a promise to be fulfilled. But it is important to keep in mind that what undergirded his critique of the Constitution was that it weakened political power; his was not an argument with any awareness that democratic government might pose a problem of its own. After having dismissed the natural rights foundation of the Constitution in the Declaration this is hardly surprising. There was nothing in the Constitution that could be regarded as a repository for the things citizens cherished; at best it was simply an empty vessel into which anything could be poured that promised greater scientific rationality.[25] But the irony of Wilson's theory of a harmonious fourth stage of constitution development was that it opened up a rift between the theory and practice of the progressive science of politics far greater than the one he thought he found in the founders. Wilson's assumption that all governments are evolving more or less along the same lines and toward the same idealized form is in reality an act of faith and not a scientific analysis. Further, from Wilson's pen it is political evolution without human agency; a curious thing for a theory of politics, and for someone who wants to write his own autobiography as the political autobiography of the regime, but perhaps appropriate for a theory of species evolution. In Wilson's theory of evolutionary development there is no serious place for prudence or folly, judgment or circumstance; it is a science of politics without real people. It is coincidentally therefore something of a paradox, although a common paradox in progressive thought, that impersonal evolution is combined with powerful leadership; in this case, presidential leadership. Real evolutionary progress in the progressive tradition requires a Promethean president unbound by constitutional restraints. And, we may add here, unbound by any restraints implied by natural law, much less constitutional law.

In Wilson's account, the president is the true source of democracy; only the president represents the American people in their unity whereas the legislative branch represents the American people in their diversity. In Wilson's theory of constitutional government it is the president who represents the future whereas the Congress is stuck in the past, like a prehistoric bug in amber. This new model president exercises power in two senses in Wilson; constitutional power and personal power. The former is relatively trivial in *Constitutional*

Government while the real source of presidential power is personal power built on public opinion. The logic of Wilson's conception of presidential power, given his definition of constitutionalism, informed the comment Richard Nixon made on presidential power in his famous interview with journalist David Frost; "When a president does it, that means it is not illegal."[26] For both Wilson as well as Nixon, presidential power, untethered by the founders' Constitution, was the solution to the achievement of a more perfect democracy and less of a problem for republican government. The president, as Wilson reminded his readers, "does not demand actual experience in affairs so much as particular qualities of mind."[27]

The higher reality of the new model presidency, of which Wilson so eloquently spoke, was the presidency of the future, not the presidency as it had been understood by either the founders or past historical experience. Such a president will not only lead his party, but will lead the nation as a whole in its unity rather than diversity. He will be a "man who understands his own day and the needs of the country, and who has the personality and the initiative to enforce his views upon the people and upon Congress."[28] In short, what Wilson seems to have envisioned was a president who looked pretty much like himself. Unlike the founders' president who was expected to lead, unrealistically perhaps, by nobility of character in the manner of a Washington, the new model president would lead by rhetorical skills, perhaps after the manner of a television evangelist; it was a quality the founders' mistrusted.

Detaching the new model presidency from the Constitution had another, unintended and unexpected consequence that has plagued the progressive model of the presidency ever since. Leadership based on public opinion is more than leadership built on a fickle and ever shifting attitudes. It masks the problem of political authority in the American system. The progressive presidency requires charismatic leadership to make the presidency work. If the president is persuasive, the problem of authority is not conspicuous. But if or when he is not persuasive, he may retain whatever residue of constitutional powers but his ability to lead is almost certain to be severely diminished, as public opinion becomes an inchoate mass. This is very much what happened to Wilson as president during the 1920 election in which the Treaty of Versailles and League of Nations became campaign issues. Rhetorical appeals were insufficient and Wilson and progressives lost big.

The problem Wilson opened up with his new model presidency was one that has plagued progressive politics since the beginning; is conflict a permanent part of the human condition, or can it be overcome by the right policies and institutional arrangements? The founders thought it was permanent and the permanence is reflected in the Constitution; progressives thought it could be overcome. Darwin regarded species competition as fundamental. And there was nothing in Darwinian evolution that made room for democracy, much less the ordinary prudence or folly that we might reasonably expect of humans. It is perhaps metaphysically useful to think about the evolution of the platypus, for example, in terms of random selection, although perhaps God, in one of his moments of whimsy, would do just as well. Human affairs, however, are a different order of magnitude.

Progressives, on the other hand, regarded democracy as a teleological solution to factional conflict rather than a problem to be managed within permanent qualities of the human condition. But democracy, as progressives defined the term, bore no real relationship to how the founders understood popular government. How could it? The founders' thought of democracy as retaining certain form with fixed principles, as valid for Plato as for their own day; evolution had changed the classic foundation for comparative analysis. Wilson's new science of politics assumed that the future would be different than the past, not only in details, but also in the fundamental nature of the human condition. Loaded with the right assumptions, the platypus may indeed seem rational, whimsical, or merely odd.

Methodology, Darwin, and the Social Sciences

In order for democracy to be the progressive solution to conflict in society, it was at least logical that progressive democracy would have a utopian foundation; in progressive terms, this meant a perfected community. It was not necessary that every individual achieve some sort of evolutionary perfection in a teleological sense, but it was necessary that that the community be a perfected society in an evolutionary sense; the undifferentiated community rather than the individual was the focus of teleological evolution, much as Darwin had envisioned. This focus on society was facilitated when Darwin had made it clear that it was the environment that shaped how biological organisms develop; genetics, for example, was not yet on the evolutionary horizon and need not concern us here as an element in progressive political science. For progressives it meant that society as a whole and not the individual person was at the center of political analysis.[29] The individual was shaped by society rather than society shaped by human nature and perfection was more dependent on reason than chance. Science would supply the reason and progressives would supply the politics.

Two aspects of the development of twentieth century social sciences stand out for particular emphasis as they relate to the scientific worldview. First, modern human sciences were shaped by a secular, progressive world view. It is scarcely surprising therefore that this world view was integral to, and perhaps inseparable from, the methodological choices always implicit in the idea of secular progress. The scientific study of politics is bound by an umbilical cord to the methodology of science, both for better and worse. Progressives have generally regarded this union of science and political analysis as a perfect marriage of theory and practice. But the perfect marriage is very much like the perfect crime; there is no such thing.

Second, the scientific methodology of the social sciences provides a laboratory for the study of how science has affected the study of politics. It would be churlish to deny their genuine contributions, as it would be to deny any improvements to our general knowledge of how political systems work in theory and practice. But the issue is not whether the scientific study of politics has in some ways advanced our knowledge of politics. It is whether the assumption that science is the only true source of knowledge is in fact a sustainable concept for any study of the human sciences. Tying the study of the human condition to any exclusive methodology to the exclusion of alternative approaches may as likely result in a decrease as an increase of genuine knowledge. This inevitably raises the question, "Is there anything important that is left out of scientific political science by the new methodology?"

Enter John Dewey

For the social sciences as a whole, no writer in his own day was more influential in calling attention to the influence of Darwin than John Dewey (1859–1952). Dewey was the foremost American philosopher of his day. His lectures at Columbia University made him one of the prize scholars of that institution and he was widely regarded as one of the dominant public intellectuals of his day. His essay, "The Influence of Darwin on Philosophy" (1910) both summarized and articulated one of the dominant strands of the Progressive Movement more clearly than any other work on the subject. To contemporary progressives, Dewey's comments on Darwin did no more than state a self-evident truth. Almost every progressive writer invoked Darwin as a metaphor, but Dewey has rightly been called "evolution's first philosopher."[30] For

Dewey, Darwin was not merely a metaphor, as it was for Wilson, but the most profound source of scientific knowledge about the human condition. Wilson may have sensed this, but his concern was politics, broadly understood, and not epistemology in any scientific sense of the term. If Darwin was correct, and Dewey never doubted that he was, it would appear that morality, whatever that might now mean, was based on biology rather than reason. It was the very antithesis of natural law. It is a fair observation of Dewey to note that he saw in Darwin the embodiment of the sort of absolute knowledge that previous philosophers had been denied.

There were several elements in Dewey's appreciation of what Darwin was saying to the human sciences that contributed enormously to his contemporary influence among progressives. First was his understanding that the epistemological nature of Darwin's theory of evolutionary causality, the idea of random selection, was significantly different than the Newtonian conception of causality; the former resembled the probabilistic mathematics in a game of chance, poker for example, whereas the latter was more like the cause-effect calculations in a game of billiards that still required a first cause to set the balls in motion. Both were true science, but biological science was also a human science in a way which physics was not. Much of what appealed to Dewey was the nonteleological component of Darwin that seemed integral to his science while it seemed only peripheral to Newton. Newtonian science still wondered why the billiard balls were in motion. Second was how this affected a theory of democracy that meshed with the emerging historicism. The indeterminate nature of Darwinian evolution restored a new foundation for choice to a science of politics that was lacking in Newton. But it was a very different basis for choice than that articulated by the American founders. The founders' understood choice to be based on a natural moral order that transcended any particular present; in politics good and evil involved matters of choice. Dewey understood choice to be based on a nature that was ultimately indifferent to choices in any moral sense. Men would become the rule makers, not God. He wrote, "The influence of Darwin upon philosophy resides in his having conquered the phenomena of life for the principle of transition, and thereby freed the new logic for application to mind and morals and life."[31] If true, it represented a transformation Dewey did not underestimate

Rule making in this new paradigm in turn meant that political science was a science in which purpose was man-made and not subject by any transcendent moral order. Dewey also well understood that the modern search for certainty required a parallel search for the methods of control. The overthrow of the classical-Christian order meant that now "the individual makes his own objective and universal truths."[32] Whatever remained of the idea of a *summum bonum*, it would have to be supplied by men, or, more specifically, intellectuals who operated as social engineers. The *summum bonum* is what social engineers, operating through the state, say it is. Choices in politics lacked any cosmic support in Dewey's scheme of things but it did not lack for intellectual support. He thought that modern science had destroyed the idea of a hierarchical universe and with it the very basis for natural law. The very idea of a final cause in any sense that referred back to a purposeful God was simply "preposterous"[33] What exists as material or efficient causality has primacy in science over unscientific speculation about either first or final causality. This intermediate causality, however, could be made a subject for science and that was where intellectuals, such as himself, entered the picture. It was in the very nature of the scientific method to focus on intermediate causes and ignore first or final causality. Without the burden of permanent principles of moral conduct, political philosophy could become public policy—a matter for expert administration. In order that administrators get policy right they would have to have a scientific foundation for their diagnosis and policy prescriptions. Scientific methodology was to be the key.

In Dewey, public policy was defined as "the things that specifically concern us." Clearly he did not think a transcendent moral order was anything that concerned us. He wrote, ". . . intellectual progress usually occurs through sheer abandonment of questions . . . we do not solve them: we get over them."[34] The scientific method applied to politics required the abandonment of questions about purpose. Dewey's point was not unique to Dewey; Darwin made essentially the same observation as an aside in his discussion of the eye as a complex organism when he noted, "How a nerve comes to be sensitive to light, hardly concerns us more than how life itself first originated."[35] But it is a reminder that what often passes for the scientific community is an attitude not usually disposed to even acknowledge questions it is not disposed to ask in the first place. It was an attitude of mind intrinsic to Marx, for example, who also recommended that we stop asking questions about first causes as a precondition for social progress, although the specific references in Marx were not published until the 1930s.[36] The prohibition on asking questions, or at least questions that do not fit a predetermined theory, became one of the hallmarks of the progressive science of politics. Dewey's methodology was designed to keep malevolent ideas out of men's minds. For someone with the intellectual standing and stature of Dewey, there was a curious lack of curiosity about what had always been regarded as the most important questions about the human condition. It is difficult to see this new attitude as resembling science if we persist in thinking of science as somehow always open to new things. But one of the consequences of Dewey's prohibition on asking certain types of questions was that it promised to make methodology in political science resemble the methodology in the natural sciences. The significance of this point can scarcely be overstated.

Dewey repeatedly affirmed his notion that science in general and human sciences in particular, such as politics, could only progress when the idea of a purposeful cosmos was abandoned. "To put the intellectual center of gravity in the objective cosmos, outside of man's own experiments and tests, and then to invite the application of individual intelligence to the determination of society, is to invite chaos."[37] In Dewey's case it would appear that his methodology reflected his secular foundation rather than the other way around. "Theory having learned what it cannot do, is made responsible for the better performance of what needs to be done, and what only a broadly equipped intelligence an undertake: the study of the conditions out of which come the obstacles and the resources of adequate life, and developing and testing the ideas that, as working hypotheses, may be used to diminish the causes of evil and to buttress and expand the sources of good."[38] The choice of good and evil reentered politics, but not a transcendent good and evil; it was a good and evil that was to be determined by social technicians who would make the rules in accordance with their purpose to give relief to the human condition; very much along the lines of a cost–benefit analysis in economics. Progressives such as Dewey typically supposed that the first question to be addressed regarding purpose is "Why is there something?" But the pre-Darwinian argument, that of Aquinas for example, began with a denial that there could be nothing. The Darwinian approach to cosmic purpose misrepresented the classical-religious tradition because they too frequently asked the wrong questions.

The progressive case for politics as a moral science for Dewey was built on the supposition that the scientific method was not only appropriate but the only viable one given the collapse of the very idea of a moral universe. "The change may relieve men from responsibility for what they cannot do, but it will promote thoughtful consideration of what they may do and the definition of responsibility for what they do amiss because of failure to think straight and carefully."[39] Knowledge in this sense means "Knowledge of the process and conditions of physical and social change through experimental science and genetic history has one result with a double name: increase of control, and increase of responsibility; increase of power to direct natural change, and increase of responsibility for its equitable direction toward fuller good."[40] Darwinian science introduces a "new logic" that "foreswears inquiry after absolute origins and absolute finalities in order to explore specific conditions that generate them."[41] Dewey is confident that this new science can explore specific conditions and generate solutions to the most fundamental social problems.

Scientific reasoning, in the human sciences as in the natural sciences, is therefore about means and not ends. How could it be about ends if there is no basis for reasoning about ends beyond the purely technical means of material and efficient cause? Dewey is quite candid about this point. It "is technical only in the sense that it provides the technique of social and moral engineering."[42] Progress remained, but it was progress on in terms of material and efficient causality; first and final causality disappeared altogether except insofar as provided by social engineers—the new type of philosophers concerned with practical things that is part of the Darwinian revolution. "The progress of biology has accustomed our minds to the notion that intelligence is not an outside power presiding supremely but statically over the desires and efforts of man, but is a method of adjustment of capacities and conditions with specific situations."[43] Adjustment to this new reality was a critical requirement for the progressive scholar. Science, at its core, meant not asking certain questions.

If political knowledge could be based on a biological understanding of human behavior alone, it should be possible, at least in theory, to expand our knowledge to the degree we could measure, with greater mathematical precision, that behavior. Afterwards, patterns or relationships could be studied scientifically and knowledge would emerge from the methodology. Scientific methodology as the new basis of authority in the social sciences would bridge the gap between theory and practice. This knowledge could, in turn, be the basis for expert administration designed for the relief of the human condition. This was the promise of Darwin in ordinary human affairs according to Dewey. "Were it not for the deep hold of the habit of seeking justification for idea values in the remote and transcendent, surely this reference to them would be despised in comparison with the demonstrations of experience that knowable energies are daily generating about us precious values."[44] The specifics of this new methodology will be taken up in Chapter IV, but its connection with Darwin needs to be noted here.

We can get a glimpse of this historicized knowledge in Dewey's 1929 Gifford Lectures, *The Quest for Certainty: A Study of the Relation between Knowledge and Action.* A systematic discussion of this work as a whole need not be undertaken here. What is of interest here is how Darwinian science shaped his understanding of methodology beyond that found in his essay on Darwin. The title "The Quest for Certainty" is significant. Dewey was not a historian who sought certainty in the study of history after the fashion of Hegel, but rather a philosopher who sought certainty in scientific method. Scientific method, rather than the state, seemed to be the march of whatever remained of the World Spirit through time and place. It seems that once the secularized world is made the end of serious study, it makes little difference what is the methodology used to pursue that end; history and science converge to serve the same function as substitutes for first and final cause.

Dewey was sensitive to the reality that the scientific method had effectively destroyed the classical understanding of purpose and with the destruction of purpose came the destruction of ordinary values. With some anguish, he wrote, "How is science to be accepted and yet the realm of values to be conserved?"[45] Values, he argued, are based on experience and experience is necessarily particular, not universal. To make values a universal experience would require a form of measurement that was itself valid across individuals and cultures. Scientific measurement pointed toward a collective, not an individual, basis for values. But the irony of scientific methodology for Dewey was its value relativism. He fully understood that different scientific methodologies could produce different pictures of reality, whatever reality might be at this point. "All materials of experience are equally real—that is, all are existential . . . To use philosophical terminology, each type of subject matter is entitled to its own characteristic categories, according to the questions it raises and the operations necessary to answer them."[46]

It was the indeterminate nature of Darwinian evolution that coupled scientific methodology and value relativism for Dewey, as well as most progressives. The values that emerged from this relativism were no less values, but they were entirely dependent on the questions the philosopher felt predisposed to ask; if questions were not asked, there were no transcendent answers to nonexistent questions. Curiously, science, it seemed, would provide knowledge that would more or less confirm our nonscientific values. The quest for certainty in Dewey boils down to a search for methods of the control of values in the public square. For Dewey, Darwin replaced the nature versus nurture argument by focusing on how we learn based on innate biological predispositions. Man was the measure and nurture was the source of values. It was a philosophy ready-made for social engineering.

Knowledge of values emerges in Dewey from the scientific study of things that can be measured. In politics, what can be measured most easily is collective behavior.[47] And collective behavior can only be understood scientifically from a secular perspective. It on such assumptions as these that ideas about secular progress have gradually crowded out religion and natural law as the foundation for values. As Dewey wrote in *A Common Faith* (1934), "Secular interests and activities have grown up outside of organized religions and are independent of their authority. This change either marks a terrible decline in everything that justly be termed religious in value, in traditional religions, or it provides the opportunity for expansion of these qualities on a new basis and with a new outlook."[48]

Science had reduced God to the god-of-the-gaps. Dewey clearly placed his faith in secular progress. But reading Dewey, one can sense a palpable unease beneath the way he faced the nihilistic foundation of his thought. Much of the subsequent development of the progressive science of politics ignored these nihilistic assumptions, or took them for granted and stopped asking foundational questions. But the problems remained and scholarship built on these foundations merely papered over what was ultimately at issue. At most, scientific discoveries in material and efficient causality revealed a more complex reality than many no doubt thought, but there is no necessary reason why more natural rights or theologically inclined scholars would have thought any of this to be unusual. What was unusual was to try to stop thinking about first and final causes as either important or interesting problems in their own right. It seems to be one of the peculiar qualities of the secular mindset.

If the outside observer detects a fundamental incoherence in Dewey's application of Darwin to morals and politics it is surely because such incoherence seems to be the inescapable conclusion. A theory that seeks to explain everything may end by explaining nothing, perhaps most especially if it seeks to explain everything by deliberately omitting to ask what may be relevant questions. It certainly ceases to resemble science in either the classical or modern definitions. Darwin suggested that natural selection was a self-regulating process. Yet the idea of social reform does not sit well with natural selection as a random process and Dewey wanted to make social reform fit the application of Darwinian ideas. In this, he seems to have been pounding the proverbial square pegs into round holes. Dewey fully understands that one cannot talk either meaningfully or for very long about politics without some discussion of good and evil entering the conversation. But where do these notions come from? Not from God, and not from a formal inquiry into the nature of good and evil in any classical sense. Good and evil for Dewey and most progressives are understood largely in material terms, which in turn make them theoretically susceptible to economic analysis and statistical measurement. Knowledge of good and evil, they thought, can be better understood as empirical knowledge that emerges from the study of human behavior. But this raises the question, how should human behavior be studied, or can it be studied meaningfully in the first place without a prior interest in the questions, for example, inherent in the natural law argument?

Knowledge emerges from experimentation and experimentations on society require a new type of intellectual who stands outside of the experiment itself. First and final causality reenter political science as choices made by a new class of what might properly be called "intellectual engineers." They are disinterested in Dewey's sense only in the sense that they are not directed by some external moral foundation for their actions, such as classical natural law or religion. Good and evil are essentially metaphors used to rationalize what we chose to do. The consequences of this line of thought did not take long to develop in the social sciences. It took the form of what was called behaviorism and its self-interpretation as "the scientific study of politics." What, if anything, does this mean?

Progressivism and Political Science

Regardless of the metaphysical barbarisms commonly committed in the name of science, no one doubts that in some sense we know more about the physical world with every passing day. Who would want to be treated today by even the best doctors of a half-century ago, much less eighteenth or nineteenth century physicians? Almost every area of modern life is affected by science and there are countless things in the natural sciences that we would not know if we relied on natural law reasoning alone. Further, for better or worse, biology seems poised to become the dominant science for the twenty-first century. Yet it is not obvious, at least on the face of it, that there has been a similar progression of knowledge about the fundamentals of the human condition since Plato or St. Augustine, for example. This would not have surprised most natural law theorists, among others. We have more information but information is not the same thing as knowledge and the mere passage of time cannot be taken as proof of any such thing. Whether the argument proceeds by a dialectical process, such as Plato, or a theological basis, such as St. Augustine, it would seem that in terms of asking the routine questions about politics, "What is the purpose of government?" and "What is justice?" are perennial questions that the progressive tradition in political science has not done a great deal to answer in a manner that avoids value relativism at its foundation. The problem is not new; advances in science may not necessarily translate into advances in morality and the disappearance of interest in first and final causes virtually ensures that scientific advances will progress without reference to morality. Questions about purpose are not incidental to methodology in political science but are integral to it.

The idea of a living constitution in Wilson, for example, never confronts the moral arguments that are always implicit in the natural law of the founders. The founders may be wrong, but it requires specific political analysis to say where, why, and how they are wrong. An argument from metaphors that merely assumes that because they wrote at an earlier point in historical time they cannot be right is not a very convincing argument. Wilson assumed what needs to be proven; apparently a common failure of any political science based on an evolutionary theory. The mere passage of time proves nothing. What Wilson's constitutional development does do, if taken seriously however, is to divert attention away from the founders' science of politics. They no longer ask the questions we want to ask and, following Dewey, they can be ignored even as we too often assume that we know all we need to know about them; they are dead, white, European males. What more do we need to know? Ignorance then presents itself as superior knowledge. Wilson at least knew what the founders had argued and rejected it; the same cannot be said of many later scholars who have accepted the Darwinian argument as articulated by Dewey. One need not read Wilson in order to intuitively understand his argument as subsequent generations of progressive scholars have demonstrated; one only need accept evolution in order to have a ready-made theory of politics.

The idolatry of science in the name of progress has not been the story of uninterrupted movement toward something better. Rather, it leaves the impression of reason interrupted. Much of the early certainty in science as the fount of all knowledge, most especially moral knowledge, has collapsed over the course of the twentieth century. There are no doubt multiple reasons for this collapse, but one of the primary reasons must be the attempt to combine scientific certainty with the value relativism always implicit in Darwinism and historicism. Science strives for certainty while the essence of the historical sense, as Auguste Comte never tired of repeating, was that everything is relative. The incompatibility of the two is more likely to result in theoretical incoherence than any advance in either. Like Freud, progressives aspired to live a life without illusions and that meant a belief in science as the foundation for such a life. But a science of politics that recognizes no transcendent purpose in politics is not a science at all; it is merely a prescription for tyranny because it does not know how or where to draw lines. Fidelity to "scientific integrity" is a thin reed for a science of politics. There is no reason, scientific or otherwise, to believe that literally everything and anything is politically possible or morally permissible as value relativism invites us to do.

Even without passing moral judgment on certain human actions that are uniquely human—prudence, folly, love, hate, and the like—it would seem that any science of the human condition would have to make some sort of room for these actions and passions. It is at this point that an irony in the progressive science of politics becomes even more obvious. It has been noted that an idea of progress means movement toward something desired. But Darwinian science implies no such thing; random selection is just random. Progress in human affairs would seem to require human agency. But random selection in Darwinian evolution seems to make human agency irrelevant. This may be because a science that explains the differentiation of species other than man is unsuited to explain what is peculiar to man. At the risk of stating the obvious, the study of politics requires the study of human beings and not the study of something else. One species of cat is pretty much like all of the others, and biology can afford to treat every cat as essentially the same; a science of politics cannot do the same because societies are not herds of cats and no two societies are ever exactly the same. Societies of cats, if that is not an oxymoron, do not have priests, presidents, and intellectuals as part of their reality.

The rationalization of life, which includes both natural law and science, is one of the driving forces of human existence, but there is nothing in human existence to suggest that anything approaching rational certainty about the nature of things is remotely possible. Such a belief is not based on reason but on a form of faith. To found a science of politics on such an assumption, even if that assumption is only aspirational, cannot help but fail to explain, much less predict, an imagined future. Further, a theory of politics premised on such a rationalization will not only fail to explain, it will, ultimately, fail to satisfy precisely because of its foundational failure. The prohibition on asking fundamental questions by methodological design will, at best, produce a science of politics that is concerned only with peripheral issues. If a religious or natural law explanation is a true or reasonable explanation, why should it not be considered and analyzed, subjected to whatever assumptions such an explanation may entail? Precluding such explanations at the outset is not very scientific. Clinging to ignorance is hardly a modern phenomenon, but explicitly embracing it in the name of progress is at least worthy of our serious attention, if only because it seems to be such an aberration in most of human thought.

A science of politics, properly understood, is not simply a series of practical and moral propositions about how things are or ought to be, although that is certainly part of it—perhaps the most conspicuous part of it. A science of politics is intended to give a reasonably accurate description of how things are. Whatever may be said of other species appropriate for the study of biology, humans have produced more varied societies, professional specializations, religions, and the like, than any other known species. Failure to recognize that the study of humans requires a science unlike that suited for, say, cats and dogs, should not be judged an advance of science but as a sort of regress.[49] Human, unlike those of other animals, are judged and described in moral terms. In this regard, only humans seem capable of acting in ways we describe as inhumane; such a word is inapplicable of application to any other species because no other species seems capable of acting according to some sort of free will that can be subject to any sort of moral reproach. Cats and dogs simply do not act immorally, whatever they may do. In this regard, Aristotle, for example, must be judged vastly superior to Darwin as a methodology for the study of politics; classical political science never fell into the trap of utopianism.

But at some point a science of politics must be prescriptive, at least implicitly, for the behavior of citizens and rulers alike. The rulers who make, execute, and judge according to law have something purposeful in mind when they act. And such purposeful behavior is seldom defined in purely biological terms. Love and hate, knowledge and ignorance, prudence and folly, duty, obligations and innumerable other qualities that are uniquely human govern the structure of any science of politics. Aristotle was correct to note that the practice of politics always involves some notion of how a particular action will affect the future; politics is purposeful and what we regard as purposeful will always reflect our foundational assumptions in this regard. Classical political science, whatever its limitations, always understood that in certain fundamental ways the future would be much like the present because the nature of the human condition always set limits to what is possible. The founders' understanding of constitutional government is one example of this and may serve as a benchmark for the differences between the founders and the progressives. The progressive science of politics, on the other hand, thought of the future as something that was not limited by any such thing as a fixed human condition. Darwin helped to reinforce this notion in their political science. Hence, there were no fixed principles of politics beyond that provided by science. Such a future may as well aspire to perfection, as Herbert Croly thought. Why not?

A thoroughly secular theory of politics, such as that of the progressives, will inevitably prescribe that citizens behave in a thoroughly secular manner; laws, customs, and policies will reflect this foundation. Biological science as Darwin defined it, evolution as random selection, applied to human society, as a whole will invariably tend toward value relativism with regard to competing social principles because there is no *a priori* basis to judge one superior to another. The basic problem is not just the idea of evolution, although that is integral to the problem, but more fundamentally the idea that a science appropriate for biology is also appropriate for a science of the human condition; Aristotle knew better.

The laws that emerge from this conception of reality will consist of an almost infinite series of those petty regulations Alexis de Tocqueville warned of that are the essence of modern secular tyranny. This sort of metaphysical atheism that is at the heart of the secular science of politics has been one of the distinguishing characteristics of twentieth century politics and we can see it reflected at the origins of the American progressive tradition. No doubt many progressives would and have denied that they embrace the nihilism always implicit in the secularized methodology of progressive political science. There is no reason to doubt their sincerity. But sincerity is not the problem; the problem is embedded in the paradigmatic quality of Darwinism that directs the search for not only the proper questions that need to be asked, but interprets the results of questions asked or ignored.

A secularized science of politics, cut off as it is from any notion of transcendent justice or any methodological means of even thinking about it, always has a problem identifying either good or evil in an intellectually coherent way. If both good and evil are outside of the scope of a political solution the attempt to treat them as if they are political in nature cannot help but distort politics. Of the two, evil is probably the more pressing concern in politics. Value relativism operates not only to make all values relative, but also to make it impossible to determine if the laws we enact have a moral foundation. A thoroughgoing secularism always runs the risk of transforming evil into something lawful and therefore acceptable. The progressive science of politics may never have intended such an outcome, but the logic of its founding assumptions has hastened such an outcome. Not because any progressives desired it, but because the language of progressivism made it difficult to recognize the sort of injustice scientific nihilism could unleash. Tyranny that promised progress did not seem like tyranny but merely "liberals in a hurry."

There is a final irony in Darwinian science as the foundation for the study of politics. From Plato onward it has always been one of the hallmarks of Western philosophy that "man has a natural desire to know." This desire to know has been one of the driving forces in Western thought. Part of that desire to know has always rested on the assumption that we live in a rational universe that is at least partly knowable through human reason. If the universe were not fundamentally rational, science would not be possible. But imbedded in the scientific methodology of progressivism is the unscientific notion that there are some things we do not want to know; it is, if we read Dewey rightly, what may with some propriety be termed "a will to ignorance" of first things. This is something altogether new in Western thought. If it were simple modesty about what sort of knowledge is possible it would not be noteworthy and would probably be a source of intellectual strength. But it is a will to ignorance combined with hubris about the nature of science that marks the modern era off from the premodern period. Whatever the defects of classical political science, and there were many, it always understood that the search for purpose in human affairs was the first order of business in a science of politics. The marriage of historicism with Darwinian science looked to progressives as the perfect marriage of philosophical theory and scientific practice. But, as we all know, not every marriage is made in Heaven; some seem to be made in Purgatory, and some others somewhere else.

Notes

1. On this distinction, I follow Gertrude Himmelfarb, *The Roads to Modernity. The British, French, and American Enlightenments* (New York: Alfred A. Knopf, 2004).
2. Karl Löwith, *Meaning in History* (Chicago: The University of Chicago Press, 1949).
3. Herbert Croly, *The Promise of American Life*, ed. Arthur M. Schlesinger, Jr. (Cambridge, MA: The Belknap Press of Harvard University Press, 1965/ Macmillan, 1909), 454.
4. John Dewey, *The Quest for Certainty: A Study in the Relation of Knowledge and Action* (New York: Minton, Balch, and Company, 1929), 26. Hereafter cited as *Certainty.*
5. Eric Voegelin, *The New Science of Politics* (Chicago: The University of Chicago Press, 1952).
6. C. Darwin to C. Lyell, Yorkshire, Oct. 25th [1859], in *The Life and Letters of Charles Darwin*, ed. Francis Darwin, vol. I (New York and London: D. Appleton and Company, n.d.), 531.
7. For the affinity of Hegelian historicism with Darwin, see Karl Löwith, *From Hegel to Nietzsche. The Revolution in Nineteenth Century Thought* (New York: Holt, Rinehart, and Winston, Inc., 1964), 217–18.
8. Woodrow Wilson, *Mere Literature and Other Essays* (Boston and New York: Houghton and Mifflin, 1896), 69.
9. Ibid., 75.
10. Woodrow Wilson, in his "Confidential Journal," December 28, 1889, in *The Papers of Woodrow Wilson*, ed. Arthur S. Link, vol. VI, 463 (Princeton, NJ: Princeton University Press, 1966–1994). Hereafter cited as Wilson, *Papers.*
11. For the context of this essay, see John M. Mulder, *Woodrow Wilson. The Years of Preparation* (Princeton, NJ: Princeton University Press, 1978), esp. 55–56.
12. See Ronald J. Pestritto, *Woodrow Wilson and the Roots of Modern Liberalism* (Lanham, MD: Rowman and Littlefield Publishers, Inc., 2005). I am especially indebted to Pestritto's work on Wilson. It is the gold standard for any interpretation of Wilson's political thought.
13. Woodrow Wilson, *Congressional Government. A Study in American Politics* (Boston and New York: Houghton Mifflin Company, 1885/New Brunswick: Transaction Publishers, 2002), 5. The preferred edition of *Congressional Government* is the fifteenth edition published in 1900 because it contains a new introduction by Wilson that offers important insights into the development of his thought. The Transaction edition is a reprint of the 1900 edition and contains a very fine introductory essay by William F. Connelly, Jr.

14. See Christopher Wolfe, "Woodrow Wilson: Interpreting the Constitution," *The Review of Politics* 41, no. 1 (January 1979): 121–42.
15. See the critique of Wilson on this point in A. Lawrence Lowell, "Cabinet Responsibility," in his *Essays on Government* (Boston, MA: Houghton, Mifflin, and Company, 1889), 20–59.
16. A full discussion of Bancroft need not be undertaken here. He is one of the unfortunately neglected figures in the development of the nineteenth century American academy. See the relevant discussion of Bancroft in Jurgen Herbst, *The German Historical School in American Scholarship. A Study in the Transfer of Culture* (Ithaca, NY: Cornell University Press, 1965).
17. Woodrow Wilson, *Constitutional Government in the United States* (New York: Columbia University Press, 1908/New Brunswick, NJ: Transaction Press, 2002), 2. Hereafter cited as *CG*.
18. Ibid., 54–55.
19. Ibid., 1.
20. Ibid., 25–26.
21. The best discussion of the role of community in Wilson's political thought is David E. Marion, "Alexander Hamilton and Woodrow Wilson on the Spirit and Form of a Responsible Republican Government," *The Review of Politics* 42, no. 3 (July 1980): 309–28.
22. *CG.*, 28.
23. Ibid., 220. For other examples of Wilson's views on the "harmonious" or "organic" community, see his review of James Bryce's "American Commonwealth," in *The Public Papers of Woodrow Wilson. College and State*, ed. Ray Stannard Baker and William E. Dodd, vol. I, 159–78 (New York: Harper and Brothers, 1925). Hereafter cited as *PPCS*.
24. For a more detailed treatment of this theme than the one found in *Constitutional Government*, see Wilson's essay "Character of Democracy in the United States," in *PPCS*, I, 104, 135–36. While the details are more developed in this essay, the basic argument is not.
25. A fine discussion of this issue can be found in Robert A. Goldwin and William A. Schambra, eds., *How Democratic Is the Constitution?* (Washington, DC: The American Enterprise Institute, 1980).
26. Marvin Kalb, *The Nixon Memo. Political Respectability, Russia, and the Press* (Chicago: The University of Chicago Press, 1994), 18–21.
27. Wilson, *CG*, 65.
28. Ibid., 65.
29. David Stove, *Darwinian Fairytales. Selfish Genes, Errors of Heredity, and Other Fables of Evolution*. Introduction by Roger Kimball (New York: Encounter Books, 1995). Stove takes no prisoners in this lively discussion of Darwin.
30. Jerome E. Popp, *Evolution's First Philosopher. Dewey and the Continuity of Nature*. (Albany, NY: State University of New York Press, 2007).
31. John Dewey, *The Influence of Darwin on Philosophy. And Other Essays in Contemporary Thought* (New York: Henry Holt and Company, 1910), 8–9. Hereafter cited as *Darwin*.
32. Ibid., 285.

33. John Dewey, *Reconstruction in Philosophy*. Enlarged Edition with a New Forty Page Introduction by the Author (Boston, MA: Beacon Press, 1948/1920), 53–76.
34. *Darwin*, 19.
35. Charles Darwin, *On the Origin of the Species*, ed. Jim Endersby (Cambridge: Cambridge University Press, 2009), 151. Hereafter cited as *Species*.
36. Karl Marx, *Economic and Philosophic Manuscripts of 1844*. Edited, with an Introduction, by Dirk J. Struik. Translated by Martin Milligan (New York: International Publishers, 1964), 142–46.
37. *Darwin*, p. 59.
38. Ibid., 68–69.
39. Ibid., 71.
40. Ibid., 73.
41. Ibid., 13.
42. Reconstruction, 172–73.
43. *Darwin*, 68.
44. Ibid., 16.
45. *Certainty*, 41.
46. Ibid., 216.
47. See Harold N. Lee, "Dewey and the Behavioral Theory of Meaning," in *Dewey and His Influence. Essays in Honor of George Estes Barton*, ed. Robert C. Whittemore. Tulane Studies in Philosophy, vol. XXII (New Orleans, LA: Tulane University, 1973), 51–62.
48. John Dewey, *A Common Faith* (New Haven, CT: Yale University Press, 1934), 83.
49. I cannot improve on Stove's comments in this regard. Stove, *op. cit.*

II

Natural Law and Historical Authority in the Progressive Project

The progressive critique of natural law in all of its facets had two distinct points of reference. The first was to found a new science of politics on the basis of the emerging science of evolution after the pattern of Darwin. This has been discussed in Chapter I. The second was to ground the critique of natural law in the study of history. These two sides of the same coin fit together seamlessly but can be separated for analytic purposes. Historicism was premised on the idea that everything is relative—that is, everything is a product of time, place, and circumstance. This was not different than Darwin in terms of the idea of progress but did rest on a different foundation of reasoning. In this sense, Darwin was the intellectual fertilizer for much of modern historicism. The distinguished historian Henry Adams may be cited as a case in point of the new mood in historical writing.

Henry Adams in the *Annual Report of the American Historical Association for 1894*, wrote, "Those of us who have had occasion to keep abreast of the rapid progress which has been made in history during the last fifty years must be convinced that the same rate of progress during another half century would necessarily raise history to the rank of a science . . . We cannot help asking ourselves what would happen if some new Darwin were to demonstrate the law or laws of historical evolution."[1] The aspiration to make history a science, as Adams hoped, may not have made the attraction of Darwin inevitable, but it certainly facilitated the transition of Darwin from a theory of biology to a methodology of how to study history.

The German historical tradition, if it did not make history a science, at least gave historians reason to believe that there were laws of history. German historicism thus led progressives to an unqualified relativism that further made any natural law political science problematic. Properly understood, history is the record of events; one may philosophize about the events, but the recording of events in some sort of chronological order is, for the most part, a matter of getting the facts more or less accurate. Historicism, however, purports to stand outside of the chronology of history and make that chronology a subject of rational philosophical knowledge.[2] Historicism purports to provide a methodology that would replace *The Federalist*, for example; something that could confront the historical record of the founders' political science head-on rather than indirectly as Darwinian science did.

The fundamental premise of natural law political science was the notion that mankind lives in a moral universe that is at least partly knowable through reason; this moral universe is integral to what we mean by the human condition. The natural order of things was roughly equivalent to the Divine order of things. This knowledge reveals rights in the form of self-evident truths, but such knowledge also presupposes duties and obligations, even if they are not so self-evident. Natural law in the American context was the preserve of the founders and any references to natural law as the foundation for reasoning about a science of politics could not help but take the founders seriously. It followed that no alternative to the founders could expect to be successful until natural law was replaced as a foundation for political science. Science was one line of attack, but science merged with historical analysis and the two proceeded in tandem. Two examples of the new historicism illustrate the mood at the time.

A professor Fred Taylor of the University of Michigan nicely stated the progressive attitude toward natural law in 1891. He wrote in the *Annals of the American Academy of Political and Social Science,* "A somewhat noteworthy feature of recent social philosophy is the apparently quite general discarding of the time-honored doctrine of natural right or natural law. To say that this theory no longer has any adherents would doubtless be too strong . . . But whether few or many, most of them seemingly are in that particularly modest mood which becomes the professors of a creed that is daily characterized as a great superstition, an exploded fallacy, a chimera of abstract ethics." He went on to assert that while he does not question the motives of adherents, reformers have uniformly accepted the notion that this idea is "a senseless obstacle to social progress."[3] Taylor's general premise was a commonplace within the progressive intellectual community.[4]

Both the tone and the substance of the progressive critique of natural law for historians were set early in such influential works as W. W. Willoughby's *The Nature of the State* (1896). The nature of the state in Willoughby's account was determined by its history and not by any founding ideas. The implications for historical analysis could not be more obvious. In it he wrote, ". . . the continuance of the use of the term (natural law) in political and legal science is improper in any sense, and, if retained, sure to introduce confusion of thought."[5] The historical record, properly understood, should eliminate any confusion of thought. And the first clarification of progressive historical analysis uniformly rejected the notion of a morally purposeful universe. The study of history did not reveal any notion that anything such as natural law enjoyed the sort of universal acknowledgement progressives assumed was a prerequisite for the truth of the idea. Further, the tendency of progressives to confuse natural law reasoning with religion or theological reasoning further obfuscated a serious analysis of American history on its own terms. How exceptional is the American experience? Does it matter?

American Exceptionalism and the Historicist Critique of Natural Law

The progressive abandonment of natural law was similar to Voltaire's remark that one did not have to be a mathematician to be a Newtonian. Progressives did not have to understand natural law, or religion for that matter, in order to reject either or both. But one could more easily abandon pre-Newtonian physics and remain a scientist than one could abandon natural law and still interpret American history. Natural law presented progressives with an obviously difficult challenge whenever they entered the public square. Natural law as expressed in the Declaration of Independence was not only the specific foundation upon which the Constitution was built, but its opening lines on self-evident truths had been memorized by every schoolchild; natural law was part of the national history.

Natural law presupposes cosmic purpose, but natural law *per se* reflects more of an intermediary purpose—something between cosmic and individual purpose. Natural law presupposes human cognition of a moral order and requires human participation before that order can be brought to fruition. Natural law for the founders was not a religious pronouncement and there is scant evidence that anyone in the founding generation thought it was. Esoteric academic arguments that a natural law republic is tantamount to a theocracy are not only antihistorical with regard to the founding but would have a difficult time exorcising natural law from the public mind. Granted the progressive exorcising of natural law from public consciousness would mean something, but what might it mean? Basically, it meant that the organization of society was responsible for social injustices; this meant that the solution to the problem of injustice was to change society. This attitude helped to cause a veritable tsunami in American political thought. It was a direct challenge to both the religious character of American society and the natural law character of regime principles.

The Enlightenment project had already tended to separate religious reasoning from moral reasoning and the progressives reflected this separation, as did the founders though to a lesser degree. But the intense secularism of the progressive tradition carried baggage that most of the founders, much less most citizens, would not recognize. Progressives tended to be followers of Rousseau in this regard though there is scant evidence that very many progressives read Rousseau seriously. We may say they were often instinctive students of Rousseau in much the same way Voltaire was a student of Newton; the source of our misfortunes according to Rousseau is not in ourselves, but in society.

The classical tradition argued that moral change began with the individual; the progressive tradition argued that moral change began with institutional change. The classical tradition argued that the state was man writ large, whereas the progressive tradition argued that man was the state writ small. The implicit assumption in the progressive critique of natural law was that progressive intellectuals had no further need of individual moral improvement since scientific reason had replaced moral reason as the basis for a just polity. In this way, progressivism aimed to change the moral compass of American politics away from good and evil as an individual struggle in the soul of every person and toward a struggle over institutional arrangements that are always external to the individual. It thus tended toward a Manichean view of the world by its very nature. This view had consequences that might have been anticipated had progressives been more self-reflective. The Manichean argument was certainly not new.

The elimination of natural law from public awareness would require a citizenry as secularized and as religiously agnostic as most progressive intellectuals. In essence, citizens would have to acquire the intellectual affectations and attitudes of most college professors.

And, to paraphrase James Madison, if every American citizen were a typical professor, every American political assembly would, at best, resemble the mob of intellectuals that makes up a typical meeting of any academic association. And by confusing natural law with religion it is not surprising that a critique of natural law increasingly became a critique of religion as well.

Absent natural law as a foundation for any political argument in the American regime, progressivism always run the risk of opening up a rift between political theory and practice as the founders designed it. The most obvious example to illustrate this point is the entire range of debates in the American regime over slavery and civil rights. It seems clear at the outset that these quarrels are either unintelligible or seriously distorted outside of the natural rights proposition in the Declaration. The progressive change in a foundational understanding of a subject so central to American political history does irreparable violence to the truth of the historical record.

To begin with, it is not obvious on the face of it that science alone can pass moral judgment on slavery or civil rights, broadly defined. To the degree that modern science has deliberately excluded first and final cause as beyond the scope of science properly understood and the problem of slavery is inescapably tied to the natural rights arguments in the Declaration, it is unlikely to be the foundation for a political science capable of probing very deeply into history. Historicism tended to make slavery a product of material forces, such as economics. Excluding natural rights as well as religion from an inquiry into American politics cannot help but make the Civil War and the Civil Rights Movement unintelligible. The historical record seems quite clear. The pre-Civil War arguments against slavery were almost uniformly cast in the language of natural law and religion, with the Declaration and the Bible as the most authoritative references.[6] The importance of these foundational arguments cannot be stressed too much.

We can see the importance of foundational agreement if we pause for a moment to think about the quarrel between Federalist and Anti-Federalist over the ratification of the Constitution; they both agreed with the purpose of government set forth in the Declaration but disagreed over how those purposes should be constitutionally shaped. We can follow these ratification debates without an extensive inquiry into their respective foundational assumptions in most cases because the two sides are in fundamental agreement. This does not make the differences unimportant, but it does affect the level of analysis.[7]

The same cannot be said of the quarrel between the founders, broadly speaking, and the progressives. What the progressives wanted was a new foundation for a science of democratic politics; one that they thought would place the regime on a more scientific, historically accurate, and therefore more secure footing.[8] Slavery and civil rights is an obvious case in point. The quarrel between the progressives and the founders is of a different order altogether than the quarrel between Federalist and Anti-Federalist, even when the issue seems practical, such as the nature of executive power in Wilson. But it is perhaps most clear in arguments over American exceptionalism. Does exceptionalism mean moral superiority?

The term "American exceptionalism" is not one that the founders used, nor is it a term used by early progressives. The founders thought republican political science was politically superior to the alternatives and republican politics required the cultivation of moral virtues, but they never denied that other forms of government were somehow necessarily lacking those virtues. American exceptionalism is more commonly associated with the twentieth century, perhaps in part as a consequence of the progressive critique. It is admittedly an ambiguous term. If exceptionalism only means that the United States is unique, then it must also be said that every regime is unique. If it means that most Americans think they are unique, that may also be a common denominator for most citizens in every regime and may have the added virtue of being true. If it means that the United States is divinely inspired, it may or may not be true, but, short of Divine intervention, it will be impossible to prove.[9] But if it simply means that the United States is founded on principles of natural law and therefore stands under some sort of judgment by our Creator, then the progressive critique of whatever is meant by American Exceptionalism should properly be understood as a critique of natural law that is unrelated to American history. The logical inference from the progressive rejection of natural law seems to mean that while the founders may have cited natural law as a foundation for the purpose of government, they were clearly wrong in some sense. Historical inquiry should demonstrate where they went wrong. Where to begin?

In the case of American politics, natural law in all of its facets is inescapably an inquiry into the nature of a regime explicitly founded on natural law. This fact is in itself unique, though perhaps not the best measure of exceptionalism. The founders were divided among themselves as to the exact nature of what might be meant by American exceptionalism. Jefferson's "First Inaugural Address," for example, saw the uniqueness of the American regime in terms of geography and republican principles.[10] Tocqueville, who is generally regarded as among the most insightful in this regard, saw the "social state" of Americans as the key to its exceptional status among regimes, both ancient and modern; the absence of a hereditary aristocracy with all that implied. Natural law did not figure in Tocqueville's analysis. American exceptionalism for Tocqueville consisted of the reconciliation of freedom with democracy, the reconciliation of religion with democracy, and the absence of an intellectual class that dominated political discourse. Neither Jefferson nor Tocqueville thought of exceptionalism as implying moral superiority and to the extent that some American politicians have drawn precisely that inference we should not be surprised if foreigners get a bit tired of hearing such bombastic pronouncements.

By contrast, progressives generally saw freedom and democracy in opposition, religion as the enemy of a more scientific and more secular democracy, and the dominance of progressive intellectuals in managing the affairs of the state as the necessary final step in the evolution of the state. Progressives saw themselves as a new aristocracy of talent derived from a scientific education. And, contra Tocqueville, they made natural law the focus of their analysis of the founders. They were not criticizing the more than occasional bombast but rather the philosophical basis of natural law. Their criticism of natural law therefore was not confined to rhetorical misuse, but rather to the philosophy itself. Natural law was self-deception, not a rhetorical misuse. The progressive critique of natural law was a philosophic critique and any defense of natural law, in the founders' sense, must also be a philosophic defense. There is no need to consider any more bombastic examples in rhetoric.

Exceptionalism as a foundational argument, as it applies to the affairs of nations, is less about what they are in some respects than what they achieve or aspire to achieve, and this is always a matter of interpretation; we always need some Archimedean point from which we may set and move our interpretative lever. Exceptionalism defined in terms of natural law may be measured by how much or to what degree the nation orders its political purpose in accordance with natural law, properly understood. In this sense, natural law truth is as much aspirational as anything else. If natural law is a truthful way to think about human affairs, we may say that all regimes, ancient as well as modern, exist under its judgment, whether or not they acknowledge it or not. The quarrel over American exceptionalism, however, is rooted in an explicit acknowledgement of the force of that purposeful judgment in shaping the nature of the regime and regime politics.

So the truth or untruth of American exceptionalism is one of the persistent themes in American history. Is the United States an exceptional regime or not? If so, how? And what might be the basis for any such judgment? We might start with a hypothetical query; if the United States were to be destroyed tomorrow by some cataclysmic event that somehow left the rest of the world untouched, would the founding principles of the American republic and its subsequent development still remain a major subject of inquiry for a science of politics? Would those principles disappear, irrelevant and unlamented, or could a reasonable person expect them to be resurrected at some point and made a subject of serious inquiry? Would anyone else want to organize a polity in accordance with such principles? Any such inquiry cannot avoid the problem posed by natural law and the Declaration. Regardless of whether it is metaphysically true or false, the persistence of the natural law argument throughout history and its iteration across time, place, and circumstance point toward a never-ending discussion.

John Dewey does not have the final word here. Actually, when specifically discussing natural law, his own methodology makes him relatively uninteresting.

In classical terms, the Declaration of Independence is well understood to be the first cause of the American political order. It states in natural law language the purpose of government in general and American government in particular. Its place as the first cause also inescapably links it to the final cause of how we judge the success of the American polity in every age. It links the past with the present as if by a moral umbilical cord that we break at our peril. It is the sole source of a creed for Americans that is intended to unite ethnic, religious, and social diversity into a single people united by allegiance to an idea and not to the ethnic, religious, or cultural unity as is true of most other nations. The Declaration, especially when it is combined with the Constitution, further links political theory and practice together in a way that is seldom found in any other example of modern government.

At the academic level, progressives have split into several major schools, and perhaps countless minor schools, on how to fit the Declaration into the founding. Despite surface differences, what they all share is a historicist point of reference. One school of progressive thought saw the Declaration as a document that embodied at least a democratic ethos that was thwarted by a reactionary movement that culminated in the drafting of the Constitution. This first school tended to see the Declaration as an early example of progress, after a fashion, in opposition to the reactionary forces that found their voice in *The Federalist.* With allowances for individual variations, this was perhaps the most common early public face of progressive interpretation. This interpretation produced numerous historical narratives that described how early democracy struggled with undemocratic forces in drafting a government, and how the undemocratic forces ultimately won. The primary aim of historical analysis in this tradition was to show how time, place, and circumstance shaped the Declaration rather than a more straightforward question of whether it was true or not, much less an inquiry into whether any of the participants were even concerned with the truthfulness of the document.

A second school of the progressive argument that took root in the second half of the twentieth century faulted the founders for not abolishing slavery, granting women suffrage, and generally oppressing minorities. The founders stood accused of gross hypocrisy and the Declaration, followed by the plain-as-the nose-on-your-face histor-ical record, was the sum of the prosecution's case. It followed that if slavery could be either defended or, perhaps worse, ignored by the natural law tradition, then the natural law foundation of the regime was morally and rationally suspect at the outset. This is an argument not to be taken lightly. But it does require understanding that natural law is a foundation for subsequent political reasoning and not the final resting place for such reasoning. There is a sense in which natural law reasoning always presupposes a rift between theory and practice and thereby requires that we keep distinct the differences between founda-tional and prudential arguments. Natural law arguments are always, by their very nature, to some degree, incomplete. Prudence is one of the reasons why it is incomplete; no one really wants to live in a perfectly just regime, except perhaps a just regime in speech. If Plato's *Republic* were politically possible, who would want to live there?

A third school of progressive thought found the idea of natural law to be simply absurd on the face of it. Natural law political science was contrary to scientific political science that had the virtue of being verifi-able through historical analysis. For this school of thought, natural law might be described as the moral equivalent of an appendix; a useless something that could be safely removed without injury to the patient. Modern natural science, most especially through Newton and Darwin, each in their own way, had destroyed, or at minimum had weakened, any notion of a morally transcendent purpose that could be a rational basis for a science of politics. A more scientific basis for political science would simply render the Declaration as obsolete, in much the same way that modern chemistry made ancient alchemy obsolete. This was the argument of the behaviorists, such as Charles Merriam and also of progressive scholars as diverse as Woodrow Wilson, W. W. Willoughby, and Carl Becker.

It is worth pausing to briefly consider Charles Beard on how historicism helped to undermine natural law. Beard reduced politics to economics in his *An Economic Interpretation of the Constitution of the United States* (1913). In it he questioned the motives of the authors of the Constitution and challenged the political philosophy that informed it as undemocratic. But what is most important here is the scientific foundation for economics that exposes both the hypocrisy and the ignorance of the founders regarding their own motives. Science for Beard seems to have meant the priority of materialism over transcendent purpose. As he read the scientific revolution, science had left historical analysis dangling over a nihilistic void, but he embraced the implicit nihilism rather than reject it. He was skeptical of the notion that there were laws of history in the same sense that there were laws of biological evolution. History was full of sound and fury, signifying what? More sound and fury?

Beard did not aspire to make history a science in the sense that seems to have inspired Adams. He wrote, "The serious application of biology . . . to current human affairs . . . (is) a sign of intellectual weakness."[11] The effect of this reality released the present generation from the absurdities of the first generation, but if science was liberating it was also fraught with hazards. It meant that the future of the Republic is not bound to follow predetermined laws, such as the Constitution presupposed. Rational materialism did not require the study of first or final cause in any classical sense. And since economic materialism was the basis for all politics everywhere, American exceptionalism was, at bottom, a chimera. Historicism in Beard's account at least flirted with nihilism. Can natural law and American exceptionalism be rescued from this apparent abyss?

Further Confrontations with American Exceptionalism

The first problem with the idea of American exceptionalism is that there is not a single definition of "exceptionalism." Nor is there any widespread agreement, however it is defined, on whether American exceptionalism is good, bad, or meaningless. Has it been a force for good in the world or a source of American hubris, or both simultaneously? In the historical record it has meant different things at different times and for different people. The most that one can probably say with some degree of confidence is that sooner or later the use of the term always refers back to the Declaration of Independence. This is as it should be. The Declaration linked freedom with justice as the proper end of government that created a tension that has, at different times, found these two principles at odds with each other. The Declaration thus appears to be the foundational principle at issue for any claims on behalf of either a defense or a criticism. But just as "exceptionalism" is a slippery term, so too is how the idea of exceptionalism shapes the progressive critique of the Declaration. The idea of American exceptionalism, whenever it is defined in terms of natural law, it most emphatically is not bound up with the divinization of the state as it was for Hegelian historicism. The divinization of the state is more commonly bound up with the progressive argument that the state is the source of the totality of our rights, duties, and even our moral well-being as citizens. It is one of the ironies of the assault on natural law that the divinization of the state has been primarily the work of secular intellectuals.

Paraphrasing Leo Strauss in this regard, it is always and everywhere appropriate to begin a discussion of any claims of American exceptionalism with a quote from the Declaration of Independence. It is perhaps the best known and most oft cited line in American political culture; "We hold these Truths to be self-evident, that all Men are created equal, that they are endowed by their Creator with certain unalienable Rights, that among these are Life, Liberty, and the Pursuit of Happiness . . ." It is the natural law foundation of the regime as ordinary Americans understand the term and as progressives have critiqued. At the same time the nature of the progressive critique suggests that the natural law argument expounded in the Declaration has more in common with the classical tradition than the founders may have thought. The founders' clearly thought they had broken with the classical tradition whereas the progressives thought they had not. There is some merit to both arguments, but the Declaration may represent less of a break than does the Constitution. There is a truth in the aphorism that "the founders built better than they knew." It may be observed that one of the functions of natural law in any context, but most especially in the American context, is that it serves to screen out political principles that are contrary to regime principles. At least those principles contrary to natural law rightly understood. To the extent that natural law ceases to exercise a hold on the American political imagination it is not surprising that the social order implicit in the Constitution seems irrational or incoherent.

As a particular American expression of natural law, the passage above needs to be compared and contrasted with earlier expressions. The most often cited statement on classical natural law probably belongs to Cicero in the first century B.C. Cicero did originate the natural law argument, but he did give it a particularly elegant expression. It also deserves to be quoted in full; "True law is right reason in agreement with nature; it is of universal application, unchanging and everlasting; it summons to duty by its commands, and averts from wrongdoing by its prohibitions. And it does not lay its commands or prohibitions on good men in vain, though neither have any effect on the wicked. It is a sin to try to alter this law, nor is it allowable to attempt to repeal any part of it, and it is impossible to abolish it entirely. We cannot be freed from its obligations by senate or people, and we need not look outside ourselves for an expounder or interpreter of it. And there will not be different laws at Rome and at Athens, or different laws now and in the future, but one eternal and unchanging law will be valid for all nations and all times, and there will be one master and ruler, that is, God, over us all, for he is the author of this law, its promulgator, and its enforcing judge. Whoever is disobedient is fleeing from himself and denying his human nature, and by reason of this fact he will suffer the worst penalties, even if he escapes what is commonly considered punishment . . ." Cicero is more explicitly an appeal to conscience perhaps than is the case with the Declaration, but the latter is no less faithfully an appeal to conscience merely because it is also a propositional statement of principle.[12] If Cicero is correct, and I think he is, it may be said that natural law does not require consent to be true, but it does require consent in order to effectively order moral behavior in the polity. In this formulation, moral consent is as much a matter of prudence as right intention.

The Declaration of Independence may be the first cause of the American regime, but it does not give any direct indication of what *form* of government would best support that purpose; how power should be organized, but merely the just use of power. It simply says that "whenever any Form of Government becomes destructive of these Ends, it is the Right of the People to alter or to abolish it, and to institute new Government, laying its Foundation on such Principles and organizing its Powers in such Form, as to them shall seem most likely to effect their Safety and Happiness." There is nothing in the Declaration itself that would necessarily preclude the founding of either a monarchial or aristocratic government if either of those forms could support the proper purpose of government. It is appropriate to observe here that natural law does not necessarily require any particular form of government. Yet Jefferson uses the term "form" twice in this sentence. Why is form important? What did he mean by it? And, from the progressive perspective, why did progressives ignore any discussion of government as a form? Progressives were not, after all, oblivious to the link between purpose and form.

In classical political science the idea of form is a theoretical principle that helps us to organize how we think about particular governments. Form tends to link different eras together in a common inquiry that makes it possible to learn from the past and not merely ignore it or scold its inadequacies. The political science of Aristotle had recognized three basic forms of just government, most commonly defined as monarchy, the rule of the one, aristocracy, the rule of the few best, and democracy as the rule of the many. This basic model prevailed through the eighteenth century. Justice in each form was purposeful action defined as rule for the common good. Equally as important for a classical science of politics was the reality that each of these just forms also had a corrupted or unjust form. Terminology was not always fully consistent across the centuries, but conceptually the unjust forms were tyranny by the one, oligarchy by the few, and democratic tyranny by the many. Any form of government was subject to corruption and injustice. Democratic tyranny, for example, was not to be corrected by making it more democratic but by making it more just, which might mean making it less democratic in some way. Natural law might suggest limits on the exercise of power, but, as Madison thought, moral persuasion would probably be least effective when it was most needed. Institutional arrangements, primarily the separation of powers that took advantage of the proliferation of factions in a republican form of free government, were intended to give morality a boost when it was needed most; what the founding generation referred to as "self-interest rightly understood."

In this context, the long list of grievances listed in the Declaration was designed to make certain, in case anyone might have missed it, that everyone knew the colonists thought the British monarchy to be a tyranny. What is important in this context is not necessarily the historical truth of the dispute between the colonists and the Crown, but the philosophical truths in the Declaration as an autonomous argument in its own right. The Declaration is an appeal to moral conscience that is not necessarily tied to either history or a legal dispute over the rightful powers of monarchial government. The founders' catalog of monarchial abuse is something akin to a legal brief in support of an overarching principle. In this sense, it is a political argument within the classical tradition even as it advances a prudential form of popular government that classical political science more typically rejected.

We may stipulate for present purposes that George III as a monarch was not a tyrant in any classical sense of the term and still recognize the truth of the philosophy contained in the Declaration. But this only raises the question in this context, "What is the best form of government?" Any form of government may be described as the material cause of the regime, but the best form for the founders was defensible only in terms defined by natural law. Each just form had its virtues and might be recommended to the degree it would support the natural rights purpose of government. If the British Crown could be said to protect the natural rights described in the Declaration, the British Crown would have to be placed in the category of a just government and a revolution against a just form would be difficult to defend. The practical question for the founders turned on which form would *best* protect the fundamental purpose of government in the light of natural law. It was on the best form of government built on natural law that the founders broke most decisively with the classical tradition. It is worthwhile to note here that any discussion of "the best form of government" is conspicuous by its absence in progressive thought. Progressives could imagine only one form—democracy.

The classical tradition most often favored monarchy for a number of reasons: most conspicuously because the classical tradition generally made knowledge of justice the prerequisite for a just regime. In strictly prudential terms, it was easier to educate one person to such knowledge than the many. All of this tended to make a popular form of government least likely to establish justice. But the founders broke with this when they made freedom the essential requirement for justice. Justice was more narrowly circumscribed for the founders than it was for Plato or Aristotle. A regime based on freedom required a different type of citizen than one based on classical justice. And more to the point, it required a form of government that was not as clearly understood by the ancients as by the American founders. But this conspicuous break by the founders with the classical forms of just government did not necessarily mean a break with the classical understanding of natural law.

Unlike the classification of regimes followed by Aristotle, the founders' collapsed democratic and republican forms into a generic type they called "popular government." The quarrel among various factions at the time was whether the new regime would be more or less democratic or more or less republican. A popular form was the only form that was seriously debated. *The Federalist* (1788), for example, clearly treats democratic and republican government as two distinct types of popular government, each with equally distinctive virtues and vices that makes a comparison possible in the first place. The eighteenth century vocabulary of political discourse did not always distinguish in historical fact what was a "democratic" and what was a "republican" regime and the terms were often used interchangeably. But they were generally quite clear about certain principles that separated them. Most importantly, the form of a democracy meant direct participation in a limited territory and the form of a republic meant representation over an extended territory. And freedom as an essential component of a just regime further required a limited government with enumerated powers.

Few scholars have ever tried to argue that the natural law of the Declaration is in all respects the same as the natural law of Cicero or St. Thomas Aquinas, for example. It is not precisely the same but neither is it is obvious that it represents the sort of radical break that some have argued. St. Augustine, for example, noted in his *Confessions,* that reading Cicero, though not his famous formulation of natural law, was the first step in his conversion to Christianity.[13] The more fundamental question is how much of a break with classical natural law, if any, does the Declaration represent? There are differences to be sure, but are the differences mutually exclusive? The natural law tradition does not have a single starting point or a single philosopher who has given it a final definition. It is not infinitely elastic, but neither does it rest on a single expression. Indeed, it is less of a definition in this regard than an appeal to moral reasoning grounded in a moral order than transcends the merely temporal.

The relevant issue here, for example, is to ask whether justice alone perfects every political order as it did in classical political science. Plato certainly thought it did and Plato may be the first recorded proponent of classical natural law. Or is justice complimented by life, liberty, and the pursuit of happiness as a vital and perhaps necessary element in justice? Does the Declaration represent a radical change or merely a corollary that compliments the classical tradition? I think it is more of the latter. If not, the rest of this chapter may be less persuasive than I hope.

The points are critical because much of the debate over whether the founders' notion of natural law constitutes a difference in degree or a difference in kind with the classical formulation. Some students on this point have argued that the difference is part of the quarrel between ancients and moderns; Cicero in this case representing the classical tradition and the Declaration the modern. They tend to see the difference as an unbridgeable chasm. The reason this gulf may seem so large is because classical natural law, properly understood, is not simply a science of politics in the narrow sense that term is commonly used; is also, and perhaps primarily, an appeal to moral conscience. The natural law of Hobbes and Locke, as primary examples of modern natural law, are a stand-alone science or politics; whatever their respective merits, neither depends on an appeal to moral conscience as part of their foundation. Both appeals to self-interest and the qualification of an appeal to self-interest "rightly understood" does not obviously change this interpretation. Charles Beard is quite at home with Hobbes and Locke. Neither Hobbes nor Locke ground their appeal to rights in a moral order that transcends the purely temporal. Certainly not a moral order presided over by what the Declaration referred to as Divine Providence.

The quarrel over the break stems from a recognition that the state of nature arguments of Hobbes and Locke produced a new form of natural rights arguments that unmistakably broke with Cicero and St. Thomas. Nature for Hobbes and Locke was at least amoral; "solitary, poor, nasty, brutish, and short" according to Hobbes and which Locke euphemistically referred to as "inconvenient." If the Declaration were simply a document based on Hobbes or Locke there would be no quarrel over this interpretation. Some scholars who have followed Leo Strauss on this point, for example, have tended to see the American founding as the triumph of John Locke.[14] This is perhaps a more plausible line of argument if first we read the meaning of the Declaration as confined to the document alone and second as the singular product of the genius of Thomas Jefferson.[15] Both points need to be questioned.

It is worth calling attention to the fact that Jefferson was not somehow alone among the founders in basing his political science on a foundation of natural law. Alexander Hamilton, one of the founders not commonly associated with Jefferson, agreed with the proposition that

54

natural law was the foundation of a just society and such a foundation was perfectly compatible with religious sentiments. One of his earliest writings, *The Farmer Refuted* (1775), was quite explicit: "This is what is called the law of nature, 'which being coeval with mankind, and dictated by God himself . . . is binding all over the globe, in all countries and at all times . . .' (Blackstone) Upon this law, depend the natural rights of mankind, the supreme being gave existence to man, together with the means of preserving and beatifying that existence. He endowed him with rational faculties, by the help of which, to discern and pursue such things with his duty and interest, and invest him with an inviolable right to personal liberty, and personal safety."[16] Hamilton penned these words before Jefferson penned his immortal lines in the Declaration. Do these two who are among the giants of the founding generation contradict each other? I think not. But they do reflect some tension between natural law and religion.

The Declaration of Independence as an Appeal to Conscience and as a Moral Proposition

We may stipulate at the outset that different students of American politics will see different implications in both the founders and their progressive critics than either saw at the time. This does not mean that one interpretation is as good as another. On the contrary, it simply means that particular ideas do not always work out the way their authors intended. We are all steeped in what Thomas Kuhn has taught about the paradigmatic quality of ideas; how they help to interpret the past and point toward a future that is always implicit in the original idea. We know that ideas have consequences, both intended and unintended. And we may reasonably believe that good ideas will usually turn out to better than bad ideas regardless of intention. Intention matters but we always understand that ideas, especially what we might call the "big ideas" always have a certain autonomy that is independent of their original intention; neither the founders nor the progressives are the sole interpreters of even their own work.[17]

It is also true that political ideas are never wholly dependent on the personal qualities of the writers who express them. The big ideas in particular take on a life of their own however much they always refer back to their particular origins. A case in point is the problem of slavery in both founding debates and for subsequent generations. It illustrates perhaps better than any other issue in American history the power of ideas to shape how very practical politics are dependent on certain foundational ideas. It is also true that no analysis of the Declaration as a historical document, whether that analysis focuses on Jefferson, historical context, sociological influences, psychological motivations, or the like, that does not ask whether it is true or not will ever quite get to the heart of the issue.[18]

Among the prominent founders it is certainly true that Jefferson was the closest to Locke in philosophical disposition. We also know that John Adams more or less drafted Jefferson to compose the Declaration because he rightly regarded Jefferson as the most gifted stylist of his time. And we further know that Jefferson referred to the language of the Declaration merely as an expression of what he called "the American mind." He was probably overly modest on this score. But this is not the end of the matter. There are at least two often overlooked elements to the natural law argument in the Declaration that are essential to a proper understanding of both the natural law as well as the progressive critique.

First of all, it is to be observed that while Jefferson must be regarded as the first author of the Declaration he is not the sole author and any reflections on what the document means cannot begin and end with Jefferson alone. Two important examples at its promulgation stand out. Whatever Jefferson may have meant by the statement "all Men are endowed by their Creator with certain unalienable Rights," his countrymen had little difficulty incorporating that phrase into a culture that was religious. It is also a truism that Americans were a people formed primarily by Protestant Christianity and whatever Jefferson may have meant did not appear on the surface to be incompatible with the dominant religious tradition. No one has seriously argued that Jefferson's "Creator" is the God of Abraham, Isaac, and Jacob. But that is scarcely the end of the argument. If, for example, citizens had viewed the Declaration as incompatible with their religious traditions it is highly unlikely that they would ever have embraced it with any enthusiasm. Most citizens had no trouble accepting the idea that natural law was equivalent to Divine law.

This popular religious connotation is reinforced in concluding phrase of the Declaration that invokes "a firm Reliance on the Protection of divine Providence" for the success of this noble experiment. This was a line inserted by Congress and is not what Jefferson specifically intended, nor in all likelihood did it accurately capture his thoughts on the subject. No cat is being released from any bag when we say that Jefferson was not an orthodox Christian by even the most latitudinarian definition of Christianity. The phrase "divine Providence" was inserted by Congress because it also captured the American mind, perhaps better than Jefferson did by leaving it out. Supreme Court Justice Joseph Story had no difficulty in 1833 saying that a wholly secular reading of the Constitution on this point was a reading with no basis in historical fact.[19] Whatever Jefferson intended, the Declaration cannot be fully appreciated or understood apart from the way it has been read by Americans. But in either case, both Jefferson and most Americans have understood this to be an appeal to moral conscience that is grounded in something more than the temporal world.

Secondly, our collective national experience with the natural law principles is not primarily confined to abstract theory, however elegantly such a theory may be stated by a genius such as Jefferson. Most of the time most citizens see natural law in operation through the imperfect political institutions that follow from the founding principles; the branches of government, the rule of law, and the political practices that follow logically and reasonably from the Constitution even without specific reference to a natural law. The form of republican government found in the Constitution is a break with the classical tradition but it does not necessarily follow that either the natural law foundations of the regime or citizen perceptions of natural law are thereby denied. It may be that the form of government represents natural law in a different manner than it would have been reflected in classical forms.

Ironically, we can see the continuity of the natural law tradition more clearly within the Constitution where their republican principles did mark a decisive break with the classical tradition expressed in terms of forms of government. The great questions of political principle in American politics have typically been framed as problems calling for a just solution within a natural law tradition. Slavery is perhaps the most obvious. Slavery is inescapably a practical problem of statesmanship at the highest level and equally inescapable as a moral problem that is highlighted by the Declaration. Slavery was a challenge to a moral conscience in a way that was reflected in Constitutional arguments and was exacerbated by the order of offices under the Constitution. It was also a foundational argument ultimately independent of the Constitution; slavery was an affront to the Declaration.

The compromise in the Declaration on the matter of slavery points toward natural law as an appeal to conscience, especially the conscience of later generations. Appeals to moral conscience do not always have an immediate effect, but they are not thereby irrelevant, even in politics. Moral reasoning based on natural law has its own autonomy independent of time, place, circumstance, or any particular individual. It is scarcely a radical assertion to say that slavery is the Achilles heel of the founders' science of politics. This is not only true in retrospect but was also sensed among at least some in the funding generation. How can we reconcile slavery with the idea that "all Men are created equal," much less the notion that they are "endowed by their Creator with certain unalienable Rights?" The simple truth is that we cannot and we also know that many of the founders were as aware of this contradiction in their principles as we are. The essence of the natural law argument, however, is not finally affected by any of these considerations. Nor is the meaning and application of natural rights in the Declaration exclusively affixed to the founding generation. Such is not the way natural rights works. Moral judgment is not merely moral judgment of past political actions; it is first and foremost an active moral judgment that is always a matter of contemporary concern however much we judge the past by such a measure.

Whether individual founders held more or less enlightened or benighted views regarding race and slavery makes for interesting historical study and is part of the historical mosaic of the founding era, but is not decisive for the principle in natural law reasoning that all men are indeed created equal, much less the notion that they are endowed by their Creator with certain unalienable rights. The absence of the term "slave" in the Constitution, the convoluted euphemisms they used in its place, and the three-fifths representation for the institution of slavery in Article I may be taken as a testament of sorts to their guilty conscience on the subject. In this the American founders were neither the first nor the last persons to profess belief in something and simultaneously find it difficult to practice. However human or even prudentially expedient such failures may be, or seem to be, they remain moral failures at some level. And rifts between theory and practice have a way of coming back to affect and confound the most pragmatic politicians. The failure of the founding generation in this one regard has certainly haunted American politics ever since.

The point here is that role of the Declaration in shaping our views of slavery and after is unmistakable. As a matter of natural law, it does not matter whether or not other regimes also tolerated slavery or were morally even more repugnant in how it was actually practiced. The Declaration was a standing challenge and a rebuke to the practice of slavery in American politics at its foundation long before the abolition of slavery. Indeed, it is a challenge to slavery everywhere and every time and every place. It was the challenge Lincoln shouldered during the Civil War. He thought that the abolition of slavery would amount to a second founding of the regime on principles derived from the Declaration; it would bring the Constitution into a closer congruence with the Declaration, and there is no doubt this provides the proper interpretation of the Civil War amendments abolishing slavery and its legacy. He was almost right. The abolition of slavery was a necessary first step in reconciling the theory of the American regime with its practice, but even Lincoln did not have the last word on the matter.

The self-evident truth remained a rebuke to the constitutionalization of "separate but equal" that followed the Civil War. The fundamental challenge the Declaration continually posed was to make self-evident truth more of a reality in the Constitution; to bring the practice of American politics into greater conformity with its founding principles. No one seriously doubts that more was involved in the abolition of slavery than procedural changes in the formula for congressional representation in Article I of the Constitution. Further, it was the appeal to the Declaration and Christianity as a matter of conscience by civil rights leaders, such as Martin Luther King that provided the moral foundation for the Civil Rights Movement in the 1950s and 1960s.

The politics of the Civil Rights Movement that led to the removal of legal segregation would be unexplainable without reference to a collective guilty conscience about the rift between the theory and practice in American government. It is a further reminder that even the briefest inquiry into the politics of slavery and race is ultimately independent of the racial opinions of the founders, Lincoln, or anyone else for that matter. The classification of people according to race defined by biology, which may or may not seem biologically reasonable, is always a challenge to a conscience that is morally formed by natural law. Whatever arguments we may make as a people against slavery and its attendant since, is not typically based on an appeal to either evolution, science, or history—at least not if we wish to get to the heart of the matter. Indeed, it is difficult to think of a critique of slavery or separate-but-equal in American politics that does not invoke the language of the Declaration.

The Declaration of Independence as a Living Document

Natural law reasoning by its nature does not admit that there can be a final, definitive *finis* as to how natural moral reasoning must or even should be applied. Unlike the methodological basis of reasoning in the natural sciences, it can never claim to be complete. Perhaps the scholar who saw this most clearly was the Jesuit theologian John Courtney Murray (1904–1967). Murray thought of the American founding not in terms of Hobbes and Locke, but rather in what he called "the Great Tradition" of natural law following Aristotle, Cicero, and St. Thomas Aquinas. The appeal to conscience was the heart of this tradition. In this context, Murray singled out Lincoln's "Gettysburg Address" as the most profound statement of the American creed as natural rights. Properly understood, it provides the paradigm of how the founders' science of politics is to be interpreted by subsequent generations. Lincoln asserted that the foundation of American government in the Declaration was dedicated to a "proposition." It is a proposition that appeals to conscience very much as Cicero or St. Thomas would have understood it. But a proposition has particular qualities that need to be better understood.[20]

Murray identified two ways the term "proposition" may be used with conceptual propriety. "In philosophy a proposition is a statement of truth to be demonstrated. In mathematics a proposition is at times a statement of an operation to be performed. Our Fathers dedicated the nation to a proposition in both of these senses." But a proposition in both of these senses presented a unique challenge for both the theory and practice of American politics. "Neither as a doctrine nor as a project is the American proposition a finished thing. Its demonstration is never done once and for all; and the Proposition itself requires development on penalty of decadence. Its historical success is never to be taken for granted, nor can it come to some absolute term; and any given measure of success demands enlargement on penalty of instant decline."[21] But Murray's formulation of the Declaration as a proposition carried with it connotations other scholars, no less dedicated to the principles of natural law, found problematic.

As students of Murray have repeatedly pointed out, the notion that this particular appeal to natural law in the American tradition was built on the premise that the Catholic religious tradition, if not identical, was certainly compatible with the nature of the American regime at its founding. Murray may be correct in this assumption, but as a thesis regarding natural law in the American regime it has had its share of thoughtful critics. The degree to which Murray is correct or incorrect on this point is very much dependent on the degree to which classical natural law may be linked to the natural law of the Declaration.

The best-known modern critique of the progressive assault on natural law is probably the work of Leo Strauss, *Natural Right and History*.[22] A reference to Strauss at this point is perhaps inevitable since that earlier introduction has been the inspiration for so much of the renewed study of the founding principles of the American regime. The question Strauss posed at the time, but could not fully answer, was whether as a people we still believed in these self-evident truths. He had his doubts. It only seemed to survive, he thought, in Catholic social and political theory. He thought the unqualified value relativism of much of America's intellectual class and reflected in the social sciences that emerged in the Progressive Movement was a bad omen for the survival of the founders' republic. Value relativism is the quicksand of free government. At the same time, Strauss thought the religious connection to natural law was untenable in the long run. Several generations of students who have taken his question to heart have hoped he was wrong, but have feared he might be right. America has invested more of its theory and practice in the truth of natural law than any other modern regime and a failure of natural law reasoning with regard regime politics would have consequences and implications beyond that of most other regimes. This may, in fact, be the essence of whatever is meant by American exceptionalism.

Nevertheless, Strauss is not wrong in general to point out that religion and natural law are not the same and each has its own integrity and logic that follows that integrity. But the very basis of American exceptionalism Strauss defended was in large measure a result of the symbiotic relationship between the natural law of the Declaration and a kind of generic religion that most Americans recognized at the outset. That symbiosis came apart during the Progressive Era when both nature and religion was seen through the lens of Darwinian biology. But, as Strauss also pointed out, whatever the disappearance of the natural law argument among progressive intellectuals meant, most ordinary Americans were prepared to accept the self-evident truth of the Declaration. The triumph of progressive social policies in the decades after Murray penned his famous defense of religious freedom in America, policies that were premised on the revolt against the Declaration in the first place, gave added weight to Strauss' concerns about probable consequences of the destruction of natural law reasoning in the social sciences. Strauss thought there was a stronger disconnect between the classical natural law of Plato, Aristotle, and Cicero, for example, than did Murray. It was a concern that also found some echo among Catholic scholars.[23]

The reason Strauss could not accept the version of natural law expressed by Murray was that the latter was too rooted in religion to suit his view of political philosophy. Strauss thought religion presented a dramatically different foundation for civil society than natural law, even as he thought religion to be the last major institutional intellectual barrier in popular politics to the value relativism of the progressive tradition. In particular, Strauss further thought the Catholic version of natural law too closely tied a Thomistic political theology to be of much value in American political philosophy.[24] Without delving into the minutiae of Strauss' critique of Murray, what he accomplished, and almost single-handed, was revive an interest in the natural rights foundations of the founders' political thought. Much of that revival by students of Strauss at least tacitly accepted the idea that the founding principles of the American regime represented a radical break with the classical tradition that was ultimately rooted in the modern natural law tradition of Hobbes and Locke. The argument has considerable merit, but still may not entirely touch the main point of Murray's thesis. More probing is in order.

The critique by Strauss presupposes a more radical break between natural law reasoning and religion than may in fact be the case. As Murray further pointed out, however, the Declaration is more than a symbol. It is a political project that is never complete. Its demonstration is never done once and for all. It can never be taken for granted. It requires development on penalty of decadence and any given measure of success demands enlargement on penalty of instant decline. This makes it more than a mere symbol and more than a Rorschach test that later generations can interpret in any way they may wish; it conveys a conviction of specific moral substance.[25] The natural right of all men expressed in the Declaration was imperiled by slavery and Lincoln was compelled by the logic of the proposition to change the Constitution, even if it meant Civil War. What Lincoln did not anticipate, and Murray only partly explored, was a new science of politics in America that would challenge both the Declaration of Independence as well as the Constitution at the level of "self-evident truths." Such a challenge, if successful, would make both the founding and the Civil War unintelligible in terms that either the founders or Lincoln would have understood.[26]

Strauss recognized the implications of this new political science that gripped the imagination of the social sciences. The founders have been accused of many things over the years, many of them mutually contradictory, but no one ever accused them of being closet Thomists. But even this most obvious point is not the end of the matter. Religion supported the founders' natural law, but they never made religion the foundation for a republican political science. The tension, which is real enough, may not be as critical in practice as Strauss thought. Murray, for example, argued that a reasoned belief in God was the prerequisite for a morally ordered polity and there is no reason to believe the founders' disagreed; natural law and religion can be kept analytically separate even as they mutually reinforce each other in practice.[27] Many of the founders were, at best, ambivalent about Christian dogmas, but few seriously doubted that religion was incompatible with natural law or that any foundation of a reasonably just civil society could dispense with religious virtues. From Washington's "Farewell Address" to numerous other examples, there is no reason to doubt that as a practical matter most of the founders not only accepted but also publically embraced this connection.[28]

Natural Law and the Declaration of Independence:
The Progressive Critique

The historicized element in the progressive critique of the Declaration is probably less well known than the progressive critique of the Constitution, in part because most ordinary Americans tend to find the Declaration unexceptional. The historical side was a debate carried on by and for academics with all of the passion and general lack of public interest academic quarrels can generate. For progressive historians, natural law apart from recorded history seemed incomprehensible. At a purely historical level of analysis the progressives had a point. As a historical fact, the state of nature described by Hobbes and Locke is a fiction, a heuristic reference rather than history, a point well understood by most of the founders. And the new historical methodology precluded historical fiction or heuristic reasoning as a foundation for truth in the human sciences. Truth in this context meant exclusively historical truth. The historicist argument saw natural law as an argument that was both in the world and of the world. Which is to say, it was a view that had no transcendent meaning; it was always bound by time, place, and circumstance.

Exactly when Hegelian and German historicism explicitly entered the American intellectual scene is not entirely clear. It is clear that Westel Woodbury Willoughby (1867–1945) was explicitly brought to

Johns Hopkins University to strengthen the German school of historical method. His *The Nature of the State* (1896) was one of the seminal works of early progressivism. It deserves a broader audience than it has received by later scholars interested in the origins of the Progressive Movement. It is one of the first systematic attacks on the Declaration and natural law by a scholar of the first order.

Willoughby's political science was straight out of the German school of scholarship. He notes that the founders' were essentially contract theorists who saw the origins of the state as a compact between the rulers and the ruled in which the people surrendered certain limited powers to the state. It was an assumption of the origins of the state borrowed directly from Hobbes and Locke. But, as Willoughby points out, there is no historical example of such a contract because "the surrender of power could only be imagined as being performed by a community acting in a single body in a corporate capacity."[29] In other words, contract theory necessarily presupposed a corporate body of people in a state in order to form a contract to create a corporate body we call the state. The contract of Hobbes and Locke is both a historical and legal impossibility. From an historical perspective, contract theory seemed to rest on a tautology; the contract established the community, but the community had to exist before that contract could be made. The notion that most of the founders might have thought of contract theory as a heuristic device never seems to have occurred to him.

But, Willoughby concluded, it was out of this tautology that the modern notion of natural law or natural right emerged. He has a reasonable point to make here and if he had stopped here he might have made a stronger point, or at least one that would have recognized a distinction between classical and modern natural law. The natural law of Hobbes and Locke was not the natural law of Cicero and St. Thomas, for example. Modern natural law was indeed a contractual arrangement made necessary by a human condition without the coercive power of the state. It was of course true that before a contract could be entered into there would have to be some sort of community that existed prior to the contract that was, presumably, not formed by a contract. This was the same distinction between classical and modern natural law made by Leo Strauss and almost every scholar since. The same question remains, however, for Willoughby as it does for Strauss. Is the natural law argument of the Declaration wholly modern, classical, or some blending of the two traditions? Without denying the clear Lockean language in the Declaration, it has already been argued that is more than Lockean in vital aspects of its intellectual structure.

Willoughby is aware of the natural law argument in Plato and Aristotle, although he skips St. Thomas altogether without a mention. This is a serious omission. He does note, erroneously, that Christianity collapsed natural law with Divine law. But if he had read St. Thomas more closely he would have been aware that St. Thomas kept natural law analytically distinct and separate from Divine law and Eternal law. His awareness that classical natural law supposed a transcendent foundation was, however, correct. In any case, Willoughby noted, that natural law lacks a means of coercion because its "actual binding force can only be upon conscience." Natural law represents what should be, not what is.[30] And since it is only conscience that supports natural law, it is "little but a name."[31] Contract theory and natural law theory with it are both historically and logically untenable as an ordering principle of politics. Government for Willoughby and progressives in general means the power to coerce and government that can only appeal to conscience is not really a government in any historically recognizable sense of the term.

Individual conscience as a motive force in politics was explicitly rejected by Willoughby and this no doubt accounts for much of his difficulty in distinguishing classical from modern natural rights arguments. Even as a stand-alone component of Willoughby's theory of the modern state, this was an argument with obvious consequences. "In conclusion, then, of this entire subject, we find that the demand for a moral justification of the State is an unnecessary one . . . The state is thus justified by its manifest potency as an agent for the progress of mankind."[32] This did not necessarily mean that there was no appeal to conscience; rather it was a "social" rather than an "individual" conscience that was the motive force in the State. Darwin taught progressives to think of the state as an organism and when they did it had consequences. Social conscience had a coercive power individual conscience did not possess because the latter was unconnected to the state. The progressive conception of conscience, at least as far as it was articulated by Willoughby, was a collective conscience that was embodied in the State.

Favorably citing the sociologist Lester Ward, Willoughby concluded, "Government is becoming more and more the organ of social consciousness, and more and more the servant of the Social Will. Our Declaration of Independence, which recites that Government derives its just powers from the consent of the governed, has already been outgrown. It is no longer the consent, but the positively known will of the governed, from which the Government now derives its powers."[33] Exactly how the known will of the governed is ascertained was not spelled out by Willoughby, but he left little doubt that this was essentially a matter of scientific inquiry. Precisely how that scientific inquiry would proceed would not take final shape until the development of public opinion polling a half-century later.

The Transition to Value and Moral Relativism

The progressive critique of the Declaration was nowhere more direct than in the work of one of the most influential progressive historians, Carl Becker (1873–1945). His most influential work, *The Declaration of Independence: A Study in the History of Political Ideas* (1922), may be read as the definitive progressive critique of both the Declaration and natural law along with it. Reading Becker is to be reminded that he was a very fine academic stylist in a genre better known for a style that has probably sent more than one undergraduate desperately seeking another major. Good academic writing is not necessarily an oxymoron, much antidotal evidence to the contrary notwithstanding. Even if one thinks his interpretation of persons and events could be improved, he generally includes a sufficiently broad narrative that the reader can reach very different conclusions without reference to another source. Becker was fine narrative historian, even if his analysis often leaves much to be desired. But most of all, Becker's critique of the natural law argument in the Declaration has remained the paradigmatic progressive critique. Becker is the one inescapable reference point for an analysis of the progressive critique of the Declaration. When Strauss wrote that the abandonment of the principles of the Declaration had led American academics into unqualified value relativism, Becker is the sort of academic historian he had in mind.

Becker popularized the eighteenth century idea of what he called a "climate of opinion"; the notion that certain ideas, such as scientific progress, Darwinism, historical consciousness, and the like, are an inescapable part of our total social–political environment. For all intents and purposes, and despite our best efforts, we are fundamentally unable to transcend this condition of our existence because our existence is inescapably historicized existence. A serious conversation about fundamentals of the human condition across time is all but impossible in Becker's historicism. The only thing we can really learn from the past is how really impossible it is to learn from the past. It might seem to be an odd perspective for a historian. As Becker wrote, "For what could any of us say to either Dante or St. Thomas? Whatever we might say, on one side or the other, it is unlikely that either of them would find it strictly relevant, or even understanding which side of the argument we were espousing."[34] The one thing we can see in eighteenth century philosophers is that they are the precursors of the progressives; all they want is a more peaceful human society, not a heavenly reward.

Value relativism was not unique to Becker. Charles Beard's *Economic Origins of the Constitution* (1913) faced a similar critique. Beard, for example, tried to finesse what he knew to be the moral nihilism of value relativism, without very much success.[35] Beard answered charges of value relativism within the context of a sociology of ideas, but he never escaped the charge of reductionism; that the founders' political arguments were always about something other than what they said they were. No less a Jeffersonian scholar than Merrill Peterson could express misgivings about Becker's value relativism, but still pronounce his work "indispensable" and "a small masterpiece."[36] But Becker explored its implications and consequences of value relativism as thoroughly as any progressive scholar and did not shrink, at least initially, from the implications of his own arguments. I say "initially" because World War II evidently caused him to backtrack his earlier arguments critical of the Declaration.[37] Men and women were dying for the principles of the Declaration and in this reality Becker sensed the limits of his own critique. By that time, however, his influence rested largely on his earlier work and his later doubts have gone largely unnoticed.

Pauline Maier, in her work on the Declaration of Independence, has referred to Becker's interpretation as "delightful (but now dated)."[38] She then suggests that the reason for this is because scholarship on the Declaration after Becker has focused on the political philosophy embodied in the document that has changed our understanding of the founders' thought in historical context. This strikes me as partly true, but incomplete as an assessment of Becker's argument, which is not her intention anyway. She places his work within the context of a history of ideas, which is certainly an academically valid perspective. But that context does not really address the central issue in the progressive critique of the Declaration; is the political of natural rights philosophy an expression of a relative truth, determined by time, place, and circumstance, or is it part of a larger truth that reaches back to St. Thomas, Cicero, and beyond? What does Becker say and why does it matter?

Becker's work may be divided into two parts. The first part is a conventional historical narrative of how the Declaration was written; the various steps in its composition, the early drafts, the final draft, and the rewording of several key sections by Congress. On this part of Becker's work, very little has been added since he wrote.[39] The second part is his interpretation of how the Declaration fits into a broad understanding of politics and society. The subtitle of the work suggests his thesis; "A Study in the History of Political Ideas." The major premise of the Declaration, "that all men have imprescriptible natural rights," ". . . was derived from the dominant social philosophy of the century."[40] Curiously, while Becker later interpreted eighteenth century philosophers as precursors of modern progressivism, the eighteenth century American founders are treated as if they were not part of the same scientific revolution that affected their European counterparts. Natural law is treated as unscientific, yet it is part of the climate of opinion that included the scientific revolution. The contradiction remains unresolved in Becker.

The founders' intellectual conceptions of natural law in the Declaration are, in Becker's words, "Illusions," but nevertheless illusions make the Declaration an object worthy of study.[41] Ideas always have consequences. The strength of the Declaration was not its truth as a philosophical proposition, but its expression of "what everyone was thinking." That there is a natural order of things was the accepted premise of most eighteenth century thinking, not only in America but also in England and France."[42] What also seemed self-evident to Becker was that modern philosophy was losing a "sense of intimate intercourse and familiar conversation with God." Quite so, I might add. God was merely a Prime Mover or Final Cause of the universe. "'Nature' had stepped in between man and God; so there was no longer any way to know God's will except by discovering the 'laws of Nature,' which would doubtless be the laws of 'nature's god' as Jefferson said."[43] Natural science had altered the way we think about nature and with it the way we think about natural law, most especially a natural law somehow tied to God. "Newton, more than any man before him, so it seemed to the eighteenth century, banished mystery from the world."[44] And with it, of course, went any foundation for transcendent purpose.

In Becker's historical account of the origins of the Declaration, the appeal to nature was born of the need to find a distinction between right and wrong, between good and evil, that modern science was rapidly finding increasingly problematic. Becker acknowledges that nature in the classical tradition of Cicero and St. Thomas was quite different than nature in the tradition of Hobbes, Locke, and Jefferson. But in both cases government could only be founded on principles that made a moral distinction. "Thus the eighteenth century, having apparently ventured so far afield, is nevertheless to be found within hailing distance of the thirteenth; for its conception of natural law in the world of human relations was essentially identical, as Thomas Aquinas' conception had been, with right reason."[45] Nature had replaced God as the foundation of moral reasoning in politics, but the results were pretty much the same. For Becker, the continuity in the natural law tradition was its insistence that reason could, somehow, distinguish right and wrong. Without this continuity and this distinction, the Declaration would make no sense.

In Becker's account of the course of American political thought, the Declaration was essentially a rationalization for the colonial desire for separation from England. There is no doubt something to this interpretation. The colonists, he thought, borrowed from Locke the ability to promote their own passions, interest, and opinions in the language of natural rights; this elevated their claim. But progressives, thanks to science and historical research, know their motives better than they acknowledged. "How should the colonists not accept a philosophy, however clumsily argued, which assured them that their own governments, with which they were well content, were just the kind God had designed men by nature to have."[46] Becker reduced the natural rights foundation of the Declaration to the capacity of even the most able statesmen to create illusions about their own motives. For the progressive science of politics, one consequence of this illusion was to create a political foundation ill suited for the modern world. The political philosophy of the Declaration had, more than any other factor, created the rupture between the theory and practice of modern government. If this foundation was fundamentally an illusion, it meant that the Constitution, which was erected on this illusion, also could not withstand the serious historical analysis.

Becker reached these conclusions with a sense of melancholy rather than triumph. "What seems common sense in one age often seems but nonsense in another. Such for the most part is the fate which has overtaken the sublime truths enshrined in the Declaration of Independence."[47] It is, however, the triumph of science over an illusion. And it is one of the truisms of progressive thought that progressive political science will be a science without illusions. If this leads to value relativism, so be it. But Becker well understood the irony in his account of the Declaration. That irony is that "the main political tendency since the nineteenth century was toward democracy, and political democracy could be very conveniently derived from the Declaration."[48] It is not because there is anything explicitly in the Declaration that suggests democracy as a preferred form of government. Quite the contrary, the Declaration is silent on the preferred form of government. But the principle of moral equality could be taken as democratic in its ethos, or so most progressives argued.

Becker saw practical reasons why the philosophy of the Declaration was central to pre-Civil War American politics. "The persistence of the political philosophy of the Declaration . . . must be mainly attributed to the conventional acceptance of a great tradition; particularly so during the thirty years prior to the Civil War." Abolitionists found the Declaration to be a ready-made appeal to higher authority that the Constitution to attack slavery. "They would obey, not the Constitution, but conscience; they would defend not the legal rights of American citizens, but the sacred and inalienable rights of all men."[49] Both the defense and critique of slavery appealed to "the natural order of things" and they could not both be right in such an appeal. What ultimately happened, in Becker's narrative, was that the concept of nature changed such that it undermined both arguments. The "fruitful discoveries of natural science, particularly the great discovery of Darwin, were convincing the learned world that the origin, differentiation, and modification of all forms of life on the globe were the result of natural forces in the material sense; and that the operation of these forces might be formulated in terms of abstract laws which would neatly and sufficiently account for the organic world, just as the physical sciences were able to account for the physical world."[50] Neither God nor any transcendent idea seemed necessary to account for the social process.[51] The laws of history had been discovered and it was simply the task of the historian to record the operation of those laws. Evidently Henry Adams was premature in thinking history had not yet achieved its scientific breakthrough.

But the "spirit of democracy" Becker attributed to the Declaration did not result in a purely democratic form of government. Why? The almost universal progressive answer, which Becker echoed, was that the democratic revolution of 1776 was thwarted by a reactionary counterrevolution that resulted in the Constitutional Convention. The progressive interpretation of modern revolutions was that they are by instinct and by nature democratic. But the laws of history, revealed by the French Revolution of 1789 suggests that for every action there is an opposite, and possibly equal, reaction; what Marxists and others called the "Thermidorian Reaction" against the original democratic temper of the French Revolution.[52] For progressives, the Constitutional Convention was the American version of the Thermidorian Reaction, without the reign of terror but representing the same reactionary aristocratic forces. Becker had helped to pioneer this interpretation with his doctoral dissertation published as *The History of Political Parties in the Province of New York, 1760–1776*, (1909).[53]

In any case, Becker wrote, "To ask whether the natural rights philosophy of the Declaration of Independence is true or false is essentially a meaningless question." By implication, historians should certainly stop asking meaningless questions. "Founded upon a superficial knowledge of history it was, certainly; and upon a naïve faith in the instinctive virtues of human kind. Yet it was a humane and engaging faith . . . (but) . . . This faith could not survive the harsh realities of the modern world."[54]

Contra Becker, one might add at this point that it is precisely "the harsh realities of the modern world" that has sparked much of the revival of interest in natural law in the latter half of the twentieth century. Whether the abandonment of the natural law tradition is directly tied to the rise of modern totalitarianism, as Strauss thought, is a topic that cannot be explored here. What can be said with confidence is that when scholars stop asking questions about the fundamental ideas that have been so fundamental to so many people over the centuries it is not obvious that a more realistic, much less ethically based, historical narrative will somehow emerge. Aristotle, Cicero, and St. Thomas, to name only the most prominent persons, may be wrong on the subject of natural law. But to dismiss them as "superficial" or "naïve" seems highly unlikely to produce a more humane science of politics.

Value relativism is typically contrasted with moral absolutism. This is how the progressives typically defended historicism. Who can be absolutely certain of these things except a madman? But this sort of Manichean distinction misrepresents the natural law argument. Natural law is not patterned after the sort of categorical imperative espoused by Kant; the search for an absolutely minimalist conception of right and wrong applicable everywhere regardless of culture. The sort of relativism taught by Becker has the effect of dissolving any distinctions between true and false, right and wrong; such distinctions are merely part of the climate of opinion at any given time. For many things this is no doubt true. But why are some things almost universally wrong regardless of the climate of opinion? Does anyone seriously believe in practice that all regimes are morally equal? What makes some morally superior to others?

Variations in moral beliefs do not prove that all beliefs are equal. Rather differences are an invitation to discover which one, if either, may be better than the other. The classical tradition of natural law, in Plato, for example, made serious disagreement the starting point for inquiry not the end point. If we really believed that all moral judgments are relative it is difficult to see how we could act rationally. Most especially when our own moral beliefs are under attack, as they were for Becker during World War II, moral or value relativism is a difficult proposition to accept. We judge our own responses to Japanese–American internment by references to natural law, which are violated by that internment, rather than the Constitution, which the Supreme Court at the time held permitted that internment. Becker's response to World War II, to summon The Declaration as a measure by which to judge what was at stake, was both appropriate and moral, but he was forced to step outside of his own truncated historical methodology, not to mention his own climate of opinion, in order to see it. That is, after all, how natural law typically works.

Self-Evident Truths and Foundations in Political Science

The first problem that always surrounds self-evident truths is that they are not always self-evident. If there were a definitive, once-and-for-all solution to the problem it would not be necessary to write essays and books trying to explore the problem. The problem is further compounded by the absence of any single or accepted authority that can establish a foundation for disagreements that do not talk past each other. But the stakes are serious; how do we understand the nature of the American regime? Is one theory better than another? Why?

The foundational critique of the American regime in what they take to be a scientific critique of natural law is the analytic starting point for the progressive quarrel with the Constitution. It is not a separate critique from their critique of the Constitution. Scholars have tended to focus on the progressive quarrel with the founders over the Constitution in part because the Constitution is typically the focal point for the great policy disputes in American politics. The Constitution is typically seen as the defining point of what is right or what is wrong with a particular policy. But the Declaration is rightly understood as the first cause of the American regime and not the material, efficient, or final cause. It is this place the Declaration occupies in an American science of politics that makes the progressive critique so important to understand. By failing to adequately distinguish from among various levels of causality progressives have generally misunderstood or misinterpreted both theory and practice of regime principles. The problem begins with their critique of natural law. Not because natural law is above criticism, but because neither the theory nor the practice of American politics is intelligible without a recognition of the role natural law plays and has played in regime interpretation.

The Declaration of Independence is undeniably a symbol. But it is a symbol meant to express certain self-evident truths about the human condition. Willoughby, Becker, and other progressives, well understood the Declaration in this way. But symbols invested with a powerful symbolic meaning cannot be created at will. Every political theory and argument will have its symbols. If the Declaration is only an abstract symbol it will necessarily have far less significance in any arguments over the nature of American political principles. We can see this most vividly in perennial arguments over American exceptionalism because such arguments cannot fail to confront the questions surrounding natural law. The Declaration stands or falls as a statement of truth in natural law. Becker is partly right; the only real question that matters is "Is it true?" If it is not true, a serious science of politics ought to abandon it and find a better substitute. If it is true, we abandon it at our peril. And if we abandon it the resultant value relativism will not have a happy ending.

Classical natural law, unlike positive law, appeals not just to reason but also to conscience; precisely that quality of the human condition so many progressives have found so problematic. How the morally formed conscience of an individual should respond in politics is always problematic. Conscience in politics seems to lack external coercion; Willoughby has a point here. It reflects moral judgment but lacks any material means of enforcement. It is always more or less an expression of our free ability to embrace things we ought not to embrace and reject things we ought not to reject. Further, it seems to be premised on a notion of sin, or at least free will, which may be one of the most ignored or rejected aspects of the modern scientific tradition. Plato had argued that injustice was a defect of knowledge, and progressives, ironically, agreed. But knowledge for Plato was moral knowledge whereas moderns tend to think of knowledge in scientific terms; which is to say that questions about first and final causality are conspicuous by their absence.

Traditional natural law typically meant that it was expounded by a competent authority; Aristotle as a philosopher or St. Thomas as a Christian. But neither classical philosophy nor religion is recognized as competent authority by modern natural science. Because natural law reasoning is always human reasoning it will always be dependent to some degree on the intellect, character, and moral authority of the persons expounding it. Imperfect men will give an imperfect account of whatever is in dispute. If natural law can lay claim to our conscience through the teaching of particular individuals grounded in the claims of a moral universe, it would seem that the secularized society of the progressive ideal is seriously wanting. Scientific method was not designed to answer questions of first or final cause and it is one of the illusions of the scientific mind to suppose that it can. Becker's broad thesis that science satisfies the modern mind as St. Thomas satisfies the religious mind is no doubt true, in a sense, but does not really go to the heart of the matter. What sort of mind is satisfied with a science of politics unconcerned with first and final causality? Probably an intellectual.

Modern society is complex in ways that neither Aristotle nor St. Thomas could have imagined. But that political reality does not negate natural law reasoning and in fact maybe an invitation to rethink it anew. It is not clear that the basic elements of the human condition have dramatically changed; we do not create ourselves, we cannot know or do everything, and we will die. In this regard classical natural law, properly understood, obliges us to be both ancients and moderns simultaneously. If natural law is only a classroom lecture, few persons would seriously dispute or defend it, except perhaps the classroom lecturer. Questions regarding first and final causes in practical politics do not go away simply because we stop inquiring into them. They merely become distorted, or go underground, only to resurface later in ways that threaten to wreck whatever measure of intellectual coherence we may reasonably expect. It will affect our understanding of justice. The ancient argument of "no *telos*, no justice" is still valid. A political science not grounded in some of the deeper truths of the human condition is not likely to produce a society fit for human beings.

Perhaps the most enduring quality of the progressive science of American politics is the degree to which progressive intellectuals ceased to defend the foundations of regime principles. Whatever intermural quarrels they may have among each other, this quality seems to define the progressive intellectual in public debate. What is deemed to be indefensible will not be defended. Any defense of regime principles in this context is axiomatically "reactionary" and clearly establishes the defender as antiscientific. One of the increasingly obvious characteristics of the progressive intellectual throughout the course of the ensuing years after the Progressive Movement is their estrangement from American political culture. Traditional America was a foreign land, where, in the words of a twenty-first century progressive, "people cling to their guns and religion and fear the other."

The alienated intellectual is not new to politics. Rousseau stands out as perhaps the archetype of this species. But it is also worth recalling here that St. Augustine was also alienated. The difference is that St. Augustine thought that alienation was part of the natural condition of man; that there is no political solution that is even metaphysically possible this side of the City of God. The modern progressive intellectual, on the other hand, is intensely secular in outlook and this shapes the way a personal sense of alienation is understood. The metaphysical solution of St. Augustine is not even debated as the progressive methodology of science precludes even asking the questions St. Augustine asked. To the extent that the secular mind can comprehend a solution, it is a political solution to be realized in the City of Man. Such has been the basis of modern totalitarian ideology.

The scientific-historical foundation of progressive political science has proven less secure with the passage of time than progressives originally thought. The twentieth century has not been kind to optimists who have based their optimism on the evolutionary progress of the human species. Many progressives were men of genius, or at least men of uncommon talent, and, as G. K. Chesterton once remarked, genius always carries a magnifying glass. Armed with new magnifying glasses in the form of new methodologies they saw many things previously unseen, or seldom seen, but somehow because of this managed to miss the larger things; things that might have been made clearer in the light of a different political science. What they needed was not just a magnifying glass, but also a telescope.

Notes

1. Henry Adams, *Annual Report of the American Historical Association for 1894*, 17–23.
2. Historicism is a subject matter that does not lend itself to any definitive, that is, final discussion. I have been most influenced by Karl Löwith, *Meaning in History* (Chicago: University of Chicago Press, 1949). A very fine discussion

of so many of the philosophic assumptions that go into the ordinary writing of history is William Dray, *Laws and Explanation in History* (Oxford: Oxford University Press, 1957). See also Friedrich Meinecke, *Historism: The Rise of a New Historical Outlook.* Translated by J. E. Anderson (London: Routledge and Kegan Paul, 1972).

3.   Fred M. Taylor, "The Law of Nature," *Annals of the American Academy of Political and Social Science* (1891): 558–59.

4.   A widely cited work at the time was the philosophical-historical critique offered by David G. Ritchie, *Natural Rights: A Criticism of Some Political and Ethical Conceptions* (London: George Allen and Unwin, 1894). Ritchie observed in his Introduction, natural rights is a theory "still, in a sense, alive, or at least capable of mischief," ix. He would probably have said much the same thing a century later.

5.   Westel Woodbury Willoughby, *An Examination of the Nature of the State: A Study in Political Philosophy* (New York: Macmillan and Co., 1889), 115. Hereafter cited as Willoughby, *State.*

6.   See James G. Basker, ed., *American Anti-Slavery Writings. Colonial Beginnings to Emancipation* (New York: Library of America, 2012).

7.   Herbert J. Storing, "What the Anti-Federalist Were For," in *The Complete Anti-Federalist*, vol. 1. Edited, with Commentary and Notes, by Herbert J. Storing, with the assistance of Murray Dry (Chicago: The University of Chicago Press, 1981).

8.   See James W. Ceaser, "The Doctrine of Political Nonfoundationalism," in his *Designing a Polity: America's Constitution in Theory and Practice* (Lanham, MD: Rowman and Littlefield Publishers, Inc., 2011).

9.   See Walter A. McDougall, "The Unlikely History of American Exceptionalism," *The American Interest* VIII, no. 4 (March/April 2013).

10. Thomas Jefferson, "First Inaugural Address," in *Thomas Jefferson: Writings*, ed. Merrill D. Peterson (New York: The Library of America, 1984), 492–96.

11. Charles Beard, *The Republic: Conversations on Fundamentals* (New York: The Viking Press, 1943), 341.

12. Cicero, *De Re Publica*, with an English Translation by Clinton Walker Keyes. (Cambridge, MA: Harvard University Press, 1928), Book III, 211.

13. St. Augustine, *Confessions*, Book 3, Chapter 4. Specifically, he cites *Hortensius*, a lost work of Cicero that he described as an "exhortation to philosophy."

14. J. G. A. Pocock, *The Machiavellian Moment. Florentine Political Thought and the Atlantic Republican Tradition* (Princeton, NJ: Princeton University Press, 1975).

15. See Michael P. Zuckert, *Natural Rights and the New Republicanism* (Princeton, NJ: Princeton University Press, 1994), and his equally impressive *The Natural Rights Republic: Studies in the Foundation of the American Political Tradition* (Notre Dame, IN: University of Notre Dame Press, 1996). Zuckert sees Jefferson as the primary author of the American natural law argument and follows that argument back to Locke and the English Whig tradition.

16. Alexander Hamilton, *The Papers of Alexander Hamilton, 1768–1778.* Edited by Harold C. Syrett and Jacob E. Cooke, Associate Editor, vol. 1 (New York: Columbia University Press, 1961), 87–88.

17. This was understood at the time and it is appropriate to point out that there were dissenters from the progressive interpretation of the Declaration during

the Progressive Movement. See, Herbert Friedenwald, *The Declaration of Independence: An Interpretation and an Analysis* (New York: The Macmillan Company, 1904). Friedenwald's critique of the trend in progressive scholarship is impressive: "Nor can the evolutionary theory of the origin of government and society, now generally accepted in some form by teachers of political science, be made the basis for any such popular uprisings as have been the outcome of the older philosophy," 206.

18.   Mortimer J. Adler and William Gorman, *The American Testament* (New York: Praeger Publishers, 1975), 11.

19.   Joseph Story, *Commentaries on the Constitution of the United States.* Reprinted with an Introduction by Ronald D. Rotunda and John E. Nowak (Durham, NC: Carolina Academic Press, 1987/1833), 639–702.

20.   In this context, attention should be called to Allen C. Guelzo, *Gettysburg: The Last Invasion* (New York: Alfred A. Knopf, 2013). His "Epilogue" is one of the finest accounts I have read explaining how Lincoln understood the Declaration of Independence as a proposition that defines the very nature of the American regime.

21.   S. J. John Courtney Murray, *We Hold These Truths. Catholic Reflections on the American Proposition* (New York: Sheed and Ward, 1960), vii.

22.   Leo Strauss, *Natural Right and History* (Chicago: The University of Chicago Press, 1953).

23.   Donald J. D'Elia and Stephen M. Krason, eds., *We Hold These Truths and More: Further Reflections on the American Proposition* (Steubenville, OH: Franciscan University Press, 1993). In particular, see Peter Augustine Lawler, "Murray's Transformation of the American Proposition," 93–108.

24.   There is one interesting and curious figure in American letters who represents, in part, precisely such an interpretive argument regarding the founders. Orestes A. Brownson, *The American Republic: Its Constitution, Tendencies and Destiny* (New York: P. O'Shea, 1865). Brownson has been a much-overlooked figure in American thought and will not be revived here. But he is interesting because his unorthodox reading of American constitutional history always has an air of plausibility, if one can only get over his skipping any inconveniences that might damage his thesis. My own judgment is that Brownson is wrong, but I must say that he makes the best case of anyone with whom I am familiar.

25.   The best recent work on the Declaration is Pauline Maier, *American Scripture: Making the Declaration of Independence* (New York: Alfred A. Knopf, 1997). Maier emphasizes the symbolic nature of the Declaration. Her discussion of the slavery debates in the context of the Declaration is one of the best anywhere. But it should be complimented by Harry V. Jaffa, *Crisis of the House Divided: An Interpretation of the Issues in the Lincoln-Douglas Debates* (Seattle, WA: University of Washington Press, 1959).

26.   An interesting example of how the loss of the Declaration of Independence as a reference point for the interpretation of the Civil War is suggested in Gary W. Gallagher, *The Union War* (Cambridge, MA: Harvard University Press, 2011).

27.   Works on this subject are numerous, but a good place to begin is Daniel L. Dreisback, Mark D. Hall, and Jeffrey H. Morrison, eds., *The Founders on God and Government* (Lanham, MD: Rowman and Littlefield Publishers,

Inc., 2004). See also, Jon Meacham, *American Gospel. God, the Founding Fathers, and the Making of a Nation* (New York: Random House, 2006). For a lively discussion of this point, see Thomas S. Engman and Michael P. Zuckert, eds., *Protestantism and the American Founding* (Notre Dame, IN: University of Notre Dame Press, 2004).

28. Works on this subject are numerous. Two recent works that support this interpretation are David L. Holmes, *The Faiths of the Founding Fathers* (New York: Oxford University Press, 2006). James H. Hutson, ed., *The Founders on Religion. A Book of Quotations* (Princeton, NJ: Princeton University Press, 2005).

29. Willoughby, *State*, 61.

30. Ibid., 105.

31. Ibid., 115.

32. Ibid., 111–12.

33. Ibid., 141.

34. Carl Becker, *The Heavenly City of the Eighteenth Century Philosophers* (New Haven, CT: Yale University Press, 1932), 4.

35. A full discussion of this point in Beard cannot be explored here. For an extended analysis of value relativism in Beard, see Clyde W. Barrow, *More than a Historian: The Political and Economic Thought of Charles A. Beard* (New Brunswick, NJ: Transaction Publishers, 2000), esp. Chapter 3, "Realistic Dialectics," 57–93.

36. Merrill D. Peterson, *The Jefferson Image in the American Mind* (New York: Oxford University Press, 1960), 305.

37. See the extended discussion in Robert E. Brown, *Carl Becker on History and the American Revolution* (East Lansing, MI: The Spartan Press, 1970). See also one of Becker's last essays, "The American Political Tradition," in Carl L. Becker, *Freedom and Responsibility in the American Way of Life* (New York: Alfred A. Knopf, 1946), 1–22.

38. Pauline Maier, *American Scripture: Making the Declaration of Independence* (New York: Alfred A. Knopf, 1997), xvi.

39. For the basic history of how the Declaration was written, Becker relied heavily on the pioneering work of John W. Hazelton, *The Declaration of Independence: It's History* (New York: Dodd, Mead, and Company, 1906). In turn, Becker's narrative was closely followed by the editor of the Jefferson papers, Julian P. Boyd, *The Declaration of Independence. The Evolution of the Text as Shown in Facsimiles of Various Drafts by Its Author, Thomas Jefferson* (Princeton, NJ: Princeton University Press, 1945), 1.

40. Carl Becker, *The Declaration of Independence. A Study in the History of Political Ideas* (New York: Random House, 1970), xi–xii. Hereafter referred to as *Declaration*.

41. Ibid., 23.

42. Ibid., 26–27.

43. Ibid., 36–37.

44. Ibid., 41.

45. Ibid., 60–61.

46. Ibid., 71, 73.

47. Ibid., 233.

48. Ibid., 225–26.

49. Ibid., 240, 242.
50. Ibid., 274.
51. Ibid., 277.
52. The modern French Marxist historian who did not originate but who did exemplify this two-phase argument is George Lefebvre, *The Thermidorians and the Directory: Two Phases of the French Revolution*. Translated from the French by Robert Baldick (New York: Random House, 1964). See also, François Furet, *Interpreting the French Revolution* (Cambridge: Cambridge University Press, 1981). See also the powerful, but controversial, interpretation by J. L. Talmon, *The Origins of Totalitarian Democracy* (New York: Frederick A. Praeger Publishers, 1960).
53. Carl Lotus Becker, *The History of Political Parties in the Province of New York 1760–1776* (Madison, WI: The University of Wisconsin Press, 1909). A reprint of Becker's first work was published in 1960 with a "Forward" by Arthur M. Schlesinger, who described the work "In research method as well as content, objectivity and interpretation it is a model of what a work of historical scholarship should always strive to be." P. V. Becker was very much a historian's historian.
54. Becker, *Declaration*, 278–79.

III

Progressive Democracy

The North Star of progressive political science always pointed toward more democracy. But exactly what democracy meant in the progressive lexicon of politics was not always obvious; it certainly did not mean precisely the form of government the founders' thought of when they used the term. How could it have the same meaning after the rejection of natural law as a reference point? Progressives used "democracy" in much of the same way Louis XIV might have parsed the phrase "Divine right of kings"—as one of the self-evident truths upon which all subsequent reasoning about practical politics was built. But whatever democracy meant for various stripes of progressive intellectuals it is clear that the term was virtually synonymous with the *telos* of History conceived as some form of secular perfection; this factor separated the progressives from the founders as much as any other point for reference. Democratic power, as progressive intellectuals instinctively understood, was unlimited power in a democratic form of government. An argument for a more democratic form of government by its very nature tends toward an argument for unlimited power, any rhetoric to the contrary notwithstanding. There is, as far as I know, no example in progressive literature of a theoretical check on power exercised by a democratic state. The notion that history is on the side of democracy does not change or significantly alter this basic calculation. But the idea of a *telos* of history was a theoretical as well as a practical problem for progressives.

The theoretical problem was to define precisely what was meant by democracy that made it "progressive" and thereby separated "progressive democracy" from the popular government vocabulary of the founders. The theoretical problem was tackled most comprehensively in the work of Herbert Croly, by far the most influential of the progressive writers who specifically addressed the idea of progressive democracy. He summed up the progressive idea when he wrote, "For better or worse, democracy cannot be disentangled from an aspiration toward

81

human perfectibility, and hence from the adoption of measures looking in the direction of realizing such an aspiration."[1] Both perfection and democracy were specifically linked in Croly in a way that has remained one of the core characteristics of progressive democracy; that linkage has affected progressives in theory as well as the practice of American politics. It is appropriate to begin with the practical problem as Croly developed it.

The practical problem was that the broad character of progressive democracy that gradually emerged was patterned on a European style welfare state system. Such a system required the concentration of political power that was hostile to the Constitution. The most admired model at the time was the German system that had been engineered by Otto von Bismarck following the unification of Germany in 1871. Progressive democracy was not commonly a socialist system in the sense that it was premised on the public ownership of the economic means of production, although it did tend to veer in that direction. It was vague, perhaps because "socialism," like the term "capitalism," was also vague. Bismarck, for example, had instituted his system of social insurance in large measure to thwart socialism in the Marxist sense. The American progressive version did likewise envision state control of the economic system by a top-down administration staffed by progressive elites who were thoroughly grounded in the scientific methodology of the emerging social sciences. Top-down rule by elites does not sound very much like democracy in any classical sense, but there it is. The logic is, however, rooted in the scientific and historicist foundations of progressivism.

Progressives and Founders: Natural Law, Representation, and Conflict

Comparing and contrasting the progressive definition of democracy with that of the founders is complicated, in part, by some ambiguities inherent in the natural law political science of the founders. That ambiguity needs to be acknowledged in order to better understand the progressive break with the founders. To begin with, as has been noted, natural law alone does not point toward any specific form of government beyond a just form. For example, the natural law foundation in the founders' political science cannot, by itself, provide a complete defense of the Constitution or even a democracy. It is not clear that the specific American polity constructed by the founders, even apart from the problem of slavery, represents either the best or the only form of popular government that can be built on natural law principles. The Anti-Federalist argument, for example, may have been weaker than that of *The Federalist* but it was reasonable and could have been adopted without doing violence to natural rights. References to natural law alone, even if one accepts the validity of natural law political science, cannot resolve any conflict between the founders and progressives on democracy. But the progressive rejection of natural law was nevertheless decisive in this quarrel. It was axiomatic for progressives that evolutionary science pointed toward social perfection and this axiom shaped their definition of democracy as surely as it shaped their rejection of the Constitution. We may start a discussion of the practical problems of progressivism with the problem of representation because it affects so many other points of departure for progressives.

The progressive idea of democracy grounded in political perfection began with a very different conception of representation. Progressives had a very different conception of who and what would be represented in progressive democracy. Who, we might ask, has the moral authority to represent "the people?" The Constitution made elections, albeit complex elections, the proper mode of selecting representatives. Progressives could not totally reject elections, but elections cannot be the sole mode of deciding who has authority to represent the people otherwise there would be no need to challenge the founders on this point. If the founders' mode of electing representatives is to be rejected, on what principle does progressive political representation rest if it is to support a democracy? No progressive author ever explicitly addressed these questions, in part because they appear to have taken the answers for granted. But it is possible to reconstruct the progressive answer to these questions by setting the progressive conception of popular elections alongside how elections had developed after the founding.

Literally, democracy simply means the rule of the *demos,* the "many." Modern democracy is no different than classical democracy in this sense. But modern democracy, represented by the founders, for example, has added the idea of representation to any definition that makes specific forms of democracy more varied than the classical experience. The Greeks, for example, thought of democratic elections as participation by citizens who were equal for purposes of participation; representation of diverse factions was understood, but not as an organizing principle of democratic government. But for progressive intellectuals, steeped in the tradition of secular humanism, only scientific reason was truly entitled to representation and hence only secular progressivism could be considered the true representatives of the *demos*. How all of this came together in the progressive theory of democracy is at the heart of the progressive revolution in American political thought. Just as the founders are more than *The Federalist*, for example, progressives are more than Wilson, Croly, and a handful of others. But just as it is appropriate to refer to *The Federalist* whenever we speak of the founders, so too is it appropriate to refer to a few progressives whenever we speak of "the progressives." In each case, we take the best examples as our reference point.

We can begin to see the differences between the founders and progressives on the issue of representation when we ask who and what is being represented in each case. Why did progressives seek a fundamental change? The problem of factions in a popular form of government is at the center of the difference. The founders thought of representation in terms of the larger problem of factions, a problem that required a solution because they rejected what they called a "pure democracy" of direct citizen participation in a city or limited territory; a pure democracy could become a tyranny whenever a majority faction might dominate it. The dilemma the founders faced was that all forms of popular government would be a form of government composed of factions. Representation of these factions encompassed the entire range of human passions, interests, and opinions.

The desideratum for a just form of popular government, as *The Federalist* emphasized, required that the potentially destructive aspects of this diversity of interests be somehow controlled and still preserve both individual and group freedom. Madison went so far as to say that the violence of factions was the reason why popular forms of government had perished everywhere. But the preservation of free government also required the protection of this natural diversity that flowed from human nature. It was a conundrum inherent in the human condition. Removing the causes of faction could only be accomplished by giving everyone the same passions, interests, and opinions or by a government that denied factions the freedom to exist in the first place. Institutional arrangements in government were therefore meant to control the effects of faction since the causes could not be removed without destroying free government. This certainly did not suggest that political perfection in any way figured into the definition of democracy.

The progressives, on the other hand, never thought of themselves as a faction because they saw a scientifically based democracy as the solution to the problem of factions. It goes almost without saying that progressives instinctively thought of themselves as the sole inheritors of the scientific tradition. This was abundantly clear in writers such as Croly. As the sole carriers of modern scientific reason, progressives were alone capable of providing representation of the true interests of the polity. The founders' institutional arrangements only served to frustrate the development of a more cooperative, collectivist national community. The republican government of *The Federalist* was designed to frustrate the concentration of power. The practical aim of the progressives was to strengthen power by concentrating it in the executive. The Constitution could not ultimately stop the progress of history, but it could slow it down. None of the progressive writers seem to have ever thought of political conflict as a permanent reality of the human condition. In marked contrast with the founders, progressives sought to remove the causes of faction rather than control their effects. James Madison could have foretold the results.

The Greek model was the basic understanding until the definition underwent a major conceptual change during the period preceding the American Revolution. In the founders' political science popular government was the generic term that referred to two forms; a republic and a democracy. Perhaps the most fundamental difference between the form of republic and a democracy for the founders was the notion that in a republic a system of representation took precedence over direct participation. What the founders' referred to as "an extended republic" supposed that the larger size of territory in a republic would preclude direct participation in the classical sense. The extended republic would help to break and control the violence of factions that had been the bane of popular forms of government since the days of Plato.

Republican government for the founders was what later generations would refer to as "representative democracy." What is at stake here is not the terminology, but the foundational principles that are the basis for the different terminologies.[2] It is one of the legacies of the progressive science of politics that the founders' distinctions between a democracy and a republic as both a theoretical and practical principle has been largely lost or forgotten and with it the difference played by public opinion. The difference between a democracy and a republic in *The Federalist* is not semantic, but rather is a difference in substance that was seldom fully appreciated by the progressives. Representation was intended to enlarge and refine raw public opinion; to make it more rational as a result of public debate. Of course it is true that public debate sometimes refined public opinion and sometimes it did not. What is essential here is to record that the founders' defense of republican government was not a critique of popular government, but it did require recognition that all forms of government are problematic. One of the blind spots in the progressive science of politics has been the progressive refusal to consider even the possibility that progressive democracy might also be a problem.

The Federalist wanted both free government and popular government and therefore argued that these two principles could not be reconciled within a pure, that is, classical, democratic form alone. This was one of the significant points of difference between Federalists and Anti-Federalists; the former were more skeptical of democracy than the latter. Progressives also seemed to favor greater democracy over a republican form of government, but their affinity with the Anti-Federalist was largely superficial; Anti-Federalists generally wanted more democracy in order to weaken the power of the national government whereas progressives wanted a national democracy for the purpose of increasing national power. In a classical democratic form of government the majority would always prevail and minorities would experience their freedom as something always subject to the whims of the majority. This is why in classical thought the moral education of the rulers was considered as the primary means of ensuring justice and the protection of minorities. None of the founders would argue that moral education was irrelevant, but to a man they also argued that morality alone was sufficient to ensure a free and just polity. Reconciling majority rule with minority rights required a new science of politics that most of the founders thought represented a sharp break with the classical tradition. Few, if any, of these classical calculations entered into a progressive science of democracy.

Whereas the ancients had stressed education as the primary means of achieving a just polity, the American founders added institutional arrangements to the mix of calculations necessary for a modern form of popular government. They did not discount education *per se* but their lack of emphasis on education may be one of the most fundamental weaknesses that can be traced by its absence in their public arguments. George Washington, for example, had proposed a national university, but the idea went nowhere at the time. And it was precisely this weakness that was exploited by the academic nature of the progressive quarrel with the founders. Progressive political science was overwhelmingly a political science that emerged from the academy rather than experience with practical politics. In this regard that it is one of the ironies of the progressive tradition that it depended on the scientific education of the elites to ensure a just form of government. It is tempting to say that the progressive conception of education in a democracy required every citizen to be a college professor to make it work. Given the common academic complaint with university administration, this seems to be a conception in need of further thought.

Progressives generally agreed that the founders, at least the founders who drafted the Constitution, were antidemocratic but they did so without a serious exploration of the differences in theories of popular government required by the founders' distinction between a democratic and a republican form of popular government. When the progressives did read the founders' critique of a pure democracy they typically assumed that the critique was consistent with classical critiques of democracy. That is, one in which only alternative to democracy was either monarchy or aristocracy. They then tended to divide various founders into one of these two antidemocratic camps. Hamilton became a closet monarchist and the Constitutional Convention was filled with latent, and often overt, aristocrats. The Constitution thus tended to be interpreted as an aristocratic revolt against the democratic impulses said to be integral to the Revolution. This was certainly the interpretation of scholars of the caliber of Carl Becker, for example.

As a result, progressives commonly thought of democratic participation without thinking through the problems of participation, representation, and personal freedom that animated the founders' concerns. This lack of breadth tended to give much of their democratic theory more than an occasional incoherence. At the level of political practice, for example, progressives never seriously developed a science of politics that might have distinguished between the principles appropriate for a participatory democracy and a representative democracy. There was no principled reason in progressive political science to limit the general powers of government. They tended to collapse republican principles into a simple passion to restrict or thwart majority rule.

In addition, progressives added an element that was not foreign to the founders but may have been insufficiently developed; the problem of a new class of democratic intellectuals who could operate within the founders' constitutional framework for ends quite contrary to the founders' intentions. This broad failure to think through the founders' science of politics systematically contributed to the progressive failure to appreciate their own theoretical limitations in defining democracy. It can scarcely be over emphasized that progressives never thought of

87

themselves as an elite or a special interest faction. How, after all, could science be considered partisan?

Herbert Croly: The First Theorist of Progressive Democracy

Herbert Croly (1869–1930) was perhaps the most influential public intellectual in the Progressive Movement. Croly was primarily a journalist who never quite completed a Harvard degree. He was awarded an honorary degree, however, after the publication of *The Promise of American Life* (1909). His most lasting influence, however, may extend beyond his particular writing. In 1914 he joined with Walter Weyl and Walter Lippmann, along with a few wealthy financial backers to found the journal *The New Republic*. Croly served as the first editor where he backed Wilson in the 1916 presidential election, later fell out with Wilson over the peace following the World War, and generally became disillusioned with politics during the 1920s. Despite some ups and downs for the journal that included early bankruptcy and the departure of Lippmann after a quarrel with Croly, *The New Republic* has remained the gold standard of liberal-progressive journalism ever since. Croly's influence represents what might properly be called the "utopian" beginnings of progressivism before it became more hedonistic in the 1960s. By the end of the twentieth century utopianism and hedonism became increasingly less distinguishable, but in the beginning the utopian impulse was paramount and not necessarily associated with hedonism. Both the utopian and hedonistic varieties, however, were predicated on the value relativism progressives took to be fundamental lesson of historical study.

Herbert Croly's *The Promise of American Life* remains one of the iconic statements of the Progressive Movement. Its importance can scarcely be overstated. Croly remains, by consensus among progressive historians, one of the original members of the progressive "brain trust." Theodore Roosevelt's campaign platform in 1912 presidential election was what he called "The New Nationalism," a phrase he took directly from Croly. In his memoirs, written shortly after his unsuccessful bid for the presidency in 1912, Theodore Roosevelt ranked Weyl and Croly as the two writers who most influenced his thinking after he left office as president in 1909.[3] Later, when Franklin Roosevelt was elected in 1932 and launched his "New Deal" the progressive intellectual community tended to see it as the fruits of Croly's work.[4] The New Deal was staffed with precisely those intellectuals who were weaned on writers like Croly.[5]

What Croly had challenged was the notion that somehow the promise of American life was self-fulfilling. This may have been a straw-man argument, but it also comprised a very real issue in the promotion of anything that smacked of American exceptionalism. It required, he argued, the direct intervention of progressive intellectuals to make it work. The American polity may be evolving in some Darwinian sense, but the pace of evolution was much too slow. Its critical link with the New Deal, for example, was Croly's proposition that henceforth the state would have to take charge of economic development even if that meant a transformation of the founders' science of politics. Among contemporaneous reviewers only a scattering of critical comments can be found. None of that contemporary criticism seems to have had a lasting impact.

Before Croly, progressives were united in their judgment that the present was worse than the future they ardently desired, but divided on what that better future might look like or how to achieve it. What has given Croly his enduring appeal among progressive intellectuals was how, more than any other single writer, before or since, he filled in the theoretical blanks of what the future of progressivism should look like. He sketched a rough picture of paradise in the progressive imagi-nation. This is important to keep in mind when we recall how political theories help us interpret contemporary, as well as past, events in. The election of 1912 is a case in point that illustrates the convergence of abstract progressive theory with practical political interpretation. It is worth a discussion because it looms almost as large as the election of Franklin Roosevelt in 1932.

Prior to 1912 both Democrats and Republicans fought for whatever elements in the electorate could be mobilized to support a majority coalition for the general presidential election. This typically meant a heterogeneous mixture of factions in each party that did not always fit well together beyond Election Day. Both parties had what could be called liberal and conservative factions. Parties could not afford to be primarily ideological or they would risk losing elections. But Croly showed progressives how to be more ideological in the construction of electoral coalitions and still win elections. It required, however, joining nationalism with domestic political reform. Properly constructed, it was a potent political force.

We can see part of this in Teddy Roosevelt's "The New Nationalism," a term he explicitly borrowed from Croly. Unlike so much campaign rhet-oric, this was not a vacuous idea in Croly's work. Croly saw nationalism as the glue of the promised progressive electoral coalition. In Croly's pen, nationalism was a necessary virtue for the organic community of Darwinian evolution. As parties became more ideological over the course of the twentieth century, however, nationalism, at least traditional nationalism, was not an easy fit in an emerging progressive argument that was at war with the founders. Nationalism meshed too closely with American exceptionalism and natural law. Nationalism suggested a permanent source of conflict between nations that threatened to make Hobbes more prescient than Marx. It certainly placed limits on what could be achieved by efforts toward world peace. Nevertheless, Croly was and remains one of the few progressive writers who attempted to forge a link between nationalism and progressivism. That attempt alone would mark him as a writer with imagination.

The split in the Republican Party in 1912 and the election of Woodrow Wilson gave the Democrats at least a temporary electoral advantage in attracting progressive intellectuals. Croly backed Roosevelt in 1912. But by the election of 1916, *The New Republic* threw whatever intellectual weight it had behind Wilson. After the war, however, progressives such as Croly broke with Wilson over the Versailles Treaty. Then came Prohibition in 1919 that left Croly disheartened with progressivism in general; he declared it a political failure. By the time he died in 1930 he was thoroughly disillusioned with electoral politics that had not turned out as he had expected. But he may have been premature in his pessimistic self-evaluation. Franklin Roosevelt's "New Deal" was right around the corner and the New Deal was Croly on steroids. The animating spirit of Franklin Roosevelt was Croly's argument that henceforth the state would guide the complete development of the regime. Croly's arguments were part of what Becker referred to as the "intellectual climate of opinion" at the time. Croly's groundwork for the modern welfare state in America did for progressives what H. G. Wells' *A Modern Utopia* (1905) had done for the welfare state in England. Croly helped to lay the groundwork for the New Deal.

A reasonable question, however, is how much progressive intellectuals such as Croly actually shaped the practical politics of subsequent elections. His father's intellectual mentor, Auguste Comte, wrote "ideas govern the world, or throw it into chaos."[6] To the degree that Comte is correct, and there is ample historical evidence to support him on this point, it is always appropriate to begin any analysis of politics with the ideas that shape political movements. It is not always clear how much Comte shaped Croly, but there is little doubt that Croly shaped progressivism. To read *The Promise of American Life* even a century after its publication is to be reminded how much of subsequent liberal-progressive thought is an echo of Croly and how many of the tensions in Croly remain tensions within the liberal tradition.

The Promise of American Life

It would be difficult to overstate the place *The Promise of American Life* has enjoyed in the library of American political thought. Yet its significance cannot be measured by sales during Croly's own lifetime. When he died in 1930, *The Promise of American Life* had only sold a scant 7,500 copies and a first edition remains one of the genuinely rare books produced during the progressive era. Its influence is not to be measured, however, by how *many* read it, but *who* read it and what they took away from it. Virtually every progressive intellectual read it for the next decade or more and his analysis of the nature of the American regime were incorporated into the foundational arguments of subsequent generations of progressive scholars.[7]

The Promise of American Life is not an easy read. More than one reader has remarked on its turgid prose and we may suspect that its routine appearance on college reading lists has confirmed the general undergraduate suspicion that "good academic writing" is an oxymoron. That said, a careful reader would not help but be impressed with the sheer breadth of Croly's analysis. However much he may be suspect in details, he seemed to make up by the range of his argument. Croly brought together a range of ideas and how they might fit together that commands a thoughtful response.

Croly's argument in *The Promise of American Life* combined a simple thesis with a complex demonstration of that thesis. It is at least an echo of Comte. It begins with the observation that progress can only be interpreted to mean movement toward greater perfection. What prevented progress toward a perfected democracy in the America, however, were two distinct strands of thought that competed against each other that had their origins in the founding principles of the regime. Both strands were covered over and obscured by the Constitution and any critique of the Constitution, such as that by Woodrow Wilson, was incomplete without tracing the origins and development of these ideas.

The first was the Jeffersonian tradition of individualism and democracy. For Croly it was the individualism of Jefferson that he objected to, not the democracy. The individualism was, of course, based on the natural law of the Declaration of Independence. The second was the more farsighted Alexander Hamilton who represented the nationalist tradition, which, incidentally, he thought was best represented in contemporary politics in the person of Theodore Roosevelt. Roosevelt combined, in Croly's view, the strong national government of Hamilton with the democratic faith of Jefferson. Roosevelt's New Nationalism would use Hamiltonian means to achieve Jeffersonian ends.

In Croly's account each of these two founders had a fundamental weakness. The weakness of Jefferson was his resistance to the growth of national power and the weakness of Hamilton was his resistance to democracy; excessive democratic individualism in Jefferson fought with excessive economic concentration of power in Hamilton. This tension between Jefferson and Hamilton was the defining characteristic of American politics since the founding. Yoking the concentration of power with democracy in the manner Croly did was a bold and startlingly original argument. Generally speaking, progressives could accept Jefferson as a democrat, even as they uniformly rejected his natural rights. But Hamilton was an absolute anathema and Croly's invocation of Hamilton as a progressive hero remains a unique, if incongruous, juxtaposition onto the progressive analysis of American politics. Croly's union of the two ultimately broke apart over the issue of nationalism and foreign policy in the 1960s. I am not aware of any other progressive scholar who has anything good to say about Hamilton; most regard him as something akin to a gumboil on the countenance of the republic.

How did Croly manage this precarious balancing act? Perhaps it was the obvious optimism in Croly that initially attracted so much attention, often from unlikely sources. It was Henry Cabot Lodge, no friend of the progressives in general, who recommended the book to Teddy Roosevelt. The thesis of a powerful, charismatic executive certainly appealed to both Teddy and later his cousin Franklin. It seems unlikely that either fully understood or was seriously troubled by the nuances of Croly's arguments. But they well understood, perhaps instinctively, its rhetorical appeal. Croly's argument may have been historically tenuous, but it had the virtue of embracing American nationalism in a way that eluded most other progressives who were critical of any hint of American exceptionalism. The fact that Croly had decoupled American nationalism from American exceptionalism was not fully appreciated at the time. In practical terms, however, it made the concentration of power seem to be perfectly consistent with the founders' science of politics, even as it undermined the logic of the Constitution.

The charismatic leader who could somehow reconcile what Croly thought to be the conflicting strains of the founding became a staple of progressive historical interpretation that reached its climax in the period from the 1930s to the 1960s. But the Hamiltonian–Jeffersonian linkage of nationalism with progressivism was eventually torn apart in the administration of Lyndon Johnson over the war in Vietnam. Much of subsequent liberal political thought may be described as an attempt to repair or at least come to terms with that rupture. It is a repair made all the more difficult by the improbable, not to say bogus, way Croly originally tried to join these two founders together. Neither nationalism nor democracy meant the same things for Croly as both terms meant for Jefferson and Hamilton. Both terms require further probing in Croly's understanding of the promise of American life.

There is no doubt that Croly's embrace of nationalism opened a potential fault line among fellow progressives. How to be patriotic and to oppose regime principles simultaneously? The answer is that Croly had made the progressive appeal to nationalism contingent upon a changed understanding of the source of patriotism. It is not the patriotism associated with the founders or any defense of original regime principles. "The higher American patriotism, on the other hand, combines loyalty to historical tradition and precedent with the imaginative of an ideal national Promise."[8] Such patriotism is tied to the vision of a perfected future and not an actual past. "The better future which Americans propose to build is nothing if not an idea which must in certain essential respects emancipate them from their past." The new patriotic American "must be prepared to sacrifice to that traditional vision even the traditional American ways of realizing it."[9] In short, progressives are the repositories of true patriotism, a higher patriotism, and not that of politicians or ordinary citizens who are mistakenly wedded to the founders, natural law, and the Constitution. The challenge and the burden which history has placed on progressives, especially progressive intellectuals, is the realization of the new democratic ideal.

Progressive Freedom, Property Rights, and the Rule of Law

Croly, like virtually all of the progressives have embraced some form of central planning of the economy. Until now, Croly wrote, Americans "may never have sufficiently realized that this better future, just insofar as it is better, will have to be planned and constructed rather than fulfilled of its own momentum."[10] New conditions, he went on, "are forcing Americans to choose between the conception of their

93

national Promise as a process and as an ideal."[11] The process, of course, was commonly defined by the Constitution. But looking toward the founders' Constitution had the inescapable vice of looking backward and could not, because of extreme individualism, adapt to new conditions. The founding principles were reactionary and could never be the basis of true progress. And the new conditions, Croly makes clear, do not depend on freedom, at least not as Americans have traditionally understood the term. Individual freedom was a necessary casualty of democratic progress. But Croly did not anticipate that any eclipse of freedom would seriously affect economic development. Any connection between the two was simply beyond his imagination.

American prosperity for Croly is not a product of political freedom but the accident of geography. Citing the American historian Frederick Jackson Turner, Croly makes clear, the days of the American frontier are over. The influence of Turner's thesis on the role of the frontier in shaping the American character and its formal disappearance in the 1890 census exerted a profound, though not always acknowledged, influence on progressives.[12] Individualistic freedom associated with a unique geography is a thing of the past, whether we fully realize it or not. The future of prosperity for more Americans will mean learning from Europeans who have already turned their back on the radical individualism of Jefferson. Croly was abundantly clear on this point. Although not an economic determinist such as the Progressive historian Charles Beard, who was skeptical of Croly's "platitudes," Croly did argue that modern industrialism was the driving force behind the need to rethink the Jeffersonian influence in the American regime. This meant that individualism, property rights, and the rule of law would have to have a new foundation. He did not advocate state ownership of industry, but he did advocate extensive and minute state regulation of industry that separated him from any notion of a market-based economy.

The American experience with prosperity, in Croly's view, "has always been absolutely associated in the American mind with free political institutions."[13] European immigrants have all been converts to this aspect of American national identity. In practice, this is what has made American democracy the antithesis of European democracy. "The fault in the vision of our national future possessed by the ordinary American does not consist in the expectation of some continuity of achievement. It consists rather in the expectation that the familiar benefits will continue to accumulate automatically." Because of the changes in the underlying social and economic conditions of American life, "the idea Promise, instead of being automatically fulfilled, may well be automatically stifled."[14] What is logically needed, therefore, is central planning on a national scale.

This conscious work of progressive democracy then evokes one of the more enigmatic comments in his work; "The American idea is no longer to be propagated merely by multiplying the children of the West and by granting ignorant aliens permission to vote. Like all sacred causes, it must be propagated by the Word and by that right arm of the Word, the Sword."[15] Here Croly seems to suggest, in unmistakable terms, that progressive democracy will require the coercion of someone, whether the few or the many is not clear, to make the thing work. Paradise does not just happen in the evolutionary scheme of things, it requires planning and, significantly, policemen to usher people through the pearly gates.

One might ask at this point, why does Croly emphasize the importance of "the Sword" in the realization of the progressive promise? It is so clearly the antithesis of free government as any of the founders would have understood the purpose of a republican form. His answer turns on the status of private property as a basis for individual freedom. The unequal and unfair distribution of national wealth that has developed under the auspices of Jeffersonian *laissez faire* individualism has created obstacles to progressive democracy. "The automatic fulfillment of the American national Promise is to be abandoned . . . precisely because the traditional American confidence in individual freedom has resulted in a morally and socially undesirable distribution of wealth." Up to a point, he notes, Jeffersonian freedom has been beneficial. But at the same time it tends to make a more equitable redistribution of wealth to all but impossible. Then comes the punch line: "The inference which follows may be disagreeable, but it cannot be escaped. In becoming responsible for the subordination of the individual to the demand of a dominant and constructive national purpose, the American state will in effect be making itself responsible for a morally and socially desirable distribution of wealth."[16] This is where the necessary powers of the state become most evident; the redistribution of wealth is a prerequisite for the achievement of progressive democracy and this cannot take place as long as freedom is an integral part of the political system.

The state alone wields the police powers and, therefore, the state alone has the legal coercive powers necessary to redistribute wealth in a more socially desirable way. Croly did not, however, explicitly make an argument for socialism, at least not socialism defined as ownership of the means of production. It more closely resembled state control through a division of economic spoils in the wake of elections. It is this quality, which gives Croly his well-deserved reputation for providing a blueprint to a progressive theory of governance. Elections would provide the occasion for a redistribution of wealth in which, eventually, the groups that receive the spoils will simply outvote the losers. But elections were merely a means to an end. The progressive state in the form of progressive democracy would determine the winners and losers in society. If it requires coercion by the government to ensure this division of the economic spoils, so be it.

Croly does not advocate egalitarian results; but he does advocate much more egalitarian beginnings. Americans have assumed, erroneously in Croly's opinion, that everyone more or less started life with equal individual rights and finished unequally more or less as a result of greater or lesser talents and abilities. "Americans who talk in this way seem blind to the fact that under a legal system that holds private property sacred there may be equal rights, but there cannot possibly be any equal opportunities for exercising such rights."[17] Unequal results are, in Croly's view, solely a manifestation of unequal opportunities. The social problem is one of equalizing opportunities at the outset. Among other things, this meant an attack on the very idea of individual liberty as a property right within the meaning of American natural rights. Progressives may have been willing to concede the notion that individual differences could account for different results in life, but they could never concede that in the nature of things good and evil were anything more than hunger and bread. Good and evil were institutional-cultural and, therefore, had an institutional-cultural solution.

And, as Croly points out quite clearly, this fundamental truth of the present social condition has certain political implications for a regime in which equality takes precedence over freedom. First and foremost, the founders' understanding of the rule of law will have to be changed. "Impartiality is the duty of the judge rather than the statesman, the courts rather than the government . . . In economic warfare, the fighting can never be fair for long, and it is the business of the state to see that its own friends are victorious." To be sure, he goes on, the state must preserve "at times an appearance of impartiality," but this is only an appearance. "It must help those men to win who are most capable of using their winnings for the benefit of society." This does not mean that everyone will be equal at the end of the day, merely that at the end of the day the winners will be chosen by the state, rather than an economic marketplace "for the benefit of society."[18] The progressive coalition in electoral politics would reward its friends who helped to elect them. It must choose sides in this contest. "A well governed state will use its power to promote edifying and desirable discriminations."[19]

The aim of progressive justice was "social justice," and in practice social justice means class justice, and class justice means class war, and class war, if the historical record provides a clue, means war without mercy. It is not clear Croly thought this through to its logical conclusion, but other progressives, such as Marxists, certainly did. Most American progressives typically shrank from the implications of Croly's argument, but the logic remained and was a challenge to be taken up by the New Left progressives in the 1960s and 1970s.

Progressive Democracy as Movement toward Utopia

According to Croly there was yet another worm in the apple of Jeffersonian democracy in addition to its individualism that needs to be exorcised in the general historical movement toward perfection. It was a worm that some might considered to be one of democracy's virtues. As Croly saw it, democracy based on individualism did not promote the sort of excellence in government that Jefferson had supposed. On the contrary, it produced what he called "a sort of apotheosized majority—the people insofar as they could be generalized and reduced to an average . . . The system, that is, has only partly served the purpose of its founder and his followers, and it has failed because it did not bring with it any machinery adequate even to its own insipid and barren purpose."[20] Excellence in a Jeffersonian democracy produced only mediocrity at best. Why? Individual equality of rights undermined the sort of excellence that could only be a product of superior education. It would therefore seem that there was nothing wrong with American democracy that a few more Harvard grads could not take care of. Or, in the case of Croly, even a Harvard dropout would suffice. In effect, it seems that the progressive state would require progressive intellectuals to make it work.

The role of the progressive intellectual followed as a direct consequence of the progressive assault on natural law as an organizing principle of politics. The progressive interpretation of the scientific revolution reduced the meaning of the universe to some sort of cosmic sneeze; it was morally empty. But politics, like nature, abhors a vacuum. What Croly instinctively understood was the need to create a new religion of politics that would capture the imagination of secular progressives. In effect, what he proposed was a divinization of politics in which progressives would find meaning by their participation in the eschatological unfolding of History. And the future of this drama was the replacement of individualism, as reflected in both religious and natural rights traditions, with collectivism. Equal rights applied not so much to individuals as it did to groups.

The system of equal rights has worked, Croly observes, for the benefit of the average citizen, but also to the detriment of general American intelligence and morals. Jefferson's "concern for equal rights could not be promoted without some effective organ of social responsibility." That organ, of course, was the state. But this has put the Democratic Party in particular at a disadvantage when it tries to grapple with social problems. Every attempt to use the state to rectify these problems even against majorities is, in effect, an assault on its own rhetorical roots as a theory of democracy. "Such must be the case as long as it remains true to its fundamental principle," Croly observed.[21] The key, of course, is to no longer be true to fundamental principles but to embrace progressive principles.

Jeffersonian democracy enshrined the rule of ordinary citizens and with it had displaced any hope for a natural aristocracy that should develop in the normal course of evolutionary development of the state. There is a sense in which we may say Washington, Jefferson, and Madison represented a sort of natural aristocracy in the classical sense of the term; naturally superior individuals who could define the nature of the polity in elevated terms. But Hamilton also had a point in his criticism of Jefferson that applied to the Southern aristocracy as a whole. Ultimately, Hamilton thought this was an example of a false aristocracy because it was built on principles contrary to the Declaration of Independence. By the time of the Civil War it was even less an aristocracy and more of a classical oligarchy—a corrupt form of rule. American progressives sought to educate talent to rule. It is reflected in Croly's condescension for the ordinary citizen that was a commonplace sentiment among most progressives. Only progressive intellectuals, the new elite, would be capable of producing the enlightened rule that would be progressive democracy.

It is here, as we peel away layers of progressive thought, that we come to the heart of Croly's science of politics and, with it, much of the liberal-progressive objection to the founders. Any serious science of politics will be built, implicitly or explicitly, on a view of human nature. If we may judge by what they wrote, most progressives certainly viewed themselves as the most evolved products of the human species. But both German historicism and Darwinian science had challenged the notion of a fixed human nature. Progressives embraced both of these arguments and in the process rejected any science of politics built on any notion of practical limits as to what is or is not possible. It was not conducive to political modesty about what is or is not either theoretically or prudentially possible. It stands in sharp contrast with the founders and a brief mention is necessary because the contrast stands out in such sharp relief with Croly.

The American founders had what may be called a "sober" view of human nature. They thought ordinary people were quite capable of greatness and nobility, especially if given sufficient freedom. But they also understood human depravity. Even the best of people could behave quite badly at times. This is why the powers of government had to be strictly limited and arranged in such a way that the tyranny of either an individual or an overbearing faction would at least find the path to power difficult, if not impossible in absolute terms. In the words of Madison, "in a nation of philosophers, this consideration ought to be disregarded. A reverence for the laws, would be sufficiently inculcated by the voice of an enlightened reason. But a nation of philosophers is as little to be expected as the philosophical race of kings wished for by Plato" (*Fed. 54*). Imperfect human nature put limits on what we can reasonably expect from any form of government.

But it was precisely "limits on human nature" that Croly, and progressives in general, rejected. Darwin had already taught progressives that there was nothing fixed in the evolution of any species, humans included. What could this mean in evolutionary terms except that imperfection itself was merely a temporary stage in movement toward perfection? Progressive democracy, he wrote, required a new and different foundation that reflected this new reality of how we understand nature; "Democracy must stand or fall on a platform of human perfectibility. If human nature cannot be improved by institutions, democracy is at best a more than usually safe form of political organization; and the only interesting inquiry about its future would be: How long will it continue to work?" The purpose of political institutions is not to control or to regulate a permanent human nature, but to change that nature by changing institutions; not merely for transitory reform, but to effect a permanent change in the human condition. He continued, ". . . the sincere democrat is obliged to assume the power of heaven. For him the practical questions are: How can the improvement best be brought about? And, How much may it amount to?"[22] Both are, to say the least, appropriate questions to ask of someone who does not try to disguise the fact that he intends government to play at god-like social engineering.

After reading Croly, it seems that a progressive utopia is a secular paradise no different, really than the material lifestyle most progressives had already achieved. The pursuit of happiness was the pursuit of material well-being. Regime happiness would naturally follow when everyone had achieved secular perfection. It was a place for Croly in which sin was not so much banished as it was ignored on the assumption that it would go quietly into the night. It was much like the modern undergraduate experience with college life. No one would fret about justice since it only required the removal of artificial barriers to make the pursuit of happiness a natural thing. What could be more obvious?

Progressive Democracy and the Solution to Conflict

It is a truism that any notion of political perfection will necessarily be devoid of ordinary political conflict. It is one of the marks of utopian thinking that politics is or will be devoid of conflict; indeed utopianism is antipolitical in precisely this sense that it envisions the end of conflict. Croly's vision of progressive democracy as a polity that at least approaches perfection must be understood, therefore, to aim at nothing less than the abolition of politics and, implicitly, any need for a theory of politics. The reasoning is clear enough, even if its congruence with reality is not. All serious political theory must, at some level, contain a theory of conflict. The end of conflict is the end of political science. Is conflict inevitable or is it not? Croly thought that it was not inevitable because he thought of progressive democracy in terms of political perfection. What is at issue here is not the political viability of Croly's argument on how conflict might be abolished, but rather the implications of his argument. The notion that conflict might be avoided by the correct application of scientific social engineering is one of the abiding assumptions of the progressive worldview in general and Croly in particular.

"Why don't people get along?" is a plaintive cry that has echoed across the centuries. Recognition of the reality of human conflict, at whatever level of intensity, was the beginning of political science for the Greeks as well as the American founders and virtually everyone in between. All of the various arguments that have been advanced for the origins of conflict, from the seven deadly sins through more modern arguments based on economics or the will to power, need not be detailed here. It is sufficient to note that classical political science and the political science upon which natural law arguments were based assumed the permanence of conflict in the human condition. An end to human conflict is one of the distinctly modern arguments and it is rooted in the idea of progress. It is not surprising that American progressives would accept and promote this view of politics.

Conflict in *The Federalist* was described as factional conflict. Factions were famously described by Madison as "a number of citizens, whether amounting to a majority or minority of the whole, who are united and actuated by some common impulse or passion, or of interest, adverse to the rights of other citizens or to the permanent and aggregate interests of the community." It was what he called "the violence of faction" which had been "the mortal disease under which popular governments have everywhere perished." They understood that a democratic tyranny was always a possibility. A solution had to be found or it would not be possible to recommend a popular form of government such as the Constitution proposed. Two solutions presented themselves for consideration; the one, remove the causes of faction, the other, control the effects. The founders opted for controlling the effects because removing the causes was contrary to their natural law understanding of the human condition.

Removing the causes of faction involved two unpalatable choices; "the one by destroying the liberty which is essential to its existence, the other by giving to every citizen the same opinions, the same passions, and the same interests." The first solution strikes at the very purpose of government, as Madison understands it. Without freedom in some degree there is simply no such thing as politics; there is only command and rule; it can be done, but only with the establishment of a tyrannical form of government.

The second solution considered by Madison, giving everyone the same opinions, passions, and interests, simply runs counter to our experience with human nature; it does not seem to be metaphysically possible this side of the grave. We have different opinions because we do not know everything and Madison well understood this reality as well as its practical meaning. For everyone to have the same opinions, passions, and interests, we would have to suppose that opinions about these things could somehow be replaced with an absolute knowledge, presumably available to everyone at more or less the same time. But the idea of absolute knowledge had already entered historicized methodology via Hegel and the German historical school. The founders opted to control the effects of faction because this was the only means of dealing with factions that also preserved a free form of popular government and could be considered theoretically possible. It had the added virtue of being a practical possibility.

Croly was well aware of the problem of factions described by Madison. His solution, however, was precisely the opposite. Progressive democracy would remove the causes of faction. Again, what made the end of conflict seem reasonable to Croly was his view of progress. Progressive intellectuals, those who had absorbed the scientific methodology that had replaced the classical conception, would be in a position to implement true knowledge of the human condition. This part of Croly's argument was perhaps implicit in *The Promise of American Life* but was quite explicit in his second book, *Progressive Democracy* (1914). The problem is not that Croly and progressives in general did not take the problem of tyranny seriously, which they certainly did. But they saw tyranny arise from different sources than the founders, which was no doubt true enough. But in the process they ignored many of the founders' most original contributions to political science and thereby opened themselves to the promotion of progressive tyranny. Their methodology and the language it spawned to describe politics made it difficult for progressives to understand that "progressive tyranny" is not necessarily an oxymoron.

The chief failure of the Constitution in Croly's account, which is in many respects an echo of Woodrow Wilson, was that it failed the test of representing the emerging character of modern society. A science of politics appropriate for an agrarian society would not suffice for an urban, industrial society. It may have been true that the violence of factions was a problem for the founders, but there was no reason why this should persist after the Civil War. The elimination of slavery had removed the primary source of factional conflict in the United States. Further, the practical effect of this change was to remove the chief obstacle to the evolution of a more homogeneous national community. For the first time in American history a greater emphasis on equality of social conditions and a lesser emphasis on individual freedom was possible. He noted with approval, "The ideal of individual justice is being supplemented with the ideal of social justice."[23] Croly did not view social justice as antithetical to individual justice, but rather as a

102

compliment to it. The crux of the matter was over how Croly viewed a democratic community versus the way the founders viewed a republican community. The founders' conception of community was one of diverse opinions, interests, and passions. Croly's conception of a progressive community was more homogeneous and thus less likely to break into factional conflict. The key point for the founders, of course, was that such unanimity of opinion could only be achieved by the elimination of freedom. Croly, however, was up to the challenge.

Croly did not believe that the national community he envisioned would evolve without active assistance—what he called "positive" representation of progressivism versus the "partisan" representation of the founders. Indeed, one is tempted to say that leadership was *the* critical element in Croly's political thought. But it is a disguised form of leadership in certain respects because it is based more on educational or pedagogical qualities than politically charismatic leadership in the more traditional sense. As such, the problem of political demagoguery is also disguised in Croly. It does not appear as grasping for personal power. It rather appears as moral leadership. Whereas the founders' had sought to control the danger of tyranny by a combination of institutional arrangements and moral leadership, Croly put all of his emphasis on moral leadership alone; specifically, the moral leadership of progressive intellectuals such as himself. But, we may ask, how would moral leadership prevail in a democratic system that elected its leaders on a partisan basis? Croly has an answer that reflects the changed meaning of ordinary words in daily use.

Under Croly's vision, "the words 'majority' and 'minority' would assume a somewhat different meaning from that which is attached to them in ordinary political discussion."[24] This alone would change how we understand the problem of conflict. The public, in the act of deliberating actively on different policy options, would be continually debating the reasonableness of the plans being offered by intellectuals using "scientific analysis" to refine their ideas.[25] By science, Croly appears to mean science both as the final end or policy option, as well as the means chosen to reach that end. The function of public debate would be that of deciding from among policy alternatives, all aiming at the same end and all equally scientific. Diversity was reduced to intermural disagreements among progressives on how most efficiently to reach collectivist ends. Demagoguery would be ruled out by the rationality of the proposals themselves; the resultant dialectic, which would involve public opinion "in a welcome struggle for existence," would transform majorities and minorities from antagonists into complimentary educators of one another. The assumption, of course, was that everyone who thought scientifically would agree with each other about ends and any disagreement over means would be resolved without serious conflict. Reactionaries were not merely irrelevant; they were to be systematically ignored in the policy process. Only majorities count in progressive democracy and only progressives represent the majority in scientific terms.

Public administration was the heart of making government a scientific extension of public opinion as expressed in the national community as a whole. But administration, while at the disposal of the executive, was not the same thing as the executive. Executives come and go, but administrators would be "scientists" in the sense of public policy "experts" who would not change with each election of a new president. Executives reflected only the temporary will of the majority that placed them in office, whereas the new administrators would be a disinterested cadre of experts who would assist the president in formulating policy choices that were presented to the public as scientific in nature. In his provocative chapter entitled "Visions of a New State," Croly wrote, "The administration becomes, indeed, the government in the English sense of the word, whose duty it is to propose desirable measures of state policy and whose authority is sufficient to carry out its measures—as long as it retains public confidence."[26]

The progressives thought that politics might be reduced to administration, which could, in turn, be the proper science for a democracy. Both Woodrow Wilson and Frank Goodnow, the first president of the American Political Science Association, had pioneered this part of the progressive argument and Croly was merely following their example. As Croly's collaborator at *The New Republic*, Walter Lippmann, put it at about the same time, "we have a right to call science the discipline of democracy."[27] Both Croly and Lippmann agreed that democracy could not reach its full potential until democracy was permanently wedded to the science represented by progressive intellectuals. Scientific administration would replace "partisan democracy" on behalf of a "disinterested public object." The very purpose of science was to settle disputes among different opinions by reducing them to a rational set of calculations for the common good. Such calculations could not be reduced to a permanent body of law, for "the really permanent element of the life of the community will be derived not from the accepted aspects of the program, but from the progressive democratic faith and ideal."[28] The scientific administrator was not a "bureaucrat," but rather an "agent of democracy." As such, the administrator "must foreshadow the completer [sic] kind of manhood ... (whose) authority will depend, as we have seen, on its ability to apply scientific knowledge to the realization of social purposes."[29]

What is required of the progressive intellectual is faith in democracy itself. "Faith is the primary virtue demanded by the social education of democracy," he wrote, and added significantly, "in case human nature is capable of salvation."[30] It was to be a faith explicitly analogous to that of St. Paul, but with the difference that salvation would come, much more scientifically, from politics. Croly may have picked up this secular religious element from his father's philosophical mentor Auguste Comte. But from wherever he picked it up, it was a logical outcome of the idea of secular progress. In Croly's version of secular humanism, the City of Man would replace the City of God as the end point of progress. It would seem that when people in general and intellectuals in particular stop believing in God they do not believe in nothing, rather they are likely to believe in anything.

The Legacy of Croly in American Politics

A hundred years after he first wrote, Croly is probably more widely read by conservatives and nonprogressives searching for the foundations of liberal-progressivism than by most liberal-progressives themselves. This is not because Croly has somehow been rejected but because the liberal-progressive tradition in American politics has built on foundations he articulated and moved on, typically without a full acknowledgement of the debt it owes him. Croly showed progressives how to understand and use the electoral process as a means to achieve the progressive state. He showed them how to translate progressive theory into progressive practice; it was a blueprint for political practice that has been the mainstay for progressive politics ever since. Further, Croly combined practical politics with a quasi-religious idealism that is so often characteristic of secular humanism. Progressives also have their gods.

Croly understood, perhaps better than most other progressives that man does not live by science alone. Progressive democracy was not only scientific, but it rested, in the final analysis on a secular faith that was the new religion of the intellectual class. It was "not merely a new method, important as a new method may be, but a new faith, upon the rock of which may be built a better structure of individual and social life."[31] Democracy was the secular god for progressive intellectuals who could no longer abide traditional religious life but still needed something to believe in.

One of the fundamental consequences of Croly's conception of democracy was that democracy as a form of government seemed remarkably unproblematic; rather, it is the final solution to all the discontents of the human condition. It is in the closing chapters of *Progressive Democracy* that we can see how the foundations of a progressive science of politics take on the attributes of a new sort of religion rather than a science of politics in the classical sense—the sense that still animated the American founders. The mysticism in Croly's idealism is largely rooted the paradox of progress itself, a paradox Croly saw but could not resolve by a strict reference to science. As first philosophy and then science have replaced religion as a framework for understanding the human condition, the spirit that once animated religion now animates the faith of progressive democracy. The hypocrisy of defending socially imperfect systems with religious faith and natural law is ultimately doomed to failure in the progressive historical narrative. But the defense of progressive democracy, because it is scientific, will not fail because its foundation is reason. It was writers such as Croly, not the original founders, who helped to create a divinized idea of the state. It was a secularized divinity to be sure, but a divinity endowed with the total powers of God nevertheless.

Croly's legacy on the theory and practice of progressivism are connected as if by an essential link that cannot be cut without damaging how we understand both the influence of Croly on the progressive tradition and the subsequent development of progressivism. At the level of abstract theory, Croly was perhaps the first progressive to openly embrace the idea that progressive democracy aspired toward perfection and acknowledge that its policies were shaped by this fact. And since the very definition of perfection precluded political conflict, the violence of factions in the founders' lexicon, Croly identified the abolition of conflict as the ultimate aim of the progressive state. The attainment of this end was the idealism of progressive politics that joined theory with practice.

Practical politics meant that progressive politicians would participate in this eschatological unfolding of history by removing property and later other sources of conflict as the precondition for a more purified form of democracy. This in turn required ever more concentration of power in the state in order to remake the national community, which tended to resist homogenization, into a more egalitarian and less individualistic community through a system of government regulation and income redistribution.

There is both an irony as well as incoherence in Croly's redefinition of democracy that reflects one of the major sources of tension in progressivism. The irony is that a new elite of progressive intellectuals will be the true rulers of the regime and the many, the actual *demos*, would rule only in appearance. This is, to say the least, more of an oligarchy and less of a democracy than most nonprogressive definitions of democracy would allow. Such a regime, in practice and in principle, is less tolerant of diversity than the founders envisioned and is the potential source of a progressive tyranny. Diversity, whatever may be left of the word at this point, is certainly not interpreted to mean tolerance for unscientific opinions.

The practical incoherence stems from the requirement that these new elites must, by the nature of the electoral process outlined in the Constitution, cultivate particular factions within the polity in order to rule. This necessarily includes major businesses and organized unions that control large amounts of wealth and votes. The very natural diversity of the national electorate works against long-term unity. The result is typically a system of transitory coalitions based on a kind of crony capitalism, often far more corrupt than the free market system it seeks to replace. The new corruption stems from the rationalization of its morally corrosive features. The idea of a free economic market as the preferred economic system for a free polity was not part of the progressive understanding of political perfection. A market economy is what the New Deal writer Thurman Arnold called "The Folklore of Capitalism."[32] The very language of progressivism makes it difficult for progressives to engage in the sort of critical self-evaluation that is necessary for the survival of free government. And the notion that economics is the key source of conflict that can only be relieved by a government redistribution of wealth carries with it the seeds of its own problems. Progressive rule requires the resources best generated by a free market system in order to carry out its policies. Progressive elites can and do win elections and rule in such a system, but if the economy does not grow enough to positively affect a wide range of citizens, and if dividing up the economic spoils begins to approach a zero-sum game, even with periodic elections, is more likely to increase rather than decrease factional conflict. It is unlikely either Jefferson or Hamilton would see any of their handiwork in such a system.

Croly gave progressives a science of politics not only at odds with that of the founders' but also, at the deepest level, with ordinary human experience. The idea that progressive democracy requires human perfection to make it work nicely illustrates one of the pitfalls of being on the cutting edge of theoretically improbable ideas. Human perfectibility as a foundation for a science of politics would seem to be such an absurdity that it could not possibly survive serious analysis. Yet it has not only survived but also thrived. How is this possible? There are a number of reasons.

The Progressive Movement measured progress in wholly secular terms. Its animating idealism for Croly meant, as it did for Comte, movement toward earthly perfectionism. The founders' constitutional system did not require perfection. On the contrary, it assumed imperfection and the Constitution was constructed accordingly. But the assault on natural law along with religion by progressives undercut any notion that imperfection is a source of ordinary human experience; perfection was an experience that was anticipated to happen in the here and now. Croly assumed that history was both secular and progressive and, therefore, there was no reason to think of government in terms of experienced human nature. Darwin's rejection of cosmic purpose had, ironically, opened the door to the notion of evolutionary perfection for progressive intellectuals. But whatever fantasies they may have privately entertained, none stepped through that door until Croly showed them that perfection was the idealism that had all along animated their political science. That vision of a perfected secular social order was akin to a revelation. The problem was that if a science of politics is untethered to any view of human nature grounded either in ordinary experience or is yoked to a philosophical foundation that recognizes no limits as to what is metaphysically possible, perfected government may seem altogether reasonable as well as inevitable. They could be Darwinians and simultaneously reject purposeless evolution. It was the best of both worlds; scientific and utopian together.

As Croly and other progressives well understood, some political means would have to be found to move toward perfection of the human condition. The idea of progress always contained the germ of teleology in some form. What teleology needed was specificity with regard to both form and process. The means would be a political party in which the Democratic Party after 1912 increasingly played that role. But most progressives also recognized that idealism had to be built on a sound scientific methodology. Croly had clearly pushed all of the right buttons that excited the progressive imagination and just as clearly laid out a political strategy for a new electoral order. He had all of the instincts of progressivism but was not intellectually grounded in the emerging methodology of the social sciences. In this sense Croly was incomplete by himself. Granted progressive democracy was the *telos* of historical progress, what was needed was a practical roadmap of how to translate theory into practice. A map of the way forward was at hand.

The Progressive Interpretation of Progressivism

Benjamin Parke DeWitt's *The Progressive Movement* (1915) was probably the first work in the progressive canon that attempted to link practical electoral politics with the utopian elements of Herbert Croly. To say that defining perfection in secular terms is a tall order risks understating the problem DeWitt faced. Perfection, even perfection that aims at justice, can be a vague concept even the best of writers. One person's perfection may be another person's nightmare. In this regard, there is probably none better than Plato, yet who would want to live in Plato's *Republic*? Certainly not the American founders, nor would most progressives, except insofar as both Plato's *Republic* and Croly's progressive democracy were both ruled by self-appointed philosopher kings. Plato at least understood that his was a city in speech and likely constructed more for heuristic reasons than for reasons of practical politics. Croly, however, had no such inhibitions. Indeed, some progressives thought that time was immanent and constructed a history of the Progressive Movement that reflected that faith in historical progress. The immanent transformation of the human condition was always latent in the idea of progress from the outset, but DeWitt made it both explicit and seemingly rational to a generation of progressives unschooled in the concept of modern Gnosticism. De Witt is not a major writer, but he is instructive precisely because he was so much in the mainstream.

DeWitt's *The Progressive Movement* is probably one of the least known of the major progressive tracts. Part of the reason for this is that it is the only thing he ever wrote. He never expanded, rethought, or defended anything that was contained in this one work. But when the work first appeared DeWitt was compared to in the same breath with Croly and not found wanting. There was something in DeWitt that struck a nerve among progressives. The laudatory review of DeWitt in *The American Political Science Review* saw the relationship between Croly and DeWitt as the relationship of theory to practice, with Croly supplying the theory and DeWitt supplying the practice.[33] This was far from faint praise. And if such praise seems excessive when DeWitt's work is compared with other progressive writers part of the reason may be that the basic historical narrative in *The Progressive Movement* is so integral to the progressive interpretation of progressivism that reading DeWitt is tantamount to reading most of the later progressive historians. DeWitt was not a first-rate thinker, but he was perfectly attuned to the progressive climate of opinion extolled by Becker. As such, he is a first-rate window into progressivism when progressivism was in its formative period.

What is most striking about DeWitt's work is how he tied the past, the present, and, most importantly, the future of progressivism into a single, coherent narrative; it has been the paradigm of progressive self-interpretation ever since. At some point a belief in progress needed "relevance" which in turn meant electoral politics in the American regime. So far, so good. Since progressives universally regarded the past as irrelevant, at best, and the present as a mere interlude, only the future could be treated as politically relevant. Not so good. If the future is not to be simply an empty basket, someone has to put something in the basket. DeWitt was that person and the something was socialism; progressive democracy for DeWitt meant democratic socialism. He was not eccentric in this view, but neither was he necessarily typical.

The Progressive Movement has been aptly described as a "quirky" book, which it certainly is.[34] What makes DeWitt a writer of consequence in the progressive library is not his originality; most of his ideas were at least implicit in other writers and can be found elsewhere. His significance is his organizational skill in bringing together the diverse strands of progressive reform and linking them together into a coherent whole for his time and later. He described for progressives what might be called "the rules of electoral politics." It was an impressive achievement and has provided the basic outline for the progressive history of progressivism ever since. Later progressive writers have extended his historical narrative, but none have significantly altered either the theme or the underlying assumptions of it. The most that later progressive writers have done is push further forward the timeline for when the perfected polity would arrive. The immanent expectation of that denouement is always latent and always just beneath the surface.

On the face of it, DeWitt's narrative is structured around the standard progressive interpretation of American politics. Part I is a perfunctory critique of the American founding. DeWitt sets collective justice as not only the alternative to the founders but as a true form of democracy. Part II is a discussion of the Progressive Movement as a whole. This is the heart of his narrative because in it he defines the goal of what progressives mean by "reform" of regime principles. It does not mean mere tinkering, he notes, the passage of a few specific policies, or even constitutional amendments. Rather, the newly founded regime will support a more European form of collectivism, which DeWitt identified as socialism.

It should be noted here that socialism in 1915 was a concept with multiple meanings. It did not have the specific historical reference point in a real regime that it would have a half-century later with Fascist and Marxist states to serve as examples. For most progressives, DeWitt included, socialism was not as much of an economic concept as much as it was a romantic concept; socialism meant the end of conflict, injustice, and all of the political ills of the human condition as it had been experienced throughout history. What made this perfection possible, of course, was the promise of the progressive methodology that tended to treat social ills as economic in origin. Progressive economists tended to eschew socialist utopias at the level of economic analysis, but were fully capable of embracing a bastardized form of socialism as a matter of public policy.

The timing of DeWitt's work could not have been better; 1915 was a particularly propitious time for progressives and DeWitt's interpretation of the 1912 presidential election was not eccentric. Describing the 1912 election as an election that "transformed" American politics is not an exaggeration. Over three quarters of the vote in 1912 was cast for candidates that easily fit the label "progressive." The four-way race presidential election of 1912 was dominated by the progressive reform agenda. Woodrow Wilson ran as a Democratic Party progressive and won with about 42 percent of the popular vote. Theodore Roosevelt, following his dramatic break with the Republican Party, ran as leader of the Progressive Party and finished a respectable second with just under 28 percent of the popular vote. Together Wilson and Roosevelt won about 70 percent of the popular vote. The Republican Party candidate, William Howard Taft, finished a distant third with about 23 percent of the popular vote. In addition, and most important in DeWitt's narrative of the future of progressivism, Eugene Debs led the Socialist Party to its highest popular vote total ever with about 6 percent and made socialism appear to be a permanent force in American politics.[35] DeWitt was enthusiastic about the outcome in 1912 because it meant, as he put it, triumphantly, "The government now seems to have won the victory."[36] DeWitt had caught a glimpse of the future and was enthusiastic with what he saw. It was just what the progressive narrative had predicted.

But the very partisan diversity of the 1912 election posed a problem of interpretation. Was there anything that united Democrats, Progressives, and Socialists, not to mention Prohibitionists and other assorted third-party factions that made up the electorate, that might transcend partisan politics? For example, did they have anything in common with progressivism as an eschatological concept? Certainly DeWitt thought so and much of what gave *The Progressive Movement* its appeal was how he demonstrated what he took to be the unity within the diversity of competing factions. As he put it, "the country had gone progressive," and the task of both the statesman and the historian was to harness progressive politics with progressive theory. What might this mean in terms of what the future might hold? DeWitt had no doubt.

The founders were superseded because whereas the thought of politics as matters of "reflection and choice," the triumph of progressivism revealed the hollowness of this dichotomy. Choice was no longer part of the progressive political equation. Politics was now revealed to be entirely unidirectional; even practical politics was no longer concerned with questions of better and worse. We now have electoral proof of what the public regards as better. The American public had decisively made the choice in 1912. And the theoretical unity of progressivism was to be measured in terms of public opinion in support of progressivism and not partisan division. All that was needed for a scientific interpretation was to show how the Progressive Movement evolved over time and how that evolution pointed toward socialism as the final cause historical evolution. Progress, according to DeWitt, was not automatic but was the work of dedicated and far-seeing progressive heroes. The present electoral triumphs of progressivism confirmed evolution as a human-directed project, at least in politics.

According to DeWitt, the Progressive Movement moved through three distinct phases or stages. This secularized Trinitarian symbolism, it should be noted, was a staple of the secular interpretation of history; it metastasized from Hegel through Marx and into the mainstream of the American progressives. The first stage was in the past and DeWitt described it as the recognition of a general economic crisis in American society after the Civil War. This stage saw the beginnings of social unrest and while progressives diagnosed the ills of society they had not yet worked-out a theory of what to do. The second stage of this broad-based crisis was the practical response that resulted in the 1912 election. This second stage was practical in the sense that political action took place within the electoral process of party politics; it focused on the very practical problem of reforming the necessary machinery of government in order to implement the progressive agenda.[37] The third stage was the goal of progressive reform, defined by DeWitt as socialism. Analytically, each stage could only be understood and interpreted in terms of its relationship with the other stages. And the third stage was the decisive stage.

The third stage, the *telos* of historical progress, was at the heart of DeWitt's description of progressive politics. It was the lynchpin of what he meant by pragmatism in politics. The United States did not need a general uprising of the masses, as Marx envisioned, in order to achieve the victory for socialism; such a victory was just around the corner. He wrote, "This view makes the third phase of the progressive movement in the nation of less *practical* importance—*temporarily*, at least—than the first or second" stages (emphasis mine).[38]

Part of what connected DeWitt to Croly on this point was that Croly had also argued that, in its own unique way, the American political order was not hostile to a dramatic reordering of regime principles that moved it away from the founders. The Constitution was, in a sense, a "living" document for progressives before it became a judicial argument. The final aim of progressive politics, as DeWitt wrote, was "to bring the United States abreast of Germany and other European countries in the matter of remedial legislation."[39] This was not the work of mere tinkering with the Constitution. "To give the federal government the power to grapple with these problems, moreover, would mean more than the mere passing of an amendment or two to the constitution. It would necessitate an upheaval of our entire constitutional and judicial system."[40] The harbinger of this transformation was the Socialist Party in the 1912 election.

DeWitt did not object to anything in the Socialist Party platform, merely that they have no practical roadmap of how to get where they want to go. The relationship of the Socialist Party to the Progressive Party is that of ends and means. "In its relation to the progressive movement at the present time, socialism may be said to be the goal toward which the movement is tending. It is an ideal which the movement hopes someday to be realized."[41] Socialists understood that their triumph would require the total transformation, if not the elimination of the founders' Constitution, but they sought that transformation as a sudden and total event. DeWitt counseled patience. The transformation had begun with the election of Wilson, but the final work was to be the result of a series of incremental and irreversible changes. The end result for progressives and socialists would be the same, but progressives appeared to behave in a more practical approach to that end.

One of the virtues of the Progressive Party was that it made factions within the parties more pronounced than the difference between the parties.[42] This in itself was progress. In the evolution of American politics, the Progressive Party "is not very different than the Socialist Party in many of its beliefs. . . . As time goes by these parties will undoubtedly grow even closer together." The reason for this convergence is clear; "Everywhere in city, state, and nation, there is a growing confidence in the socialization of certain services."[43] Socialists tend to be "all or nothing" in their politics, and this, DeWitt, thinks, is the source of their political weakness. Progressives, on the contrary, believe that legislation freed from the corruption of special interest factions will mean, "no class legislation will result and the best interest of all will have to be observed."[44] The gradual socialization of the economy is inevitable, according to DeWitt, but this process requires the spadework of countless local initiatives. Socialism and progressivism are two sides of the same coin, but progressives are more practical. Progressives recognize responsibility for their actions in a way socialists do not; "Responsibility brings sanity and judgment and the principles of the ideal system become greatly modified when put to the practical test."[45]

Socialism had two fundamental appeals for DeWitt that were not always present among other progressive writers, Croly, for example. First, and perhaps foremost, it would remove the causes of factional conflict that were the root cause of political corruption. Second, it was paternalistic and collectivist in its ethos. At the heart of the socialist agenda, as DeWitt saw it, was its emphasis "in the desirability of extending the functions of government in the interests of the individual and looks upon the removal of corruption and the simplification of government as a mere means to that end."[46] The "Socialist Party, by limiting its demands to a single proposition; i.e., that the community should own the means of production and distribution, has grown with amazing rapidity."[47] But socialists partly misunderstood the appeals of these demands. Socialization of the economy essentially meant the replacement of politics with administration. Woodrow Wilson would agree. No one complained about a government monopoly of the post office or municipal services, for example. There is no reason to believe that the gradual expansion of government into other areas of the economy would not be greeted with similar acceptance; progressive administration was a cure for the mischiefs of faction that had eluded the founders.

DeWitt fully recognized that American culture supported the founders' Constitution and militates against the concentration of political power. But this only means that the third and final stage of progressivism, the socialist end, cannot be achieved at present. Recognition of this reality is the bedrock of progressive pragmatism. "This makes the third phase of the progressive movement in the nation of less *practical* importance—*temporarily* at least—than the first and second."[48] In making the case for socialism as the final phase of progress, it is important to keep in mind that DeWitt was neither unique nor eccentric among progressives who saw some form of socialism or state control of the economy as the final *telos* of progress. The future was on the side of the progressives and all that was needed was a bit of patience that DeWitt thought to be the very essence of progressive pragmatism.

Progressive Democracy and the End of Constitutional Government

In 1914 William Walling could write confidently that it was time for progressives to move beyond mere tinkering with the capitalist system and fully embrace not merely the idea of the socialist state, but take practical steps toward its realization. Government is, Walling wrote, the engine of progress; "the extension of the functions of government to relieve distress . . . is important not so much because of what the national government is doing or can do in enacting remedial legislation, as it is because of what it seemingly ought to do and people generally expect that it will do."[49] While there is no public opinion polling on attitudes "to relieve distress" at the time DeWitt, Walling, and Croly wrote, there is no reason on the face of it to doubt the reality of widespread support for such an attitude. And the expectation in general is not unreasonable. But "to relieve distress" is an ambiguous term that is not easily defined, even in economic terms. The relief of economic distress, however it is defined, is not the only purpose of government and, as the founders understood, diverse interests must somehow be balanced in the common good.

There is no need to inquire into the motives of those progressive intellectuals who built the foundations of progressive democracy;

their stated arguments are clear enough to judge at least some of their passions. It is appropriate however to consider the broad implications of the progressive argument to concentrate political power in the state and subordinate the founders' Constitution to the visions of a few secular intellectuals. Perhaps Alexis de Tocqueville is our best guide on this point. Tocqueville thought that the concentration of power in the state and the host of petty, complicated rules that flow from that concentration is the primary source of modern tyranny that he most feared. But this was not the end of the matter for Tocqueville. He observed that freedom and citizenship in America was associated with an attachment to local communities with their private associations that were a bulwark against the concentration of power by the national government; the national community was an abstraction that was typically engaged only during times of national crisis. This was the difference between freedom and tyranny because the difference between citizens and subjects was largely a matter of where they looked for sources of authority as well as assistance in times of distress. Local communities were where people knew each other by name, addressed each other by name, and could practice self-government. They were the source of American democracy.

In national communities citizens know each other only by abstract associations, such as political parties, and contact is necessarily impersonal; contact was through representative institutions that may be reasonable enough and they no doubt contributed to the common good, but they are not the primary venue for self-government rightly understood. Abstract contact tends to produce abstract thought and abstract thought, especially if it is not grounded in some sort of practical political experience, tends toward ideological thought. Self-government can become an abstract notion at the national level as the government usurps individual freedoms more properly exercised at the local level. The national government depends on the rule of law to preserve the national community as a republic, but it is the nature of the local community that preserves, promotes, and facilitates a self-governing democracy. If the Constitution as the source of law turns out to be a living document with no permanent principles that bind citizens and representatives alike, the rule of law will tend to become arbitrary at best and capricious at its worst. And if Tocqueville is right on the distinction between free citizens and subjects, it does not seem unreasonable to observe that progressive democracy involves a definition of democracy more appropriate for subjects than for free citizens. It is one of the marks of progressivism as an ideology that the tensions are not merely unresolved but inseparable from progressivism as an ideology.

The concentration of power in the nation state will, by its very nature, require administration rather than self-governing citizens to make it work. This concentration of impersonal power was integral to the progressive conception of pragmatic politics. Progressives are surely correct that the establishment of a national democracy will necessarily entail more than tinkering with the Constitution. The difference between a republic and a democracy is clear on this point; a republic may encompass a larger territory, but democracy requires a smaller geographic unit to make it work. We may observe here the tired but true axiom that as the state tends to become larger, the individual tends to become smaller. Further, it is not only the size of government but also the changed function of government that fosters this transformation of the individual citizen into a subject. Limited national government would seem to be a prerequisite for the republican government promoted by the founders; a national democracy will not be a democracy within the definition of the sort of popular government debated at the founding. The broad definition of progressive democracy may well encompass the modern definition of representative democracy, but to the extent that such a democracy is true to its own principles and it seems unlikely that the sort of self-government citizens personally experience will be one of its chief features.

Notes

1. Herbert Croly, *The Promise of American Life* (New York: The Macmillan Company, 1909), 454. Hereafter cited as *Promise.*
2. Paul A. Rahe, *Republics Ancient and Modern: Classical Republicanism and the American Revolution* (Chapel Hill, NC: The University of North Carolina Press, 1992).
3. Theodore Roosevelt, *An Autobiography* (New York: Charles Scribner's Sons, 1915), 25. The decisive link between Roosevelt's ideas he dubbed "The New Nationalism" in 1912 seems strained, this reference in his autobiography to the contrary notwithstanding. First, Roosevelt's heroes, such as Andrew Jackson, were not the heroes of either Weyl or Croly. Second, the publication chronology of their works and Roosevelt's "New Nationalism" does not seem to jibe. It seems more likely that he read Weyl and Croly more or less after he had already made up his mind and he found their ideas compatible with his own. But even if they are merely compatible and not entirely causal, their compatibility is itself revealing and needs to be taken seriously.
4. Most conspicuously, see Arthur M. Schlesinger, Jr., *The Age of Roosevelt: The Crisis of the Old Order* (Boston, MA: Houghton Mifflin and Company, 1957). Every page is another vote for the New deal.

5. One of the most interesting books to trace this influence in the New Deal is the highly charged but revealing work, Jonah Goldberg, *Liberal Fascism: The Secret History of the American Left from Mussolini to the Politics of Meaning* (New York: Doubleday, 2008). My own view is that Goldberg stretches a few points in order to support his general thesis. But his discussion of New Deal intellectuals is well worth serious analysis.

6. Auguste Comte, *Auguste Comte and Positivism: The Essential Writings*, ed. Gertrud Lenzer (New York: Harper Torchbooks, 1975), 83.

7. For example, Arthur M. Schlesinger and Dixon Ryan Fox and a few other progressive historians produced a twelve volume series in the late 1920s and early 1930s under the broad title *A History of American Life*. The volume on the Progressive Era by Harold Underwood Faulkner was appropriately entitled *The History of American Life: The Quest for Social Justice 1898–1914*, vol. XI (New York: The Macmillan Company, 1931). It is an example of progressive historical writing at its best. Every line is a hymn to Croly.

8. *Promise*, 2.

9. Ibid., 5.

10. Ibid., 6.

11. Ibid., 7.

12. Frederick J. Turner, *The Significance of the Frontier in American History*. Annual Report of the American Historical Association for the Year 1893 (Washington, DC: Government Printing Office, 1894).

13. *Promise*, 10.

14. Ibid., 17.

15. Ibid., 21.

16. Ibid., 23.

17. Ibid., 181.

18. Ibid., 193.

19. Ibid., 195.

20. Ibid., 188.

21. Ibid., 188–89.

22. Ibid., 400.

23. Herbert Croly, *Progressive Democracy* (New York: The Macmillan Company, 1914/New Brunswick, NJ: Transaction Press, 1998), 148. Hereafter cited as *PD*.

24. Ibid., 321.

25. See Eldon J. Eisenach, *The Lost Promise of Progressivism* (Lawrence, KS: University Press of Kansas, 1994), 78.

26. *PD*, 295–96.

27. Walter Lippmann, *Drift and Mastery: An Attempt to Diagnose the Current Unrest* (New York: Mitchell Kennerley, 1914), 285.

28. *PD*, 358.

29. Ibid., 376.

30. Ibid., 424–25.

31. Ibid., 25.

32. Thurman W. Arnold, *The Folklore of Capitalism*. With a new introduction by Sidney A. Pearson, Jr. (New Brunswick, NJ: Transaction Press, 2010/New Haven: Yale University Press, 1937).

33. *The American Political Science Review* 9, no. 3 (August 1915): 579.
34. William Schambra, "Saviors of the Constitution," *National Affairs*, no. 10 (Winter 2012): 91–107.
35. See Lewis I. Gould, *Four Hats in the Ring: The 1912 Election and the Birth of Modern American Politics* (Lawrence, KS: The University Press of Kansas, 2008). Sidney M. Milkis, *Theodore Roosevelt, the Progressive Party, and the Transformation of American Democracy* (Lawrence, KS: The University Press of Kansas, 2009).
36. Benjamin Parke DeWitt, *Progressive Democracy. A Non-Partisan, Comprehensive Discussion of Current Tendencies in American Politics* (New York: The Macmillan Co., 1915/New Brunswick, NJ: Transaction Publishers, 2012), 114.
37. Ibid., 21.
38. Ibid., 167.
39. Ibid., 24.
40. Ibid., 163.
41. Ibid., 99.
42. Ibid., 71.
43. Ibid., 97–98.
44. Ibid., 92.
45. Ibid., 86–87.
46. Ibid., 89.
47. Ibid., 106–7.
48. Ibid., 167.
49. William Walling, *Progressivism—And After* (New York: The Macmillan Company, 1914), 162.

IV

The Methodology of Progressive Political Science

The quantitative study of politics quickly became the culminating logic of progressive scholarship. It is difficult to see what could better join the study of the human condition with pure science than quantitative analysis. For the full impact of the progressive methodology on the study of politics one need go no further than the latest issue of *The American Political Science Review*. For progressives, this was a natural development in the sense that quantitative analysis seemed to be science in the purest meaning of the term. After all, numbers don't lie (we hope). At the outset of the Progressive Movement Charles Merriam, widely regarded as the father of behavioral political science, set the tone when he wrote, "Political science as such is or aims to be scientific in method and result."[1] The "and result" is especially telling. In, Merriam's account, political science, sociology, and even history, became scientific only when it replicated the methodology of the natural sciences. The progressive assumption has always been that the results would be commensurate with the methodology.

But quantitative analysis in the social sciences comes with a caveat that is not as evident in the natural sciences. The natural sciences, with biology in the case of man, do not typically study objects endowed with free will. It is not as obvious on the face of it, in spite of what so many progressives assume, that there is a clear and self-evident connection between the natural sciences and the social sciences or, if there is a connection, the precise nature of that connection. What if the connection creates a pseudoscience of politics? It is a question progressives have never seriously addressed and which critics, such as myself, are obliged to be specific regarding whatever objections may apply. The problem of a quantitative approach to the study of politics is not that it fails to address certain questions, but that the methodology, by its own assumptions, precludes asking the traditional questions that are, or were, at the heart of political science. It reinforces the tendency of progressivism, made specific by Dewey, to impose a prohibition on asking certain types of questions; questions of first and final causality are beyond the scope of quantitative studies. This is by design and needs to be more fully understood.

The problem is most obvious when we consider the traditional heart of politics, questions of what is just and what is unjust. Historicism had already reduced all such questions to one of value relativism. But value relativism matters more in politics than it does in biology; a preference for dogs over cats, or vice versa, is typically regarded as a matter of taste. No one thinks that choosing one atomic structure over another involves a moral choice. But the differences in regimes can be a matter of life and death while differences in species are simply curiosities. In any case, it is far from clear that the quantitative study of politics without the assistance of natural law, for example, can get to the heart of questions about justice and injustice, good and evil. Historicism taught progressives that few, if any, ideas are universally held and if they are not universal, they cannot be necessary. And if they are not necessary in general, they cannot be necessary in any particular case. Natural law would seem to be much to specific to ever be a universal principle. In practical terms, that meant that much of the case for a progressive science of politics that will replace the founders stands or falls on the strength or weakness of quantitative social–political–historical analysis.

The Status of Public Opinion and Voting Studies

For the quantitative study of politics both public opinion analysis and voting studies were and remain the most conspicuous subjects of the new methodology. This is scarcely surprising. Both lend themselves to statistical analysis in ways most other aspects of politics do not. But quantitative political studies have their own biases that are typically obscure and the obscurity masks how the methodology contributes to the bias. Quantitative studies purport to bypass ideological concerns and go directly to facts independent of biases or preferences. This is partly true, but the exceptions are substantial. Facts and opinions are not always as easily separated as might be assumed. The quantitative study of politics has always faced the problem of finding a foundation for a preference of one value, or one opinion, over another. Most conspicuously, why prefer democracy, however it is defined? Is value relativism baked into the cake of quantitative politics?

Quantitative analysis of statistical data by itself is not necessarily progressive, liberal, conservative, classical, or any other particular political persuasion. Properly understood, it is a tool best utilized to focus on material and efficient causality in politics; this is not an improper focus. But by itself, quantitative political analysis has nothing to say about either first or final causality beyond providing some way to measure how the best laid plans of mice and men may all too frequently become a cropper. One of the problems with quantitative analysis, at least in the terms the early progressives sought to harness it to the study of politics, was that the methodology often drove the research rather than the research determining the appropriate methodology. Leo Strauss had a point in his critique of quantitative and behaviorist political science as it had developed by the 1960s and much of his critique remains valid. But there is no obvious reason why quantitative analysis cannot help in the study of politics from a classical-natural rights perspective, as long as the study is rooted in asking the necessary questions about purpose, justice, and the like.[2] The particular problems associated with the quantitative study of politics are, however, rooted in the methodology that claims more than the study of politics can admit by the very nature of the human condition. In other words, peculiar problems of progressivism generate peculiar problems in methodology.

First of all, the quantitative study of politics and society does not take place in an intellectual vacuum. This is not the place to compare and contrast various scholars who have utilized quantitative research for liberal or conservative ends. It is sufficient to note that scholars on almost any side of an issue can and will use whatever data may be found in quantitative research to support their position. In this sense, much social science research is at least as likely to be driven by an agenda that is independent from science as one derived from it. This is neither surprising nor sinister. It is merely a reminder that scholars, even the most fair-minded, are typically engaged in their work to a degree not always appreciated by outsiders; this very natural engagement is very frequently subject to all of the ideological biases that plague everyone else. This is certainly true of progressives as well as their critics. When any work is presented as "the latest social science findings," such findings should always be taken with a proverbial grain of salt. Scholars are just as capable of having ideological blind spots or self-deception as anyone else. But what quantitative methodology is most likely to obscure is the importance of first or final causality. The primary concern here is how the progressive use of scientific methodology, primarily quantitative research tools, helped to obscure some of the most important political questions and why this matters. The scientific study of politics is bound by the logic of the progressive paradigm to its methodology of science, both for better and worse.

Public opinion and voting studies are the crown jewels of the progressive argument in the social sciences. Further, they have become the public face of academic political science. And there is no doubt that much has been learned about public opinion and voting behavior since each have received increased emphasis following World War II. It would be churlish to deny their genuine contributions, as it would be to deny any improvements to our general knowledge of how political systems work in theory and practice. But the issue is not whether the scientific study of politics has in some ways advanced our knowledge of politics. It is whether the assumption that science is the only true source of knowledge is in fact a sustainable concept for any study of the human sciences. Tying the study of the human condition to any exclusive methodology to the exclusion of alternative approaches may as likely result in a decrease as an increase of overall knowledge. Such seems to be the case with the modern social sciences. A science that explicitly makes man the measure of all things seems destined to make value relativism one of its core components and man the measure will be a dead end for any subject that requires reflections on good and evil. The quantitative study of politics is a case in point.

James Bryce on Democracy and Public Opinion

The importance of public opinion in the progressive science of politics begins with James Bryce's enormously influential *The American Commonwealth* (1888). This work was the touchstone for the progressive debates about public opinion and modern democracy. The reason for this is not primarily because Bryce was a "progressive" in the meaning of the term used here, but because his work covered so much intellectual territory that it helped to define for scholars of his era and after how they should think about linking political theory with practice. Its influence on progressives, both popular and academic, can scarcely be overemphasized. His work went through numerous editions and for progressives it easily replaced Alexis de Tocqueville's *Democracy in America* as the most oft cited reference for the study of American government by a foreigner. In particular, Bryce's section "Public Opinion" was perhaps the first systematic discussion of public opinion that is recognizable in modern terms. This fact alone gave it primacy of place in the library of progressive thought unlike any other single work on the subject of public opinion.

Bryce captured the imagination of progressives on the subject of public opinion more than any other writer when he wrote, "We talk of public opinion as a new force in the world, conspicuous only since governments began to be popular." The American founders might have said much the same thing, but Bryce broke with the founders by arguing that the quality of opinion rather than institutional arrangements marked the difference between free government and despotic government. He acknowledged that measuring public opinion was more of an art than a science and for this reason democracies required some sort of representative assembly. Modern democracies could not dispense with these assemblies because they were the only way public opinion could be determined between elections. Such assemblies, however, were less than the ideal democracy in which public opinion "would not only reign but govern."[3] What Bryce proposed as the ideal democracy was one in which the rule of public opinion would bypass representative institutions, such as those under the Constitution, although it must be said that he did not pass through that door himself. The time was not quite ripe. What is perhaps most striking in Bryce is how he instinctively adapted the historicist model of political interpretation and how that model shaped his foundational understanding of what democracy was really all about.

According to Bryce, the evolution of government showed it passing through four distinct historically identifiable stages with ideal democracy as the last stage—that is, democracy ruled entirely by enlightened public opinion. The problem, as Bryce saw it, was that all existing democracies were locked into the third stage of representative democracy in which public opinion was registered through voting, political parties, and referendums. In Bryce's scheme, the governing of a regime by public opinion alone would be the fourth and final stage; the end of the history of democracy, so to speak. But what made this fourth stage a practical impossibility, as he saw it, was the technical impossibility of ascertaining the public's will on a continuous basis. It might have been possible in the world of the Greek *polis* where citizens assembled personally to make decisions, and size was the overriding factor. But the size of modern nation state made this a technical impossibility. The democracy of the final stage remained an abstraction. And Madison had made this simple fact one of the cornerstones for a republican as opposed to democratic form of government. The final stage, in Bryce's view, could be reached only "if the will of the majority of the citizens were to be ascertainable at all times, and without the need of passing through a body of representatives, possibly without the need of voting machinery at all."[4] Public opinion in the perfected democracy was intended to close any constitutional space between the rulers and the ruled that had been so carefully crafted by the founders in a republican theory of representative government. In the ideal democracy, the Constitution would be subordinate to public opinion and the space between rulers and ruled would disappear.

Bryce's argument was a view of democracy coincided precisely with the progressive argument. Woodrow Wilson authored a lengthy review of *The American Commonwealth* that praised Bryce effusively. Wilson considered Bryce's selection on public opinion to contain "some of the author's best analytic work."[5] And Wilson well understood the implications of Bryce's argument, even to the extent that he seems to have incorporated Bryce's four stages of political development into his own three stages of development that appeared later in his *Constitutional Government*. The similarities are unmistakable. In Wilson's work, "The difference between a constitutional system and an unconstitutional one is that in a constitutional system the requirements of opinion are clearly formulated and understood, while in an unconstitutional they are vague and conjectural."[6] Wilson echoed the progressive complaint with the Constitution that institutional arrangements, such as the separation of powers, render public opinion "vague and conjectural." The most important consequence of this was that it made political leadership all the more difficult. Wilson's and the progressive notion of presidential leadership could be enhanced if somehow it could unambiguously stand at the head of an aroused public opinion. At a practical level, this emerged as the progressive link between public opinion and executive leadership.

Wilson's theory of executive leadership was built on the mobilization of public opinion that would overwhelm constitutional government altogether. His final stage of democracy was when "the leaders of the people themselves become the government, and the development is complete."[7] In his address before the Virginia Bar Association in 1897, Wilson said, "Policy—where there is no absolute and arbitrary ruler to do the choosing for the whole people—means massed opinion, and the forming of the mass is the whole art and mastery of politics."[8] In the words of one scholar, the interpretation of public opinion was the core of Wilson's idea of executive leadership.[9] Between Bryce, Wilson, and Croly, the modern conception of progressive democracy emerged with public opinion as the lynchpin political leadership; public opinion was the power behind the throne of democratic leadership. Nevertheless, Bryce had put his finger on the central problem of making a pure democracy on a national scale a reality; the technical impossibility of obtaining a continuous measurement of public opinion. But the technical solution was immanent. And, as we might expect, the solution required progressive intellectuals to make it work.

Public Opinion Democracy and Constitutional Democracy

The idea of historical development culminating in a perfected democracy reflected the secular idealism that was always inherent in the progressive critique of natural law. In a very real sense public opinion became a substitute for natural law in the public square. If secular history was evolving toward a more perfect democracy it followed that tracking public opinion was tantamount to tracking the eschatological unfolding of history as movement toward a perfected democracy. The significance of public opinion in this context again can be seen more clearly if we compare and contrast how public opinion fit into the founders' constitutional system with the democratic theory of the progressives.

The founders had also understood public opinion to be the ultimate political power in a republic. But they constructed their theory of republican government in such a way that the authority for the exercise of that opinion was conferred by the Constitution. Further, the Constitution helped to create a space between the government and public opinion that, they hoped, would help enable the reason of the public to prevail over the passions of the public. Public opinion represented power, but not necessarily truth and certainly not necessarily reason. But, as Bryce and his progressive followers made abundantly clear, the aim of progressive democracy was to subordinate the Constitution to popular opinion rather than the other way around. This was made easier because the adoption of the scientific method in the human sciences and the corresponding critique of natural law banished the notion of truth statements in the first place. Truth claims of this sort seemed to be a mask for various forms of elite control of political power, as later deconstructionists would have it.

For progressive intellectuals during this formative period, public opinion and not the Constitution was the final authority on how power would be exercised. The realization of progressive democracy, as Wilson and Croly well understood, required the concentration of power and public opinion was the ultimate power in a democracy however democracy might be defined. The space between public opinion and government had to be eliminated under ideal conditions, or narrowed under less than ideal conditions. The progressive view of the authority for the new claims of public opinion came from the scientific measurement of opinion and not from constitutional arrangements. Elections were, at best, an imperfect means of measuring public opinion because diversity was the culprit inhibiting a unified, organic community.

How to study public opinion and voting in was not as readily apparent to the early progressives as it appears to later generations. Since the middle of the twentieth century public opinion and voting studies have become the public face of modern political science. By the latter half of the twentieth century, citizens became schooled daily in the latest Gallup Poll findings and the ubiquitous pre- and postelection voting studies that are an inescapable part of the mass media punditry. In addition, it must also be said, both public opinion and voting studies may properly be considered the finest products of the scientific science of politics. It is testimony to their importance that the modern study of modern American politics is largely inconceivable if it does not include this sort of quantitative research at some point; virtually everyone routinely makes use of such research, at least insofar as it supports their own positions.

The first academic studies of public opinion focused on public opinion as it was manifest in terms of referendums, initiatives, political parties, elections, and representatives at each level of government. Opinion was typically studied in the context of how it affected various institutions. A reasonable question, however, is whether there is such a thing as pure public opinion apart from any institutional structure? There was a difference of opinion among the first students of public opinion as to what this pure opinion would look like. When Lawrence Lowell, then president of Harvard University, wrote one of the pioneering works on public opinion, *Public Opinion and Popular Government* (1913), he found each of these institutional modes of opinion expression to be unsatisfactory.[10] The more scholars thought about public opinion, the more complex it seemed to be. One of Lowell's insights was that the scientific measurement of public opinion required the study of psychology rather than politics. Pure opinion, it seemed, was independent of politics, and certainly independent of institutions. Ironically for progressives at this point, the study of public opinion seemed to point in the direction of individualism and not collectivism.

There was no consensus among the early progressives on the proper foundation for a scientific study of public opinion beyond science itself. Walter Weyl, a colleague and professional economist at the *New Republic*, in his enormously influential *The New Democracy* (1912), thought of public opinion in economic terms, which he described as "consumer sovereignty."[11] Herbert Croly in his *Progressive Democracy* (1914) echoed the notion that the Constitution had to be judged undemocratic because it did not adequately allow for the full expression of public opinion. He knew public opinion was not fully represented, and this was at the heart of his critique of constitutional government. In Croly's words, "the future of democratic progressivism depends upon the truth of its claim that the emancipation of democracy from the continuing allegiance of any specific formulation of Law, and its increasing ability to act upon its collective purposes."[12] In other words, the institutional structuring of public opinion by such devices as the separation of powers and the constitutional rule of law were clear impediments to a more pure democracy. What eluded Croly and other early progressives was a scientific methodology for the study of opinion. Finding certainty in the study of opinions was certainly elusive.

Walter Lippmann was one of the first writers to think systematically about the problem of public opinion and democratic theory within the progressive tradition, most notably in *Public Opinion* (1922) and *The Phantom Public* (1927). It is interesting to note in this context that he did so with scarcely any reference to opinion polling, which is to say, absent what we think of as quantitative analysis. What Lippmann questioned was whether or not raw public opinion, precisely because of its psychological complexity, could serve as the basis for authority in democracy. For Lippmann, the source of any such authority was in the scientific interpretation of opinion by a specially educated class of intellectuals who could take the raw opinion of the many and make sense of it. Pure opinion could not govern. His thesis on public opinion was relatively simple: In order to make public opinion the authoritative basis of democracy, public opinion would have to be made rational, or at least more rational than it was likely to be in its raw state. For Lippmann, public opinion was less of the rock that Bryce had imagined and more of a construction built on sand that began to slip through our fingers the more we tried to grasp it. Theories of representation did not seem adequate to interpret, much less to channel, public opinion.

In order for public opinion to be made rational, Lippmann thought it would have to pass through the hands of professional administrators. The public influence on government should be understood as more procedural than substantive. As long as the government produced results that were in line with public opinion, the people would have no reason to complain. Administrators, at least those properly schooled in the methodology, would be able to minimize the distorting effects of popular passions. The people as a whole were not competent to decide every technical issue of policy that arose; the very complexity of modern society required experts who specialized in various areas that required technical expertise. And what was true of industry was also true of politics. Understanding the nature of public opinion required what he called "the machinery of knowledge."[13] Exactly what Lippmann meant by "the machinery of knowledge" is not always clear, but at a minimum it seems to have meant the mobilization of academic "experts" who understood the complexities of public opinion better than elected politicians. This shifted the problem of gathering and organizing the study of public opinion to the academic community.

Lippmann's elevation of an intellectual class to the true governing class in modern democracy was at least consistent with the general thrust of progressive political science. Using Aristotle as the model for a classic science of democracy, Lippmann conceded, or perhaps stipulated for the sake of argument, that every Athenian citizen had sufficient knowledge to manage the complex affairs of the classical democratic regime. But he doubted that this was possible in a modern regime. The issue here is not whether he read Aristotle accurately, but that he sensed that modern democracy represented a political terrain in which past traditions would shed little, if any, light. This "steadfast love of fixed principles" was simply not suitable for a complex modern regime such as the United States.[14] Lippmann accepted the critique of the Constitution as an undemocratic document that reflected the economic interests of the original founders, but he thought it could be made more democratic "in spirit," as Jefferson had done, if only organized public opinion could be brought to bear on public policy.[15]

Lippmann was sufficiently astute about political realities that he acknowledged the difficulty of drawing practical conclusions from his practical analysis. Government by experts was his uneasy conclusion, but inescapable and demanded by the nature of modern politics. "If democracy is to be spontaneous, the interests of democracy must remain simple, intelligible, *and easily managed.*"[16] These experts, as

Lippmann conceived them, were neither "liberal" nor "conservative" in the usual sense in which those terms are used. They would be apolitical social scientists whose motives would mimic laboratory scientists. "The social scientist would acquire his dignity and his strength when he has worked out his method."[17] They would organize and staff what he called "intelligence bureaus" for each branch of government and present their "facts" to policy makers but would not be part of the policy making process. "The real sequence should be one where the disinterested expert first finds and formulates the facts for the man of action, and later makes what wisdom he can out of comparison between the decision, which he understands, and the facts, which he organized."[18] Such a view, of course, depended on the unstated assumption that public administrators would be the most impartial and trustworthy interpreters of scientific facts.

Lippmann thought "the democratic fallacy has been its preoccupation with the origins of government rather than with process and results . . . For no matter how government originates, the crucial interest is how power is organized."[19] The purpose of this organization is not to burden every citizen with the demand that he have an expert's opinion on every issue "but to push the burden away from him toward the responsible administration."[20] It was, as Lippmann described it, an appeal to science and reason over superstition and outmoded theories of democracy. "This is not because mankind is inept, or because the appeal to reason is visionary, but because the evolution of reason on political subjects is only in its beginnings."[21] The new and emerging understanding of public opinion was, in Lippmann's view, the beginning of a new science of politics that would finally replace that of the founders after so much frustration.

Quantified Public Opinion and Modern Democracy

The progressive argument for democracy pushed the study political cal science in the direction of public opinion analysis as the practical heart of politics. This, however, raises a question. Which came first, a fundamental change in the way democracy was defined by Bryce, Wilson, and Croly, or the technical revolution in the form of public opinion polls. Certainly the two reinforced each other, but the emphasis points toward the former; a new progressive conception of democracy preceded the quantitative study of politics. It seems unlikely that modern opinion polling would have significantly altered the arguments of *The Federalist*, for example; modern polling might have reinforced for the founders the need for some different or additional form of constitutional space between the governed and the governors. But for progressives opinion polling became central both for the study and practice of politics and crowded out every other consideration. The reasons for this were twofold; one, based on the role played by modern science, and two, how modern science facilitated the concentration of power in the progressive state.

Any emphasis on democracy as a form of government cannot escape thinking about public opinion. This axiom is as true for the founders as it was for the progressives. But even thinking about public opinion has baffled more than one observer. As V. O. Key, Jr., one of the great pioneer scholars on public opinion famously observed, "To speak with precision of public opinion is a task not unlike coming to grips with the Holy Ghost."[22] And scholars such as Charles Merriam were correct to observe that advances in mathematics were bound to provide scholars working in the human sciences with new tools for social analysis. With or without the progressive arguments, the nineteenth century scientific revolution in mathematics, particularly advances in statistical analysis, would have opened up the quantitative analysis of public opinion and voting in ways the founders could not have imagined. In this sense, science really was neutral in the collection and generation a new type of facts not available outside of quantitative methodology. How that collection of facts would change politics, however, was anything but neutral. The very idea of scientific neutrality applied to political analysis faced its most critical test in the study of public opinion. If it did not work here, where would it work?

The concept of nature in any age is always dependent on some metaphysical assumption; such assumptions cannot be avoided. Natural science is as dependent on these assumptions as much as any theory of natural law, even if the assumptions are buried deep in the methodology. Modern natural science, for example, always assumes that nature is rational, or obeys rational principles that are at least partly knowable by reason. If nature is irrational, or if it cannot be known, even in part, by reason, science would not be possible. No one believes gravity is a social construct. Both natural law and science can only be explored by theoretical assumptions that are prior to the exploration itself. It follows that both concepts may best be thought of in the same way we think about Christmas toys; some assembly is required before they can be used as intended. And, like Christmas toys, sometimes the directions get lost or are hard to follow.

The requirement that some theoretical assembly is required before we can study politics is, of course, the soft spot of any theory; facts never speak for themselves any more than the parts of a toy necessarily tell us just what the assembled object will look like. In this sense, methodology often will tend to reinforce whatever preconceived theory may be brought to bear on any particular subject. Most students of public opinion were aware of this, but virtually all thought such biases could be controlled by methodological refinement. To a limited extent this is no doubt true. But the progressive belief in scientific neutrality created the blind spot in the developing methodology; both first and final causality were considered to be beyond the scope of science, rightly understood. Realistically, scientific neutrality that deliberately excludes or ignores certain questions by design will necessarily bias the final analysis.

The study of politics cannot easily escape concerns about purpose and if the questions excluded are serious questions about purpose, the consequence will result in a serious analytic distortion. The working assumption of most students of public opinion analysis is that factual information is a precondition for scientific knowledge. But we cannot know what we need to know until and unless we ask the right questions; factual information, in both natural and human sciences, is better understood as a by-product of the questions we ask. To obscure this sequence is to create either a pseudoscience or, at best, a very incomplete science. And if an incomplete science claims to be complete, it can too easily become a pseudoscience.

It may be stipulated that the study of democracy necessarily requires the study of the opinion(s) of the *demos*. Whoever controls public opinion controls the levers of power. This is why demagoguery is a political problem peculiar to democracy. In the case of the progressives, scientific neutrality in methodology masked the political pursuit of power by progressives; the real power behind the throne of electoral politics was the power to manipulate or interpret public opinion. Few progressive students of democratic public opinion have ever thought that mass opinion represented truth with a capital "T," but all have recognized it as the unifying force in the progressive theory of democracy. Further, although less clearly articulated, the assault on the Constitution required a new source of practical authority, which progressives found in the science of progressive democracy. A scientific analysis of public opinion would make public opinion not only the source of power but the source of authority as well. What true democrat could quarrel with the will of the majority?

Public opinion analysis thus emerged as integral to the progressive assault on the Constitution as defining the form of government. It also implied an assault on fixed rules for government. Rules that limit majority rule are automatically suspect in any form of democracy. And one of the characteristics of government by simple majority rule would be the eclipse of fixed principles derived from a corrupted past. The study of public opinion in this context may be described as an attempt to find new rules for the study of popular government that were fixed in science rather than law. Public opinion as the ultimate source of political power did not change between the founders and the progressives, but the progressive attack on the Constitution did change the source of authority. Authority was now to be found in scientific methodology and not the rule of law. If the scientific measurement of public opinion clashed with the clear meaning of the Constitution, it was the latter that had to give way.

Absent the Constitution, with all that implied, what remained in practical politics for progressives was the power of public opinion. And practical politics meant the mobilization of public opinion in a way that would overwhelm any constitutional limitations on the exercise of that power. In this process, the founders' distinction between the reason of the people and the passion of the people, both of which they thought are contained within the concept of public opinion, was lost. Opinion can be measured, more or less, in quantitative terms, but not reason, and an opinion does not somehow become more or less rational by the scientific means of measurement. Opinion polling can measure the spectrum of opinion, but no matter how accurately that spectrum is measured methodology alone cannot determine whether or not one opinion is better or worse than another. Natural law or religion might suggest at least the direction of one such measure, but if either or both are excluded *a priori*, all that is left is a spectrum of opinion with no obvious way to help decide if one opinion is better than another.

The reduction of political science to quantitative measurement may not have been inevitable, but it was certainly logical given the starting point of science defined in largely mathematical terms. If public opinion could somehow be studied by the methods of economic analysis, for example, then the new science of politics could be built on a scientific foundation that would be wholly mathematical. Unlike natural law, the new foundation would be ethically neutral and, therefore, the results would be scientifically unassailable. The goal was a true "political science" that would not be the oxymoron that almost every college undergraduate instinctively thinks it is.

From the outset the quantitative study of politics has promised, or perhaps more accurately threatened, to replace the older science of politics in *The Federalist* that scholars such as Charles Merriam typically referred to as "normative" or "wisdom" political science, which they never tired of alleging were unsupported by empirical facts. On the surface, the basic reasons for this attitude are not difficult to fathom. With opinion polling and the new science of politics has been able to generate a form of evidently factual information that otherwise would not exist as something knowable and in the process to transform that information into a normative power to be reckoned with. Some scholars have thought that this revolution has impoverished the study of American politics by focusing on relatively trivial things that can be quantified at the expense of significant things that cannot so easily, if at all, be quantified—"that it fiddles while Rome burns," as Leo Strauss once put it.[23] But, as another scholar put it, "The modern state is an edifice built on numbers."[24] Public opinion polls are part of those numbers and, hence, part of that edifice.

Much of the methodology of modern public opinion polling is built on the assumption that quantitative measurement can make a sharp distinction between facts and values. We may not know whether X is better than Y, but we can know percentages of popular support for X and Y and make our political calculations accordingly. This assumption was integral to Max Weber's insight that the utilization of numbers in modern politics represents a rationalization of political life that has roots much deeper than the polls themselves. The roots were in the fact-value dichotomy of epistemology that emerged out of Enlightenment rationalism and through it was linked the rise of modern democracies. By the "rationalization" of politics what Weber meant was the tendency of modern politics to quantify certain types of information for the purpose of achieving certain specific, short-term goals. This numerical rationalization, he thought, came at the expense of serious thinking about the purpose of government that had previously been the first question in a science of politics. The practical effect of this, Weber thought, was the bureaucratization of all modern governments that blurred the classical distinctions between different forms of government; monarchy, aristocracy, and democracy were all the same in their bureaucratic foundation; progressives did not necessarily disagree.

In practice, Weber thought, this bureaucratization of modern government not only made classical typologies of regimes irrelevant, but that instrumental reasoning, as opposed to philosophical reasoning, was paramount in modern democratic thought. Weber well understood the moral dead end of purely instrumental reasoning, but offered nothing to replace it. In his famous essay, "Politics as a Vocation," delivered originally at Munich University in 1918, he explicitly denied that what we call the modern "state" could be identified in terms of its professed ends. But the lesson Weber drew from this distinction was that facts were "dead" without some corresponding "value" that was the basis of interpreting facts, and science could afford no such foundation. This led him to the notion, commonly and rightly associated with Nietzsche, and less systematically by Woodrow Wilson, that values were something asserted by charismatic leaders who were the real builders of the modern state.[25] The quantification of public opinion into the source of political power in the modern state was fraught with consequences that Weber understood but could think of no defense to control. This increased the likelihood of political demagoguery with nothing to control that demagoguery but the moral character of the leader. But if all moral reasoning is merely opinion what serious control can be expected? This was the conundrum Weber faced and was unable to resolve. The progressives fared no better and for much the same reasons.

George Gallup and the *Pulse of Democracy*

It will be helpful here to briefly consider the development of quantified public opinion through polling. The first opinion polls were referred to as straw polls, in which newspaper reporters typically went out and interviewed ordinary people for their opinions. Examples of these straw polls can be found throughout nineteenth century journalism. At first these unscientific straw polls and more scientific polling overlapped and not everyone in academia thought opinion polling was the precise science later generations came to accept.[26] The presidential election of 1936 remains perhaps the most famous example of both the overlap between straw polls and quantitative polling and the reason why the quantitative methodology of polling emerged victorious. It was no contest and the reason was clear to everyone.

The most famous straw poll in the early twentieth century was the *Literary Digest* poll aimed at predicting presidential elections that began in 1920 and lasted until its disastrous failure in 1936. The mechanics of straw polling at this level were a disaster waiting to happen. The *Literary*

Digest poll failed because it used a methodology of asking readers to mail-in their intended presidential vote that was later supplemented with telephone interviews in 1936. Still, the technique seemed to work more or less as the poll accurately predicted every election through 1932. But in 1936 the *Literary Digest* predicted the election of Alf Landon over the reelection of Franklin Roosevelt. In fact, Roosevelt won with about 60 percent of the popular vote. Something was amiss in polling.

What seems to have happened is that the people who read the *Literary Digest,* and mailed-in their postcards, probably voted for Landon while the overwhelming majority of those who did not read the *Literary Digest*, which was, after all, almost the whole of the country, voted for Roosevelt. Readers of the *Literary Digest* were hardly a random sample of the American public. Further compounding the methodological problem, telephone interviews were less reliable in 1936 that they might have been earlier or later because large numbers of people gave up telephones during the Great Depression. More people actually had telephones during the 1920s than the 1930s. The *Literary Digest* folded-up shortly thereafter and its polling fiasco is the stuff of folklore for every student of modern public opinion polling.

The *Literary Digest* failure, in its own way however, marked the beginning of mass opinion polling. In 1936 a somewhat obscure pollster, George Gallup, got the electoral percentage for Roosevelt right almost to the decimal point. His previous opinion polling went from a curiosity confined to the editorial pages of the *Washington Post* to an overnight sensation. This elevated commentary on Gallup's "scientific poll" to a subject integral to the presidential election itself. Polls had become, permanently it seems, part of the public discussion of electoral politics. How did he do it?

George Gallup's personal background was in applied psychology. But he was sufficiently grounded in the political philosophy of the progressives that he conspicuously made Bryce's *The American Commonwealth* the organizing principle for the study of public opinion. Bryce had defined the problem of how public opinion ought to be linked with a democracy and Gallup did not challenge it; instead he embraced with the passion of a missionary. In the process, however, Gallup did, differ in some respects from other progressives. He was more respectful of the founders than most progressives and does not seem to have regarded the Constitution as an obstacle to good government; he certainly did not consider it merely as undemocratic document designed by economic elites looking out for their own interests. On the contrary, Gallup defended scientific opinion polling on the grounds that it would enable Americans to complete the democratic project begun, but never completed, by the founders. It was an echo of Wilson's theory of constitutional development, but without the condescension. Gallup was an optimist who combined a textbook faith in the good sense of the American public with complete confidence in the power of scientific opinion polling to translate that common sense into good government.

This optimism and faith is reflected in his *The Pulse of Democracy* (1940), one of the overlooked but significant works in the development of public opinion analysis. It is well worth a serious reading because it fits so well into the progressive paradigm of the place of public opinion in the construction of a progressive democracy. It is the first complete construction of a philosophy of democratic government built on the quantitative measurement of public opinion. And while Gallup's own methodology has been superseded by a better methodology of random sampling, his scientific assumptions have not. It merits a close reading for its assumptions, analysis, and aspirations. Gallup retains the optimism of the progressive science of politics before the next half century began to erode so much of that initial confidence.

The theoretical failure of the founders, at least in Gallup's view, was not that they were somehow opposed to democracy *per se*, though he did accept this progressive view in an offhand way, but rather that the tools necessary to implement a true democracy in an extended republic were unavailable at the time of the founding. The defenders of what Madison called a "pure democracy" were unable to refute his practical observation that participatory democracy was impossible in any territory as large as the United States. Madison had, of course, critiqued participatory democracy on both practical as well as philosophical grounds, but Gallup focused on the practical objections that he thought to be decisive. What Gallup brought to his work was a theory of democracy that blended seamlessly with Bryce, Wilson, Croly, and the progressive tradition in general. Gallup believed that the final stage of democracy, the complete rule of public opinion, was at hand, or at least immanent, and public opinion polling would be the midwife of this final stage of development.

When Gallup surveyed the status of public opinion polling as it had developed in the 1920s and 1930s, especially in popular consciousness, he could not help but be struck by the gap between academic and business polling, which was his own background, and journalistic polling, which was impressionistic and biased by its straw-poll methodology. The 1936 election had suddenly made scientific polling respectable to the public-at-large; the old straw polls disappeared almost overnight. Gallup's own methodology was suspect among his peers and its details need not be explored here. It is sufficient to note that both Gallup and his academic critics thought advances in science were the solution to whatever shortcomings there might be in opinion polling. At this juncture, Gallup fit, or at least articulated, the progressive paradigm better than most academics.

In 1940, it was far from obvious that the future of world politics would be marked by a democracy triumphant, either that of the founders or the progressives in their more lucid moments. The motivation for Gallup was what he took to be the pressing need to defend democracy against the twin threats of Nazi and Soviet totalitarianism. The passage of time has not dimmed his ultimate concern, and he stated it with characteristic boldness in his opening chapter:

> "Throughout the history of politics this central problem has remained: shall the common people be free to express their basic needs and purposes, or shall they be dominated by a small ruling clique? Shall the goal be the free expression of public opinion, or shall efforts be made to ensure its repression? In a democratic community, the attitudes of the mass of people determine policy. But public opinion is also important in the totalitarian state. Contemporary dictators must inevitably run through the minds of their people—otherwise they would quickly dispense with their elaborate propaganda machines."[27]

Gallup saw public opinion polling as a bulwark against modern tyranny from whatever quarter.

Gallup wrote that from this challenge to democracy "sprung two fundamental questions to which the answer must be given. *Is democracy really inferior to dictatorship? Can democracy develop new techniques to meet the impact of this strange new decade?* Such questions are not academic."[28] The promise of opinion polling was that they would answer, unequivocally, "yes" to both questions. Gallup certainly understood the principled questions of ordinary political science. Opinion polls in the wake of the 1936 election have "demonstrated their accuracy that public opinion can be measured; there is a growing conviction that public opinion *must* be measured." Scientific sampling of public opinion had reached the point whereby it could provide the "machinery" necessary for measuring public opinion on a daily basis, if desired.

What Gallup called "the tempo of the swift moving age" demanded "continuous and rapid measurement of public opinion at all times." One cannot help but be struck by the singleness of purpose that animated Gallup's commitment to democracy, as he understood it. It was this singleness of purpose at the troubled time he wrote that gives *The Pulse of Democracy* its almost missionary flavor.

The Gallup Poll came of age during the administration of Franklin Roosevelt and the New Deal. We can gain some insight into how Gallup thought polling would change the legislative process by looking at what he saw as its most important feature; a more precise knowledge of what the public wanted in legislation. Whereas earlier progressives tended to see any pro-business legislation as a reflection of a constitutional defect in the way economic interests were represented, Gallup saw pro-business opinions as a defect of knowledge by representatives. He repeatedly emphasized that elections alone can never be the sole channel for determining the direction of public opinion; too many electoral variables such as partisan identification, mobilization of factions, and the like will affect elections that give a distorted picture of public opinion. Polls would help the busy legislator sort out the difference between special interests and the general public. In essence, Gallup saw polls as supplementing elections as a source of knowledge for legislators about public opinion.

The more accurate polls became, Gallup reasoned, the more elected representatives would become dependent on them for their instructions regarding the great issues of the day. He was very much aware that opinion could be wrong, but measuring wrongly held opinions merely meant that opinion polling could be the touchstone for the proper education of the public. Polls do not by themselves determine what people think. They are more like a seismograph that simply records opinions that are necessarily formed elsewhere. This could mean the sort of majority tyranny the founders feared, but Gallup denied that majority tyranny has ever been the most serious threat to American democracy. "The real tyranny in America will not come from better knowledge of how majorities feel about the questions of the day which press for solutions. Tyranny comes from ignorance . . . (and) . . . arises when the media of information are closed."[29] The promise of scientific polling was to educate both the public and their representatives in a way that closed the gap between the educated few and the uneducated many that had bedeviled Croly, Lippmann, and other progressives.

Vox Populi, Vox Dei?

The science of public opinion polling has changed a great deal since Gallup correctly called the 1936 election. But the changes have been, for the most part, technical changes in the collection and analysis of data, not the foundational assumptions about the role public opinion ought to play in a democracy.[30] What is most significant about *The Pulse of Democracy* is that while technology is much improved, the fundamental theory of how public opinion fits into progressive democracy is fundamentally unchanged from Bryce through Gallup and beyond. But clouds have appeared on the horizon. Most contemporary pollsters, for example, are far less certain than was Gallup that polls can be as accurate and precise as he thought. Both Gallup and later pollsters are aware of how the finer points of opinion polling, such as question wording and question sequence can affect the outcome of polls. Later pollsters have learned, often from painful experience, methodological pitfalls that await the unwary.[31] To this extent, later opinion polling is probably more modest in its pretentions than it was at the outset when Gallup wrote.

What the foundational assumptions of *The Pulse of Democracy* provides students of American politics is one half of two distinct sciences of American democracy; one half based on polls and the other half on the Constitution. Both arguments have existed uneasily side-by-side ever since. In this sense Gallup, and his successors may be said to have completed the theory progressive democracy inaugurated by Bryce, Wilson, and Croly, but he has by no means completely vanquished the constitutionalists. It is no doubt true that additional technologies, motion pictures, radio, television, and the Internet have changed the face and texture of American politics in ways the early progressives did not anticipate. But it is also important to understand that these technical changes are in the nature of a superstructure and not a foundation for the progressive science of politics. Polling as a neutral research tool is not the same thing as polling that is intended to support a change the nature of the American regime.

George Gallup, on the other hand, and the army of academic pollsters who followed in his wake, could foresee a technology that would collapse the constitutional space between citizens and government in a way the founders could not have envisioned. Whatever remained of Madison's philosophical arguments about size as the determining factor for a participatory democracy, opinion polling threatened to make them obsolete by modern technology. The practical side was no doubt as valid as ever, but the practical side was placed under severe stress.[32] The result of this stress has been something of a particularly modern hybrid of participatory democracy. A preference for Constitutional government over the hybrid participatory democracy represented by opinion polls tends to be a minority argument and minority arguments have a precarious status in a popular form of government. The violence of factions remains in progressive democracy, despite its aim to eliminate the causes, but without the mitigation of constitutional space that might help to refine and enlarge the opinions that divide them.

It is not clear that opinion polling has managed to escape the classical dilemmas of public opinion in a participatory democracy, but it does seem more obvious that opinion polling has put a new edge on these controversies. It is now technically possible to imagine a system that instantly registers mass public opinion on a continual basis. In the 1992 presidential campaign, for example, third party candidate H. Ross Perot proposed to establish a system that would do just that under the campaign slogan "I'm Ross, you're the boss." Although Perot was not very clear about any specifics of such a proposal, his personal link as CEO of a company that represented cutting edge technology in the United States added credence to his slogan. Perot seems to have instinctively realized, at least implicitly, that public opinion polling can, in a unique way, concentrate the full weight of public opinion on government policy that weakens the rational for representative government as well as the separation of powers. This is a trend that seems likely to accelerate in one way or another since the philosophical objections to a pure democracy have been weakened over the course of the twentieth century.

The democratic theory implicit in public opinion polling is an effort to reduce the theory and practice of a liberal democracy to a simple proposition; the translation of majority opinion into public policy. In part this is accomplished whenever pollsters force public opinion into preconceived categories, such as race, class, or gender, that may achieve a degree of mathematical certainty but at the same time tend to lose much nuance and genuine diversity. The diversity, for example, comes not so much from the opinions as from the preconceived categories. From the perspective of the founders, the price tag for this mathematical certainty is high. The price is the moral reasoning in natural law that while just government is based on the consent of the governed, it also falls under the judgment of "Nature and Nature's God." Such reasoning does not easily lend itself to the quantified rationality of opinion polling. Science as the source of authority, even under the impact of Kuhn's theory of scientific paradigms, is not typically debated in terms of majority and minority opinions.[33] And a theory of democracy divorced from moral reasoning is unlikely to produce a democratic theory capable of maintaining the sort of democracy that Gallup and so many others have taken to be the norm—a democracy worthy of the affection of its citizens.

The proper definition of democracy is critical because our evaluation of its health and performance is largely a product of that definition. The variety of available definitions, however, does not mean that the term "democracy" is infinitely plastic or that one definition is as good as another, or that such questions are "abstract" because they defy quantification. For example, if democracy is defined solely in terms of participation, either as Madison understood the term or as it has come to be defined by opinion polls, procedural changes will have a different connotation than if democracy is defined in terms of representation. Proposals that enhance participation may undermine representation. Public opinion analysis will, as a consequence, take on a different meaning within the context of each definition. Each context will prejudge how we evaluate constitutional institutions. Congress is perhaps the most conspicuous example for both the founders and the progressives.

The institutional performance of Congress is invariably evaluated in terms of whether it should be a deliberative institution or merely reflect public opinion. If it is to be the latter, then we may want to follow the logic of Wilson, Gallup, and Perot and remove the deliberative function of Congress altogether. If the function of Congress is merely to be the place where public opinion is registered, is not obvious on what grounds a bicameral legislature can be defended. Part of any defense would have to include some defense of refined public opinion. What would Congress have to deliberate if its sole or primary function is to simply translate public opinion into policy? At some point, it seems, even Perot would have to sort out contradictory expressions of public opinion, asymmetrically distributed throughout the nation, that simultaneously support more public services and less taxes.

The dilemma of democratic theory that came out of Bryce and the Progressive Era, broadly understood, is not that it is "wrong" in some theoretical sense or that it cannot be implemented (perhaps) in a practical sense, but that it is a theory that is in conflict with the political science found in the Constitution. Further, it is difficult to imagine just how public opinion by itself can be a foundational argument for a just democracy. Public opinion can be and often is the basis for just or right political action whenever that opinion is based on something that is itself based on something just or right; a quality provided by natural rights reasoning, for example. But by itself public opinion requires a foundation to rest upon or it will, as Lippmann discovered, slip like sand on a beach as the high and low tides come in and go out. Whether Bryce or the founders have the better argument is not in itself to be decided by public opinion polling but rather by a serious inquiry into the strengths and weaknesses of each; the sort of inquiry that is the particular province of political science properly understood. Scientifically measured opinion is still opinion, and unlike ordinary natural science reasoning that does not depend on majority and minority views for its truth, political opinions are something that will provoke factional conflicts whether majority or minority.[34]

The philosophical trap of scientific political science in the progressive mold is that it cannot tell us whether one course of political action is morally superior to another. It cannot give us a reference point from which to make moral judgments about the things we do. At most it can provide a rude cost/benefit analysis. The problem is rooted in the foundational assumption that political science can be a science after the model of the natural or physical sciences. If this is a false assumption, it follows that it is a false science; it cannot really be empirical with regard moral actions that are the heart of real politics. And if it is a false science, it cannot be falsified by reality. No quantitative study of politics can ever falsify progressivism. That said, it is nevertheless true that scholars have become increasingly sensitive to these shortcomings of quantitative political science.

Progressives and Founders on Public Opinion

It is a banal but nevertheless significant observation to make at the outset that the quantitative study of public opinion and voting would not have been possible at the time of the American founding. The development of mathematics in the nineteenth century, most especially the mathematics of probability, opened the door to this new mode of study. This makes it difficult to compare the political science of the progressives with that of the founders. But that does not mean that there is nothing to be gained by asking what the founders' might have said regarding these studies. The analysis of how a particular party or candidate put together a majority coalition for any particular election is significant information that is helpful for trying to understand contemporary politics. No doubt any of the founders who ran for office or even wrote about politics would appreciate this sort of information. But what is of more pressing interest is the foundational arguments and how they affect analysis.

We may concede that something is gained by these studies, but we are also obligated to ask if something is also lost. We may also ask whether what is lost is worth the corresponding gain. Is there anything of general or specific importance that the quantitative study of the social sciences has omitted? We need to again take up the beginning of the progressive view of how and where public opinion fit into progressive democracy.

We may gain some sense of how opinion polls have changed our understanding of modern democracy by returning to how the founders might have responded to public opinion polling. In particular, how are polls a challenge to republican government as the founders' designed it in the Constitution? A hypothetical answer might take any number of forms, but if we focus on their approach to the extended republic as a point of departure we may catch a glimpse of the change and the difference it makes. Madison thought that the geographical extent of each of the American states, much less the states joined in a single union of states, made participatory democracy unworkable; it was impossible for all of the citizens to assemble in a single place, as they had done in Athens, and make whatever decisions had to be made. And whenever citizens did meet in a town square the result was most likely to be conflict between different citizens with different opinions. As a matter of general public opinion almost everyone wants peace, justice, prosperity, and the like, but there is no agreement on how to achieve any of these goals, much less sort out priorities among them if there is a clash. Public opinion on specific issues is unlikely to reflect harmony. The very real political effects of this reality regarding public opinion were the great problem of democracy.

The problem of popular government, as Madison famously said, was the problem of the violence of factions. In a free government different opinions would arise about what ought to be done and conflict was inevitable as factions fought over these opinions. It was a problem that sprang from the nature of public opinion in a free society. It is worth repeating that his solution was to control the effects of faction rather than the causes since trying to control the causes and still maintain a free government were mutually incompatible concepts. The difference between controlling the effects of faction and removing the causes is the difference between free government and tyranny. His defense of a republican form of government over a more democratic form was premised on two separate arguments that encompassed a practical view of how public opinion operated in a popular form of government; one theoretical and the other practical.

The theoretical argument was that a representative system, because of the constitutional space between citizens and representatives, would "refine and enlarge" raw public opinion and give reason a better chance to prevail. That argument could be made with or without modern opinion polling. It gave representatives a measure of independence even as periodic elections kept them tied to their constituents. Republican government was both popular and more insulated from the democratic demagoguery that was the bane of classical democratic systems.

The very practical problem with what Madison called a "pure democracy" was inherent in the classical definition of a democracy. A pure democracy, one in which the citizens assembled in person to make the laws, was not practical in a territory as large as any of the individual states, much less in United States as a whole. The question, "Why did England, France, or Spain not have a democracy in the eighteenth century?" virtually answers itself by the classical definition of a democracy; they were all too large in size to facilitate every citizen meeting somewhere to pass the laws. But this is precisely the point at which opinion polling challenges the founders. Many Anti-Federalists were skeptical of Madison's arguments and would have preferred a more democratic government, but that argument tended to preclude or greatly weaken a national government in the first place. They could not overcome the practical objections to participatory democracy any more than Bryce a century later. Bryce was forced to concede Madison's point and accept a representative system as a less than perfect ideal of democracy. A constitutional space between citizens and governing representatives in a state the size of the United States presented seemingly insurmountable obstacle to a true democracy. All of these calculations by the founders changed with the progressives. This is particularly clear when we think about the linkage of public opinion with voting.

Images of Voting

It is entirely reasonable and logical that the study of voting behavior has been intertwined with the study of public opinion. In contemporary political science, the two are virtually inseparable. And both raise regime level questions about how the American polity operates in both theory and practice.

It should be clear by now that the American regime was designed at its founding in such a way that understanding subsequent American politics also requires understanding both the theory and practice of how the founding principles work, or don't work, as the case may be. In this sense, both theory and practice are not separate categories appropriate for analysis, but together form a continuum of analysis and the two parts can be separated only at the risk of misunderstanding theory or practice—or perhaps both. It is also true that the modern academic study of political science, the overwhelming progressive influence notwithstanding, has no single defining theoretical foundation; different theories using different assumptions is perhaps its most conspicuous feature. The study of voting behavior and democracy is a case in point. The former is typically thought of as the study of practical issues whereas the latter is more commonly thought of as a philosophical question, unsuited for genuine empirical analysis. But this all too frequent distinction is rooted in intellectual amnesia regarding the progressive origins of modern public opinion studies. Theory and practice have never been as separated as much of modern political science has assumed. The separation, however, is one of the reasons why it has been so difficult to reconcile voting studies with the founders' democracy. Even more than public opinion, the quantitative study of voting lent itself to a mechanistic interpretation of politics; the multiple variables than compromise an explanation of voting can be modeled in much the same way the natural sciences model physical phenomenon. The progressive separation of the process of government from the purpose of government precipitated this approach.

Studying the process without an explicit acknowledgement of the purpose of government is unchartered territory for any science of politics from Plato through the American founders. But, that said, it did not mean that progressive scholars were unconcerned with the purpose of government, albeit more narrowly conceived than that of the founders and the natural law tradition. The social scientists who were developed within the progressive university system were frequently caught up in the politics, which so much of their work necessarily involves; they were interested in shaping the future for which they had staked their professional lives. The ideal of scientific neutrality should have reduced the impact of ideological commitment, but it did not and it was naïve to think that it would. Concern for the purpose of government was smuggled in the back door of scientific analysis by making democracy the purpose of government. It is hardly surprising, given this working assumption, that elections would be a major concern as well. A great deal of attention has been focused on linking public opinion with voting in the context of a theory of secular progress toward democracy as the eschatological fulfillment of History.

On the face of it we might think that integrating voting studies with democratic theory in the classical sense might find a common ground in a common concern with the health of the polity. But nothing could be further from the truth. Integrating public opinion and voting studies with a normative theory of democracy has been sporadic at best. In part, the problem of integrating the quantitative study of public opinion and elections with the American regime is a problem that seems to be inherent in the progressive science of politics. The progressives insisted that a scientific political science could separate facts from values.[35] But when scholars who worked within the scientific paradigm of quantitative political science attempted to read values back into their data the result was not always an improved mix. Some of the early voting studies are an illustrative example.

Paul Lazarsfeld and his colleagues pioneered the first voting studies in academic political science that utilized quantitative techniques in the 1940s. The methodological assumptions, however, followed the work of Charles Merriam who had founded what was known as "the Chicago School" of political science. These early studies all took place against a backdrop of the rise of Nazi Germany, World War II, and later the Cold War era, all of which paced extraordinary demands on every aspect of the American polity. Lincoln had speculated at Gettysburg whether such a regime as ours might ultimately endure and events in the first half of the twentieth century certainly rekindled those fears. In the words of Lazarsfeld, "the world scene made many people wonder to what extent social events are within the control of various individuals who make up society."[36] These early voting studies reflect a well-founded sense of urgency about the simple survival of a liberal democracy, such as the United States. What had happened in Germany between 1933 and 1945, to say the least, called into question the Enlightenment belief in progress. "Could it happen here?" was a question on everyone's mind. And if it could happen here, might it be by a democratic means in the form of voting a tyrant into office? These were not idle questions then or later.

American democracy had defeated German totalitarianism and Japanese militarism in World War II, but democracy as a form of government seemed more precarious in 1945 than it had a mere decade earlier. After all, in a very real sense, Hitler had been voted into office by a reasonably democratic means, a reality that challenged the facile notion too often in evidence in the progressive science of politics that progress was inevitable and unidirectional. What if Plato was right after all, that democracy was, or at least could be, the last political stage before tyranny? The question of how all of this barbarism had happened thrust the means of maintaining a reasonably just and decent form of democratic government into the forefront of post-World War II political science. Following the German experience, public opinion and elections seemed to be the Achilles heel of democratic regimes. Why was this so and what, if anything, could be done about it?

Lazarsfeld was in many ways representative of this first phase of those scholars who specialized in voting studies.[37] The challenge Fascism represented to American democracy seems to have been continually on his mind and either explicit or implicit throughout his academic work. During World War II he conducted a number of political studies for the government that were aimed at understanding the enemy and strengthening free government; both noble enterprises. Total war had come to include even the social sciences in ways heretofore unimagined. After the war, when he returned to academic life, he began to think about voting and public opinion in terms of the requirements placed on voters to elect representatives who would, in turn, reflect the moral principles of a decent society.

At one level, his problem was a classical problem of "citizen virtue"; what kind of citizen was necessary to maintain this particular regime? In a democracy this seemed to imply voters who would embody democratic principles. The defense of democratic government required nothing less. Plato had argued that every form of government would reflect the dominant political type in that regime; democracy would reflect the collective character of the many. German democracy would reflect German voters and American democracy would reflect American voters. What could be more obvious? But the progressive argument for democracy, the arguments of Herbert Croly, for example, had changed the academic understanding of democracy. Which democratic principles should the voters embody?; The republican principles of the founders or the new democratic principles of the progressives?

When Lazarsfeld thought about these things it is evident that he did not fully grasp the founding arguments. His commitment to quantitative political science seems to have obscured from his view the nature of the classical tradition. When Lazarsfeld referred to "classical democratic theory" he meant a democracy in which citizens would cast what he referred to as a "rational vote." By a rational vote what he meant was that the voter had a fairly sophisticated level of information about the various candidates, the issues involved, a basic knowledge about how the political process as a whole worked, and some sense of the consequences of the choices involved in a voting decision. In short, the rational voter would closely resemble a political science professor with a progressive disposition.

Rationality in terms of these first voting studies was defined as rationality in terms of means. The end, a liberal democracy, was always implicit but the scientific methodology precluded any serious inclusion of ends in the model used for analysis. The study of rational voting in terms of means seemed to be neutral with regard to ends, but the study of means divorced from ends carried enormous implications. It was a methodology with at least potentially serious problems if it was allowed to stand alone. The focus on means alone as the definition of a rational voter was obvious at the outset. Even apart from questions about data collection, Lazarsfeld could not find any significant number of voters who met his definition of a rational voter. If the survivability of a reasonably just government depended on rational voters its future was bleak to say the least. German and American voters could each be equally rational in terms of means but in the act of voting could reach quite different and incompatible ends. This was part of the conceptual problem that began with Lazarsfeld's definition of "classical democracy"; no definition of democracy in any previous political science required or even anticipated the rational voter of Lazarsfeld's construction. If Lazarsfeld's study was a critique of classical democracy, the best one could say of it was that it had no serious contact with classical political science or that of the founders.

The idea of the rational voter received another setback, perhaps a permanent one in the eyes of most students of voting, as a result of studies conducted by the Survey Research Center at the University of Michigan in the 1950s; the quantitative methodology used was different from that of Lazarsfeld, but the results were about the same. The idea of a rational voter, at least as originally conceived, was largely a myth. The most famous product of the SRC, what came to be called "the Michigan School" of voting studies, was *The American Voter* (1960).[38] The study was based on a detailed examination of presidential elections in 1952 and 1956; it has been updated using the same methodology several times and with pretty much the same results.[39] The overwhelming reason why voters vote the way they do, according to *The American Voter*, is party identification, although the authors were careful to point out that party identification is itself a product of other factors, such as family, education, economic calculations, and the like.

The conclusion of the SRC voting studies seemed to be a conceptual breakthrough in the ability of quantitative political science to provide a clear foundational principle from which elections could be classified. Following the Michigan model, elections could be classified according to three broad types; maintaining, deviating, and realigning. Later some scholars added dealigning to the typology of elections but this modest addition did not alter the basic framework. The definition of each type was derived from the saliency of party identification in explaining election results and voting patterns. If the majority party wins, it is a maintaining election; such as 1960. If the minority party wins, it is a deviating election; such as 1952 and 1956. If there is an election that is a consequence of a long-term change in the majority/minority party voter identification, it is a realigning election, such as 1932. Realigning elections are rare, but perhaps the most significant for an extended analysis. A dealigning election would be one where both parties lose party identifiers and the election turns on something other than party identification.

This typology of elections captured the political science profession for the next half-century before it came under serious challenge by a new generation of students of American politics. The problem was not quantitative analysis of electoral data *per se*, but the inability of political scientists grounded in a methodology borrowed from the natural sciences to adequately explain just what it was that they were looking at; did the American voting patterns, as explained by the SRC, support or undermine American democracy? This was essentially the same question Lazarsfeld asked, with the difference that Lazarsfeld was worried and the SRC was formally neutral, whatever personal reservations many had. The typology of elections derived from the Michigan School, for example, took a serious hit by scholars who made the fairly simple observation that from the end of World War II through 2012 there were nine deviating elections and eight maintaining elections.[40] Perhaps even more importantly, most quantitative voting studies had not begun to address the question of whether the voting coalitions that emerged from the New Deal Era, the era of progressivism on steroids, was corrupting the republican nature of the regime.[41] This was the sort of question that voting studies might illuminate, but the question itself was outside of the framework of science as progressives had defined the term.

The problem of scientific political science in the progressive tradition has its origins in the effort to be neutral in terms of value judgments. Classical political science, for example, might say that the leaders whom it elects reflect the nature of a democratic regime. In this sense Lincoln's speeches, the Gettysburg Address and his Second Inaugural reflect something about the nature of American democracy at the time. The same perspective on the election of Bill Clinton and his parsing the meaning of the word "is" when confronted with a sex scandal also reflects something about the changed culture of the regime. More to the point, a science of politics that cannot make a value judgment between these two is not a political science with much value, either in abstract or practical terms. And science by itself cannot arbitrate; the issue is moral, as everyone recognizes, and moral judgment is the very heart of political judgment.

There is no such thing as "value free" research; most frequently such research is the prisoner of some unspoken, theoretical consideration or assumption rooted in a particular research tradition. It is not so much that such studies are "wrong" in some methodological sense; the problem is that we cannot tell by public opinion and voting studies alone whether the American political system is working well, badly, or some mixture of the two. Questions that seek to probe what we mean by purpose, for example, need some Archimedean point on which to stand; and whatever the truth of Darwin as a biological science, Darwin as a political science could not escape the value relativism that was inherent. There is no place to stand that is not continually shifting. Empirical political science, such as what typically appears on the pages of *The American Political Science Review*, for example, demands a certain type of scholar to follow the reasoning involved. The methodology alone is sufficient to effectively remove the analysis from the attention of the ordinary citizen. If the subject were theoretical particle physics, for example, we would not expect most people to follow the science. But such political research as it represented in academic journals is almost as often a barrier to the trained academic as it is more serious problem as it is for the ordinary citizen.

At a minimum, a political science that is useful beyond Machiavellian calculations will be a political science that can illuminate regime level problems and issues. Voting studies have certainly given us a better understanding of the dynamics of particular elections and some level of understanding regarding the continuities as well as the changes between elections. Voting studies have helped us to look for trends that may, or may not, show-up in the next election. No serious candidate for national office thinks they can mount a successful election campaign without someone on the staff that a technically capable of understanding the quantitative data that is the stuff of electoral studies. But that is not the same thing as providing regime level analysis. Classical political science had a number of problems, but providing a principled calculus for guiding politicians in the direction of maintaining regime principles was not one of them. By themselves, voting studies do not provide any such calculus. Scientific neutrality does not help us to know whether we are collectively better off, worse off, or about the same as in the past. It does not offer anything beyond Machiavellian guidance for either citizens or leaders.

Admittedly reading the *American Political Science Review* makes it easier to think in terms of random selection. This is just a passing observation.

Understanding why citizens vote the way they do is integral to understanding the practice of American politics in terms of material and efficient causality. But exploring the question of whether people are voting for purposes that may be described as better, worse, or irrelevant is a more important question that is analytically prior to the more mechanistic questions. A methodology designed for value neutrality is unlikely to properly frame, much less begin to evaluate the larger questions. The opposite of expecting mathematical precision in such analysis is not the abandonment of reason but the recognition that certain types of questions require a different mode of reasoning; political science, as Aristotle observed, does not lend itself to mathematical reasoning. It is not trite to observe that asking the right questions is sometimes as important as the answers we get; questions beget more questions and shutting down political inquiry, as Dewey thought, seems unlikely to advance a science of politics.

Democratic Theory Revisited: Measuring Tolerance

Most scholars who worked in the field of public opinion and voting studies were well aware that their work did not address questions about first and final causality in politics. And most were well aware of the limitations of the democratic theory that Lazarsfeld used as the baseline for his study of rational voting. But whatever his limitations, Lazarsfeld had raised an important question. What kind of citizen is necessary to maintain a reasonably decent democratic form of government? Since rational voting behavior did not seem to have much of a future, what other qualities might be important; most especially qualities that might lend themselves to quantitative measurement and statistical analysis? One of the most common progressive answers was "tolerance" and it is worthwhile to look at the subject of tolerance as a democratic virtue in the progressive notion of democracy.[42] If tolerance is a virtue in democracy, as most progressives regard as a necessary foundation, public opinion analysis ought to be able to give some rough measure of citizen tolerance. And progressives in general came to think of tolerance as the highest, possibly the only social virtue.

The most widely cited study of citizen tolerance to appear immediately after World War II was by Samuel Stouffer, *Communism, Conformity, and Civil Liberties* (1955).[43] It was, if anything, less optimistic about widespread tolerance in American society than even Lazarsfeld had been about rational voting. But it remains an instructive study for any exploration of the place of tolerance in the progressive mind.

The notion that tolerance is the pavement on the road to democratic freedom is not as obvious as it has so often seem to the progressive mind. The idea of tolerance as a primary democratic virtue is subject to the same criticisms that may be leveled against the rational voter. The Founders certainly thought citizen virtue was one means of promoting freedom, and they just as certainly advocated a level of tolerance, up to a point. None of the original founders regarded tolerance, aside from religious tolerance, as a necessary virtue for a republican form of government. Religious tolerance would, hopefully, defang one source of conflict. But the founders' conception of republican virtue envisioned citizens who would fight to defend republican principles, of which natural law was an integral part.

The Constitution provided what Madison called "auxiliary precautions" for the protection of freedom in the event citizen virtue broke down at some critical moment; if passion overwhelmed reason. The Founders thought natural law reasoning was what we might call a first order of citizen virtue; toleration would be, at best, a second or third order virtue, because when it was most needed, it was least likely to operate. Institutional arrangements were a necessary part of a popular form of government because we cannot depend on the constant operation of virtue alone to maintain a decent polity. Which means, as a practical matter, a theory that views more democracy as a cure for the ills of democracy will tend to be either unrealistic as a protection for minorities or a harbinger of democratic tyranny, or both.

Progressive political science turned to tolerance of what came to be called "cultural diversity" as the first order virtue in the maintenance of democracy. They tended to see tolerance as a way to avoid precisely the factional conflict that Madison thought to be the fatal disease under which popular forms of government have everywhere perished. This was not surprising. Progressives had made democracy the *telos* of Darwinian political development, which in turn meant the supremacy of simple majority rule. If a decent democracy was entirely dependent on public opinion it was imperative that public opinion be virtuous. The value relativism of progressive methodology had worked to make tolerance the one virtue compatible with science. But the notion that tolerance is the road to freedom is not as obvious as it seems to most progressives.[44] Tolerance in progressive thought was a prelude to cultural relativism and both rest on the same foundation of value relativism that seems to be inherent in scientific methodology as defined by the progressive tradition. If we ask what sort of citizen is necessary to make progressive democracy work the answer seems to be a "tolerant" one.

In the context of the eighteenth century, tolerance was generally associated with tolerance for different religious confessions. This was the context of the founders' arguments for the separation of church and state. They did not seriously think religion could be denied a place at the table of public debate because they well understood the distinction between "church" and "religion." This distinction, while salient for the eighteenth century, is absent from progressive speculation that tends to collapse separate notions of church, religion, and natural law into a single idea. The distinction between natural law moral reasoning and toleration is clearer if we ask whether toleration is an adequate foundation for the sort of moral reasoning exemplified in the Declaration of Independence. The answer is reasonably obvious. Whatever one may say about the Declaration, it does not elevate tolerance into either a moral or political virtue because tolerance, by itself, is a question-begging proposition when compared with natural law. The republican tolerance of the founders will tend to support a republican form of government, whereas progressive tolerance will tend to support a progressive form.

Tolerance does have a pedigree in the foundations of the modern liberal state. John Locke made religious tolerance one of the pillars of classical liberalism that ties the founders to the progressives. His plea for tolerance masked his larger point that religion was largely immune to reason and therefore could not be made the rational basis for politics.[45] In any case, the separation of church and state, which is accepted by progressives and the founders alike, does not dispose of this particular problematic, as anyone who has read the cases and controversies over the "free exercise" clause of the First Amendment understands. Moreover, and it cannot be emphasized too strongly, the founders wanted to keep church and state separate, but not natural law and the state. When the progressives collapsed religion and natural law into a single idea that was opposed to science, the progressives radically altered the founders' distinctions. The progressive linking of tolerance to democratic government may, in fact, exacerbate the problem of maintaining a free government precisely because the value relativism as the progressive foundation of tolerance. Stouffer's conception of the problem is a case in point, but by no means the latest.

Tolerance made its appearance as a progressive virtue in the wake of the early years of the Cold War. As one scholar put it, "the practice of American politics was emerging from a deeply troubled period." And the troubles were decidedly rooted in the anticommunist prejudices of the American public. The American public opinion was "most notable for its strand of virulent anticommunism . . . Anticommunism was a form of ideological prejudice, a belief that functioned to suppress other values and prejudices." The problem for progressives was that this prejudice was rooted in the character of American citizens: "Unlike other forms of bigotry and intolerance, anticommunism amounted to an item of genuine consensus in American politics."[46] Suddenly, democratic government was incompatible with progressive democracy. Many liberal-progressives at the time felt the full force of a democratic majority directed against them and it was a majority that did not typically draw a fine distinction between liberal-progressivism and Communism. This reality prefigured a later tendency of many progressives to back off from some aspects of progressive democracy and into a greater reliance on the judiciary to accomplish the same goal. But means matter, and policies imposed by judicial rulings will not have the same reception as policies that reflect the consent of the governed. Croly's reliance on the sword to lead the many into the progressive paradise might suddenly seem more prescient.

The problem with tolerance as a principle of political science is that it always runs the risk of being conceptually incoherent. Does, or should, democratic tolerance extend to demonstrably undemocratic political parties built on principles openly hostile to regime principles?

156

And if it does, is the tolerance a matter of principle, that there is no fundamental difference between Democrats, Republicans, Fascists, and Communists that are worth quarrelling over? Or is tolerance a matter of prudence at some level, knowing that Communists are not going to win any elections anyway, why bother trying to suppress them? To what extent would tolerance extend to a Ku Klux Klan Party or American Nazi Party? One could easily make a plausible argument that what doomed German democracy in the Weimar period was that both German citizens and their elected representatives, for the most part, lost the moral capacity to make moral distinctions of this sort and lost free government in the process.[47] Linking tolerance with the preservation of free or even decent democratic government would seem to be a theory in need of further theorizing somewhere outside of the halls of academia.

The problem of tolerance as a foundation for progressive democracy does not require a detailed exploration into the political nature of Fascism, Communism, or the KKK, or any more benign political party, important as these questions are in their own right. The issue is the basis for an inquiry into what principles are necessary to maintain American democracy that does not cause harm to fundamental moral principles—principles that the founders engraved into the heart of the American regime. At one level of analysis, this was the concern that motivated George Gallup, Paul Lazarsfeld, and Samuel Stouffer alike. The problem of tolerance arose in the progressive tradition because many scholars instinctively understood democratic government to be as much a moral enterprise as a political one. This remains one of the central tenants of classical liberalism that the founders endorsed. But their moral foundations are very different and therein lies the source of the conflict.

What also seems clear, based on the historical evidence as well as the inherent logic of tolerance as a stand-alone principle, is that a morally neutral political system is neither possible as a practical matter nor desirable if it were. To make something as problematic as tolerance a fundamental purpose of democratic government is to construct a science of politics divorced from any historical experience. The irony of a political science built on historical progress yet ignorant of even recent history should not be lost here. In the final analysis, no one really believes that one value or one political culture is pretty much the same as another. And no science of politics should be predicated on something no one believes.

It can be stipulated that some degree of tolerance is no doubt a useful virtue both in the ordinary contact citizens have with one another and among representatives in the policy-making process of any government, although respect may be a more desired virtue. But a difference in degree is also the difference between boiling and freezing and a serious science of politics ought to be able to appreciate the difference, even if it cannot precisely locate the precise point when tolerance becomes a vice rather than a virtue. Tolerance at the level of an organizing principle will not easily be able to examine the true health of a regime; we would not know whether we are boiling or freezing. Would a growing support, or tolerance for, the Communist Party or the KKK, or both simultaneously, mean that the country as a whole was growing healthier or somehow sicker? As James Madison observed in *The Federalist*, "An elective despotism was not the government we fought for." He could make this case because he did not for a moment believe that simple majority rule alone was sufficient for a decent form of popular government. A serious science of politics appropriate for any democratic regime will require recognition of the problem of an elective despotism—one of the central problems in the constitutional design of the founders. Public opinion and voting studies can measure the degree of popular support for political parties of all types and descriptions. But by themselves cannot answer regime level questions; are such movements good, bad, or irrelevant to the health of the polity?

Notes

1. Charles E. Merriam, *Civic Education in the United States* (New York: Charles Scribner's Sons, 1934), 39.
2. One of the most interesting, and overlooked, accounts of how what may be called "the idolatry of methodology" has had a detrimental effect on the social sciences is Irving Louis Horowitz, *The Decomposition of Sociology* (New York: Oxford University Press, 1993). Horowitz focuses on sociology, but most of what he says could equally apply to any other social science.
3. James Bryce, *The American Commonwealth*, 3rd ed., rev. (New York: The Macmillan Company, 1895), 258.
4. Ibid., 258.
5. Woodrow Wilson, "Bryce's 'American Commonwealth,'" in *The Public Papers of Woodrow Wilson. College and State*, ed. Ray Stannard Baker and William E. Dodd, Vol. 1 (New York: Harper and Brothers, 1925), 164. Hereafter cited as Wilson, *Papers*.
6. Wilson, *Constitutional Government*, 21.
7. Ibid., 28.
8. Wilson, *Papers*, I, 339.

9.   Jeffrey K. Tulis, *The Rhetorical Presidency* (Princeton, NJ: Princeton University Press, 1987), 125. I think Tulis is correct on this point. I would only add that I also think the origins of the rhetorical presidency are even deeper than Tulis indicates. I have tried to trace it here to Bryce, but further inquiry might find even older roots from which Bryce may have drawn his inspiration.

10.   A. Lawrence Lowell, *Public Opinion and Popular Government* (New York: Longman's, Green, and Co., 1913).

11.   Walter E. Weyl, *The New Democracy: An Essay on Certain Political and Economic Tendencies in the United States*, with a new introduction by Sidney A. Pearson, Jr. (New York: Macmillan, 1912/New Brunswick, NJ: Transaction Press, 1998).

12.   Herbert Croly, *Progressive Democracy*, with a new introduction by Sidney A. Pearson, Jr. (New York: Macmillan, 1912/New Brunswick, NJ: Transaction Press, 1998), 154.

13.   Walter Lippmann, *Public Opinion* (New York: The Macmillan Company, 1922/New Brunswick, NJ: Transaction Press, 1998), xix–xx.

14.   Ibid., 274.

15.   Ibid., 276–84.

16.   Ibid., 270. (Italics mine.)

17.   Ibid., 373.

18.   Ibid., 375.

19.   Ibid., 312.

20.   Ibid., 399.

21.   Ibid., 414.

22.   V. O. Key, Jr., *Public Opinion and American Democracy* (New York: Alfred A. Knopf, 1961), 8.

23.   Herbert J. Storing (Ed.), *Essays on the Scientific Study of Politics* (New York: Holt, Rinehart, and Winston, 1962), 327.

24.   Nicholas Eberstadt, *The Tyranny of Numbers: Measurement and Misrule* (Washington, DC: American Enterprise Institute, 1995), 2.

25.   See Robert Eden, *Political Leadership and Nihilism: A Study of Weber and Nietzsche* (Tampa, FL: University Presses of Florida, 1983). In particular, see Eden's introductory chapter that links Weber and Wilson on the nature of modern leadership.

26.   One of the most interesting critiques of the influence of opinion polling on American democracy followed the less than stellar performance of the Gallup Poll in the 1948 election. Lindsay Rogers, *The Pollsters: Public Opinion, Politics, and Democratic Leadership* (New York: Alfred A. Knopf, 1949).

27.   George Gallup and Saul F. Rae, *The Pulse of Democracy: The Public Opinion Poll and How It Works* (New York: Simon and Schuster, 1940), 6–7. Although the name Saul F. Rae appears on the title page of this work, it was the name George Gallup that gave the book its place in the subsequent debates over public opinion and American democracy. We will not be remiss, therefore, if we refer to the work in terms of its primary author, George Gallup.

28.   Ibid., 9.

29.   Ibid., 269, 272.

30. By far the best account of this development remains that of Jean M. Converse, *Survey Research in the United States: Roots and Emergence 1890–1960* (Berkley, CA: University of California Press, 1987). Hereafter cited as *Survey Research.*

31. Perhaps the best discussion of the myriad of problems pollsters routinely encounter is Herbert Asher, *Polling and the Public: What Every Citizen Should Know,* 5th ed. (Washington, DC: CQ Press, 2001). The work has gone through multiple editions and is updated routinely.

32. This point is made with considerable force and insight by Harvey C. Mansfield, Jr., "Social Science and the Constitution," in *Confronting the Constitution,* ed. Alan Bloom (Washington, DC: AEI Press, 1990), 430–31.

33. Kuhn, *op. cit.*

34. Martin Diamond, "The Dependence of Fact upon Value," in *As Far as Republican Principles Will Admit: Essays by Martin Diamond,* ed. William A. Schambra (Washington, DC: AEI Press, 1992), 309–18.

35. Martin Diamond, "The Dependence of Fact upon 'Value,'" in Schambra, *op cit.,* 309–18.

36. Paul F. Lazarsfeld, Bernard Berelson, and Hazel Gaudet, *The People's Choice: How the Voter Makes Up His Mind in a Presidential Campaign* (New York: Columbia University Press, 1948), vii.

37. Converse, *Survey Research.*

38. Angus Campbell, Philip E. Converse, Warren E. Miller, and Donald E. Stokes, *The American Voter* (New York: John Wiley and Sons, Inc., 1960).

39. See, for example, Philip E. Converse, "Information Flow and the Stability of Partisan Attitudes," in *Elections and the Political Order,* ed. Angus Campbell, Philip E. Converse, Warren E. Miller, and Donald Stokes (New York: John Wiley and Sons, Inc., 1966), 136–57. The major follow-up study by the Michigan School is Warren E. Miller and J. Merrill Shanks, *The New American Voter* (Cambridge, MA: Harvard University Press, 1996).

40. See David R. Mayhew, *Electoral Realignments: A Critique of an American Genre* (New Haven, CT: Yale University Press, 2002). Sean Trend, *The Lost Majority: Why the Future of Government Is Up for Grabs and Who Will Take It* (New York: Palgrave Macmillan, 2012). See also Theodore Rosenof, *Realignment: The Theory That Changed the Way We Think about American Politics* (Lanham, MD: Rowman and Littlefield Publishers, Inc., 2003).

41. There are a hopelessly large number of polemical treatments of this subject and listing more than a handful would be fruitless. But, as an example, the most balanced work, and one that is based on a very subtle analysis of electoral data, is Jay Cost, *Spoiled Rotten: How the Politics of Patronage Corrupted the Once Noble Democratic Party and Now Threatens the American Republic* (New York: Broadside Books, 2012).

42. This was the answer to Lazarsfeld promoted by the too often overlooked work by Peter B. Natchez, *Images of Voting: Visions of Democracy.* With an Introductions by John C. Blydenburgh, Jr. and Sidney A. Pearson, Jr. (New Brunswick, NJ: Transaction Publishers, 2012/New York: Basic Books, Inc., 1985).

43. Samuel A. Stouffer, *Communism, Conformity, and Civil Liberties. A Cross-Section of the Nation Speaks Its Mind* (New York: Doubleday and Company, Inc., 1955).

44.   The best, and most succinct, refutation of the notion that value relativism can lead to tolerance remains Bertrand de Jouvenel, *Sovereignty: An Inquiry into the Political Good* (Cambridge: Cambridge University Press, 1957), 288–89.

45.   The works on Locke are too numerous to list here. The work that is most pertinent for the idea of Locke's conception of religious tolerance is John Locke, *Questions Concerning the Law of Nature* (Ithaca, NY: Cornell University Press, 1990).

46.   Peter B. Natchez, *Images of Voting: Visions of Democracy* (New Brunswick: Transaction Publishers, 1912/Basic Books, 1985), 141.

47.   See Eric Voegelin, *Hitler and the Germans* (Columbia, MO: University of Missouri Press, 1999).

V

Progressivism and Its Discontents

The American founders erected a cathedral of philosophic thought about politics on a foundation of science that appears increasingly problematic. Not because it is wrong in some sense, but because it represents a political science progressives in particular do not know what they do not know. It is starting to look very much like the venerable cathedrals in Europe; tourist attractions filled more often with picture snapping foreigners than with worshipers. The original function of the buildings seems unfamiliar to many. This is perhaps the inevitable result when the statues and stained glass windows are seen as merely works of art and not as symbols of a living reality. When Athens and Jerusalem have been amputated from the modern world discontent will likely be the order of the day. The discontent will likely be in the form of intellectual incoherence. Socrates has just been handed the hemlock.

Progressivism, like all political philosophies, has its discontents that are in large measure a product of its foundations. What we may refer to as the discontents of progressivism stem from two analytically distinct but related factors, one practical and the other theoretical. The theoretical problem is that the Constitution was never designed to support the political logic of the modern welfare state that is the culmination of the progressive project. Because the progressive argument at this level is aimed at the Constitution, it is not surprising that much of the focus has been on the judiciary. This has, in turn, led to court decisions that occasionally overturn, sometimes thwart, and always frustrate the logic of progressivism at various points. The progressive response to this has been what has come to be known as the "living Constitution"; it is an idea that found its earliest and most complete expression in Woodrow Wilson. In effect, the living Constitution would make the founders' Constitution null and void as an independent source of restraint on government and make whatever might be left of the idea of a constitutional government simply an exercise in political power; power exercised in the name of a newly defined democracy, but raw power nevertheless. Restraints on government, such as they might be, would be supplied purely at the discretion of whoever exercises that power. Do we really want anyone to exercise that much power?

The second discontent of progressivism is practical, but like all practical ideas, it has origins in the theoretical mismatch of progressive ideas with the founders' Constitution. Making progressive political science compatible with the political institutions established by the founders' Constitution is an enterprise worthy of Prometheus. But such is any science of politics that aims to change the nature of the regime without also changing its founding institutions. One way to reflect on some of the consequences of how foundational arguments have affected practical politics is to briefly consider the theory and practice of progressivism at the point of its first major triumph in constructing the modern welfare state, the New Deal under President Franklin Roosevelt.

The Progressive Movement achieved its greatest triumph in practical politics with the election of Franklin Roosevelt in 1932; the presidency of Woodrow Wilson and the outlines of the election of 1912 may be described as more of a curtain raiser for the New Deal. The New Deal has remained the iconic representation for progressive moment ever since. It is therefore the most appropriate place to begin to understand progressivism in practice with an eye on the theory that preceded it. And is so often the case when abstract political theory meets practical politics there is a paradox in the juxtaposition of the two. How theory and practice are joined is always something of a puzzle but whenever theory and practice seem to present a puzzle, we are obliged to ask "why?" John Chamberlain nicely captured this paradox in a work that bore the provocative title, *Farewell to Reform: Being a History of the Rise, Life and Decay of the Progressive Mind* (1932). It is a serious work that deserves to be more widely known by students of the progressive mind.

Chamberlain thought that he stood at the end of the Progressive Movement in 1932 because it seemed to him that the foundational arguments of progressivism had reached an intellectual dead end; a point in which the very term "progress" inhibited serious political in-quiry. The idea of liberal-progress, he reasoned, had lost its authority to interpret politics because political development did not look like progressive theory. He wrote, "What was the 'technique of liberal failure'? It was . . . the unwillingness of the liberal to continue with analysis once the analysis had become uncomfortable."[1] The question Chamberlain posed was how could progressivism develop politically if its foundational assumptions were so myopic, faulty in some way, or somehow question begging? He thought that it could not; action follows thought as surely as lightening follows thunder. How could a flawed idea still advance politically?

Chamberlain was too much the rationalist in this case. What he had not fully reckoned with was the degree to which progressivism had been transformed from a search for the truth of things into a political ideology that only occasionally touched political reality. When theory becomes ideology, paradoxes are resolved as if by magic. Triumph in the New Deal effectively ended any further progressive elaboration of its foundational structure at a point when it was still an academic enterprise and had not yet systematically confronted the reality of governance in the American constitutional system. When it did try to reconcile theory with practice, in the work of a writer such as Thurman Arnold, the result was to add yet another layer of abstract theory that did little to clarify the issues Chamberlain had raised. With Arnold it is the gap between theory and practice that is interesting.

Reading Chamberlain in the twenty-first century would seem, on the face of it, an exercise in nostalgic futility; the great triumphs of progressive politics still lay in the future to a degree Chamberlain did not fully reckon. But such a reading would miss the heart of what is involved in the progressive science of politics that was inaugurated with such confidence in the nineteenth century. Chamberlain thought progressivism had come to a dead end because it had intellectually exhausted the implications of its founding principles. This may be true in the sense that the foundational arguments of progressivism had not changed in any substantial way since the beginnings of the Progressive Movement. But progressivism remains as a political force to be reckoned with. Why?

What Chamberlain underestimated was how the progressive foundation in nineteenth century science could produce a labyrinth of superficially diverse political arguments that nevertheless remained connected to the roots of progressivism. It is one of the curiosities of progressivism, however, that the political triumph of progressivism in the New Deal tended to spawn increasingly abstract theorizing about politics. One might think that when theory meets a messy practice theory will have to adjust, and indeed it most frequently does. But not always in ways that are predictable. Progressivism still remains more of an aspiration than a reality after more than a century following its origins. The reason seems to be rooted in the rejection of natural law and the embrace of science as a foundation for politics. The very idea of progress tends to create a Manichean view of politics in which some vast sinister conspiracy is continually thwarting a true democracy. Further, perfection as the model for a progressive democracy is bound to disappoint. The disappointment can be intellectually ameliorated, however, by not asking any foundational questions, as Dewey so astutely advocated. As long as history is ultimately on your side there is no need to question foundational assumptions.

A good place to see how progressivism has managed to avoid confronting foundational assumptions and yet continue the progressive tradition is to consider the progressive interpretation of progressivism that came out of the New Deal. If it had not been for the political triumph of progressivism in the New Deal we might read Chamberlain differently; progressivism might have been stillborn or relegated to the status of a passing period of American history. The Great Depression was the opportunity many progressives had been looking for to put their theories into practice. Subsequent practical experience did not spark any reconsiderations, soul searching, or willingness to consider alternatives. This makes the foundational story of progressivism, for all intents and purposes, complete with the New Deal.[2] All that remains are the policies of perfection without the corresponding assumption of perfection.

The economics of the New Deal have been challenged and defended, but that is not the issue here. The inquiry here is not into the economic arguments but rather how the New Deal cemented the transformation of the American regime as a matter of progressive interpretation.[3] In the progressive tradition, the New Deal is the iconic symbol of the progressive theory and practice of politics and Franklin Roosevelt is the sainted hero who made it all possible. And as with religious icons that become objects of veneration, the veneration so many progressive intellectuals have vested in the New Deal can make even a sympathetic critique seem to the true believer as heresy at best or apostasy at worst. Nevertheless it is appropriate at least to suggest a philosophical continuity in the progressive tradition that begins with writers such as Woodrow Wilson and continues through the twenty-first century. The continuity is not entirely a matter of particular policies, although it does include policy issues, but more importantly the philosophical foundations of the progressive tradition; self-evident truths are the starting points that seem to mark all political quarrels.

The Folklore of Progressivism

There are a number of potential windows into the New Deal that explore progressive theory and practice, but one of the most interesting is that of Thurman Arnold. His iconic work in this regard is *The Folklore of Capitalism* (1937), which was in turn a more developed and nuanced version of an earlier work *The Symbols of Government* (1935). The reason why Arnold is of particular interest is because a close reading of his work illustrates several of the dominant characteristics of the progressive paradigm in historical–political writing. First is, the tendency to reduce political categories, such as justice, freedom, and the form of government, to something else; categories such as economics, psychology, or sociological variables such as race, class, and gender. In Arnold's case, the reductionism is in the form of psychology. Second is the self-interpretation of the role of the progressive intellectual in the transformation of American politics; a role that is characterized by a pathological altruism that seems to be denied to nonprogressives. Wilson's belief that his own autobiography is somehow the autobiography of the regime is not peculiar to Wilson alone among progressive intellectuals.

Like so many works in the progressive library, Arnold's thesis was a fairly simple one, but he fleshed out its implications perhaps better than any other. It was the idea that all of what we call political reality is, in the final analysis, simply a linguistic construction. In politics, there is no "there" there except as a linguistic symbol; there is no obligation the present and future owe to the past because all of pragmatic political reality is contained within an eternal present.

Arnold is not as well known to later generations as he was in his own day, which is unfortunate. His credentials as being in the forefront of New Deal intellectual can be briefly sketched, and they are impressive. Arnold was a prominent law school professor at Yale when he first came to the attention of New Dealers. From 1935 until 1937, Arnold spent his summer vacations as a trial examiner with the Securities and Exchange Commission chaired by William O. Douglas, who later served on the Supreme Court from 1939 to 1975. His job in this capacity was to help prepare legal briefs showing that New Deal policies were indeed constitutional. It was a logical and prestigious assignment for a high-profile law school professor. But this was only the beginning of his illustrious career.

What seems to have most impressed Arnold during this time was how much his legal briefs were merely rationalizations of New Deal policies that were barely connected with the Constitution in any traditional sense. Progressive theory and practice seemed to be divorced from the received understanding of law. Shortly after this experience, Arnold took a sabbatical from Yale to serve as an assistant to Robert Jackson who was then head of the Tax Division of the Department of Justice and who also served on the Supreme Court from 1941 to 1954. In 1939, Arnold resigned from Yale to become assistant attorney general of the Antitrust Division of the Justice Department. After what can best be described as a five stormy years in the Antitrust Division, President Roosevelt appointed Arnold to the U.S. Court of Appeals for the District of Columbia in 1943. It certainly appeared that he was being groomed for a Supreme Court appointment. In 1945, however, he resigned from the Court and formed one of the powerhouse law firms in Washington, DC that included Abe Fortas, who, it should be noted, also served a brief and controversial tenure on the Supreme Court from 1965 to 1969. Arnold always traveled in good company among Washington insiders. His law partner Fortas always regarded Arnold as a "genius" and that seems to have been a common attitude among New Dealers.[4]

Nevertheless, psychology as a reductionist argument is more problematic than economics, for example, which is the more common progressive argument. Early public opinion analysis hinted at psychology as the proper foundation, but it never really took hold as an organizing principle. Psychology tends to be subjective analysis whereas economic aspires to be more objective. How Arnold, almost single handed, helped to make psychology a progressive stronghold in progressive political science is worth an extended look. A brief background on the progressive interpretation by Arnold is in order. While praise for *The Folklore of Capitalism* was near universal among New Dealers, there were areas of dissent from Arnold's thesis. One that must have stung came from renowned Princeton University scholar Charles Corwin, one of Arnold's former teachers and one that he singled out in his memoirs as among the most stimulating, who compared it, no compliment intended, to Plato's "Noble Lie."[5] On the other hand, progressive historian Louis Hartz, for example, thought Arnold to be well within what he saw as the liberal consensus that reached back to the founding of the regime.[6] But Hartz, like most progressives, did not take the founders' science of politics seriously and easily misinterpreted its foundational assumptions when compared with the foundations of the progressive tradition.

Arnold's account is curiously sparse with regard to any serious analysis of the founding principles of the American regime. Croly's account of the founders is seriously flawed, to say the least; he simply dismissed their work as "folklore." The New Deal was the new order of regime principles. Progress had reduced the founding symbols of political order, natural law as basis for thinking about moral principles in politics, to that of an obsolete genre. It was, therefore, "natural that the country whose theories of government are the most unrealistic in the world" would have difficulty dealing with the Great Depression; nonprogressives "were making plans for a paper government that had no real existence."[7] Regime principles derived from the founding were theoretically irrelevant but in practice were a hindrance to the new order.

His argument on the founding, while sparse in its own way, is more interesting than Croly, for example. The dilemma of the American system for Arnold was that it is founded on a rational principle and any changes to that principle would inevitably be cast as a conflict between good and evil. This was not the "fault" of anyone, he wrote, but "simply illustrates the law of political dynamics."[8] It was not that Arnold thought the Constitution was irrelevant, as many of his contemporaries thought him to be. But whenever laws that he took to be necessary did not match established constitutional interpretation he adopted an attitude that came to be called a "post-realist" legal theory; a theory of law that focused on the symbols of government and viewed law in anthropological terms rather than the "legal realism" that saw law as the formal façade for economics.[9] The idea of a "living constitution" was beginning to take a more complex shape.

The administrations of Theodore Roosevelt and Woodrow Wilson raised the curtain for progressives on how government should be managed, but never quite managed to achieve the final objective. It was Franklin Roosevelt who managed to come closer than anyone before or even after in melding progressive theory with practice. And there were few defenders of the New Deal and its politics more widely respected in his own day than Arnold. *The Folklore of Capitalism* touched a nerve as much as it touched the intellect; it was the perfect title for a polemical defense of the New Deal combined with a near perfect theoretical defense, at least for true believers. What Arnold did was to take the notion that practical politics was, at bottom, about the manipulation of public opinion through the psychological symbols of political, economic, and social reality. Further, he embodied the progressive conviction that these symbols could be rationally manipulated by those intellectuals who best understood that social reality was no more than a symbolic construct. Such was the real essence of pragmatic progressivism, as he understood it. The full implication of his argument was perhaps not as obvious initially as they were later.

Arnold's thesis is that ordinary human needs require some sort of political and economic organization that is represented by symbols and creeds that are fundamentally neither political nor economic in their origin. Their true origin is better understood in psychological terms than the traditional categories of political science and economics that he describes as "folklore." Further, these traditional symbols can become an impediment to political change, especially in times of crisis, because all such symbols serve as a conservative drag on activist government. Political theory, properly understood, consists of understanding the function of these symbols and political action or practice requires the manipulation of these symbols. *The Folklore of Capitalism* thus emerges as a study of the relationship between theory and practice in the manipulation of symbols. He wrote, "An objective study of government is necessarily troubling to the intellectuals of our time because the prevailing mental picture of our folklore compels us to deny the facts before us."[10] Paraphrasing Marx, Arnold observed, "Economic theology is the opiate of the middle classes."[11]

Much of what makes Arnold so important in understanding the development of progressivism was his conviction that the success of the New Deal in economic terms would depend on expressing its policy in symbolic terms that would resonate with the public. His purpose in combining both political and economic categories into a common folklore was to break the grip each had on our collective imaginations. Once this traditional folklore was exposed as an illusion, a new science of political economy could be constructed on the foundation of a new civic culture. First came the deconstruction of traditional categories of political science, and then would come a new science of politics that was necessary before a science of economics could be constructed that would support it. The new science was to be the work of an intellectual class of "planners" and their work was to be independent of constitutional laws, which he often used as a synonym for "politics," and market economics, both of which were nothing more than folklore in the first place.

The very practical political problem, as Arnold understood it, was to consciously reconstruct a new symbolism of politics that would reflect the progressive attitude toward the American polity. This is what the progressive tradition has meant by the term "pragmatism" in politics. The New Deal historian Arthur Schlesinger, Jr., wrote, somewhat vacuously, "For Roosevelt the technique of liberal government was pragmatism."[12] Progressivism was by its very nature defined as pragmatic, which, by implication, made the foes of progressivism reactionaries and ideologues. Howard Zinn, among the most Left historians in the progressive tradition, wrote, "Both in *The Symbols of Government* . . . and in his more famous book *The Folklore of Capitalism*, Arnold came closer than any other writer to an exposition of what has come to be called the 'pragmatism' of the New Deal."[13] If anything, Zinn regarded Arnold as too much a pragmatist because he never embraced the neo-Marxist argument that politics is built on a superstructure of economics. The reason, however, is that Arnold was not an economic determinist that has been one of the continuous threads of progressive thought.[14]

In Arnold's account, whatever we think about government and politics is always based on symbols derived from the past. But the future is what is important. Trying to apply fixed symbols to an ever-changing reality is not merely impossible it is self-defeating because the correspondence between our mental pictures and what is actually happening grows ever wider. It is a psychological critique of the founders that parallels Woodrow Wilson's constitutional critique. But whereas Wilson had used Darwin as the model for science, Arnold used psychology as the cutting edge of modern science. In a sense, Arnold began where Wilson and Croly had left off. After all, if the founders' science of politics was as irrelevant as Wilson and Croly had argued, what else could they be except lingering symbols of an obsolete folklore?

Much of what gave weight to *The Folklore of Capitalism* was the psychological attitude Arnold expressed as much as his political analysis. The problem of finding a solution began with his observation that no one wanted to be branded a communist or a fascist, for example, even though few people outside of the academy had any idea of what these terms meant. These were merely symbols and fear of offensive symbols was a problem rooted in the nature of a democracy where the many may know what they want but have no idea of how to achieve it and are in turn ruled by passions attached to ever more antiquated symbols rather than to reason. Nevertheless, political pragmatism required a certain fealty to these symbols, as well as the conscious creation of new symbols that would replace them. "The reactions to the French Revolution and the modern German, Russian, or Italian revolutions differ only in that the vocabularies are different." Such revolutions are, he says, "the modern equivalent of heresy."[15] In the case of the revolution taking place in America, Arnold wrote, "What Roosevelt represents to the great majority of the electorate cannot be so easily formulated because no authoritarian literature has developed . . . to explain him as a symbol."[16]

The point Arnold was trying to make was not that the communist or fascist revolutions should be emulated by Americans, or that he could be identified with either, both of which he charged with demagoguery. But rather that the symbolism by which all revolutions interpret themselves is little more than a mask to hide the reality behind them. The reality of the revolutions sweeping Russia, Germany, and Italy was that behind the facade of political ideologies the machinery of government was moving toward a planned economy and the inevitable concentration of power that was a prerequisite. There is considerable truth to this observation. Broadly speaking, Arnold thought this to be a phenomenon analogous to the need for a new social–economic structure the New Deal was trying to construct. It is a fundamental principle of human organizations, he wrote, "that when new types of social organization are required, respectable, well-thought-of, and conservative people are unable to take part in them. Their moral end economic prejudices . . . compel them to oppose any form of organization which does not fit into the picture of society they have known in the past."[17]

Arnold and the New Symbolization of Progressive Theory and Practice

Arnold was not content to merely theorize about the progressive argument in political science. Much of what gives him his enduring appeal as an interpreter of the New Deal and progressive politics in general derives from his unique role in one of the most significant presidential administrations in American history; certainly the most significant after the Civil War. Other writers had tried to combine progressive theory with progressive practice, and perhaps Wilson is the most important. But Wilson expounded his theory before he became president and much of the commentary on Wilson has focused on whether or to what degree his subsequent experience modified or altered in any significant way his academic theories. Arnold was different in that his theory followed his practical experiences. In its own way, this sequence reversal has only added heft to Arnold's progressive credentials.

The Constitution for Arnold was less of a living document reflecting a serious science of politics than a symbol. He described the Constitution as a creed whose chief purpose is to serve the psychic needs of the American people. As with Wilson, Arnold regarded the English Constitution as superior to the American Constitution and for much the same reasons; the English Constitution concentrated power in the name of democracy. In practice, the American constitutional system had become dysfunctional; British government had evolved whereas American government had not. But the practical problem was not to waste time trying to replace it, but rather to alter its symbolic meaning. Arnold did not use the term "living constitution," but his argument was premised on the notion that the Constitution had no fixed meaning. The end of the founders' constitution would come with a newly constructed symbolism that referenced the Constitution as a symbol, but drained it of all fixed meaning. The old words remained, but no longer had the same meaning.

What Arnold added to Wilson's constitutional critique was a psychological argument. The basis for Arnold's departure from Wilson and earlier progressive critiques of the Constitution was not merely that he did not take the founders' political science seriously, but rather because, ultimately, Arnold did not take any science of politics seriously. Reality was merely a psychological construct that was reflected by symbols. As such, these existing symbols were merely folklore and too individualistic to serve as a guide for statesmen trying to cope with real issues. Folklore was an obstacle to be overcome. What Arnold made abundantly clear was the notion that in the practical politics of the New Deal that followed was inseparable from the theoretical argument. But the theoretical arguments had to be slightly altered to reflect the newfound political reality.

Arnold's most long lasting achievement in the progressive tradition was in how he consciously, and effectively, transformed progressivism from a broad political theory into a political attitude that could be partly divorced from its philosophical foundations whenever necessity required it. This was a new pragmatism. The foundations remained as implicit building blocks, but the symbolic character that Arnold described no longer had to be defended or explored. In the wink of an eye, had let the cat out of the bag that all politics was just a symbolic cover for power. Dewey had paved the way for willful ignorance in this regard, but it was writers like Arnold who understood the power of symbols to move nations, for good or ill. To the extent that "progressivism" became a symbol, in Arnold's terminology, it ceased to be anything resembling a science of politics in terms either the founders or even some of the early progressives might have understood. But as a symbol, it could serve as a mask for more concentration of power.

Because creeds, even purely symbolic creeds, reflect culture, the real problem for the political pragmatist, according to Arnold, is not to try to change culture, which he thought may be futile, but to do what needs to be done and appropriate the symbols of the nation for whatever purposes the policy maker desires; he wrote, "let me designate the heroes of a nation and I do not care who writes its constitution."[18] Pragmatism, unlike other creeds, is the real universal truth of politics. Faced with similar problems, Arnold believes that practical people will deal with them in pretty much the same way unless one of the national creeds intervenes to distort political actions. It is antiquated symbols, coupled with national heroes are national devils, that is the practical problem for policy makers; their task is to put themselves on the side of the heroes and the opposition on the side of the devils: "Move Communism or any other kind of creed into this country, keep the present hierarchy of tutelary divines, and one would soon find that the dialecticians and the priests were ingenious enough to make communistic principles march the same way as the old ones."[19] In short, quarrels over different forms of government, different conceptions of justice and tyranny, freedom and oppression, have no practical reality; there is no "there" there. It is the symbolic historical narrative that counts and not any reality behind that narrative other than raw power.

There was no doubt in Arnold's mind that the New Deal was best understood as akin to a religious movement. "The process of creating abstract realities out of polar terms and surrounding them with scholarly definition has always accompanied the decline of great religions. It is not surprising therefore that in a time when private property and rugged individualism are more myths than realities we should find law and economics more theological than ever before in our history."[20] All organizations, but most certainly organizations that maintain themselves within the context of the folklore of capitalism, do not maintain themselves by an obvious show of force but by reference to creeds and symbols. New Deal policies will succeed when the symbolism of the New Deal conforms to the symbols the nation implicitly accepts as legitimate. In effect, the New Deal will succeed when it becomes the civic religion of the United States. When historians make the New Deal the culmination of the progress that began with the American Revolution the new symbolism will match the new reality of political organization.

The emerging New Deal creed, Arnold observed, will function much like religious creeds of the past, but it will be wholly secular in its nature. He wrote, "Men cannot face the world without some sort of religion. In other words, we lack a *religion of government* which permits to face frankly the psychological factors inherent in the development of organizations with public responsibility" (italics mine).[21] He took for granted that symbols were mutable and ultimately the symbols of government and religion were, essentially, interchangeable. He had earlier written, "The history of the symbols of government is a succession of romantic but unnecessary sacrifices of human life or comfort in their honor."[22] Hard choices can be obfuscated by symbols, but behind those symbols is the certain reality of new power arrangements; a new political order needs new symbols. To drive this point home, he wrote, "Actual observation of human society . . . indicates that great constructive achievements in human organization have been accomplished by unscrupulous men who violated most of the principles we cherish."[23]

The practical implications of Arnold's thesis were never far from his mind. In a series of lectures Arnold delivered at the University of Omaha in 1942 published as *Democracy and Free Enterprise* in which he wrote, "What we need is a new vision" of economic organization in which everyone "sees the constructive possibilities in a new political order."[24] Since this new political order is only experiencing its birth pangs in the New Deal, its final form will necessarily be in the future. But Arnold has no doubt that it will be more scientific and more rational than what has been the case in the past: "the same folklore which justified freedom to experiment on the part of industrial organization offered the greatest handicap to similar activity on the part of the Government, even in fields where governmental activity was most imperatively needed."[25] The traditional distinction between public and private, while purely symbolic in the modern commercial republic, is the culprit and chief obstacle in forming the new civil religion. Public policy needs to be understood the way the folklore of capitalism has previously understood capitalism. For the government, the problem is that it "possesses no acceptable bookkeeping to convey to the public the idea that . . . expenditures are a source of public wealth."[26]

The implication is the irrational "general belief that taxes are a necessary evil, to be resisted so far as possible, turning the learning of taxation into an amazing and complicated metaphysics."[27]

Arnold thought that one of the consequences of the war was that the government management of the war effort would reveal to a skeptical public the superior merits of government planning over free enterprise.[28] New Dealers would use the language of constitutionalism, natural rights, and the like, which was the symbolic language of the American founding, but there is no doubt the New Deal represented the replacement of the *ancien regime*, the constitutional regime of the founders. The new political order is based on a new foundation because the reality of power behind the old symbols will be transformed.

The new reality is a foundation Arnold described as the difference between "objective" and "rational" diagnosis. "Rational diagnosis" is folklore, but "objective diagnosis" is grounded in scientific rationality. Among other things, objective diagnosis promises more accurate prediction in politics that will make the policy-making process more scientific. He wrote, "I will illustrate the increased ability to diagnose and predict which this platform gives by describing the kind of diagnosis and prediction which resulted from the pioneer work of the late Professor Edward S. Robinson of Yale, a psychologist who chose to observe law and economics."[29] What Professor Robinson taught Arnold was, from the point of view of an outside observer, the language of law and economics was essentially "literature," and fictional literature at that. Words tend to be used more for their emotional impact than for their descriptive utility. That is why words such as "communism," "fascism," "socialism," "capitalism," and the like are used so promiscuously and without ever really describing what is happening. Language for Arnold was plastic and was as likely to obscure as illuminate political reality. He had a point, although perhaps not entirely as he intended.

The Social Philosophy of Tomorrow

It would not be a mistake to read the progressive interpretation of the New Deal as a subtle endorsement of socialism. Arnold certainly seems to have leaned in the direction of some form of socialism. Yet, it seems also true, as Strauss pointed out, that the abandonment of natural law as a foundation for political argument in the American regime has left its mark in other ways as well. Philosophical nihilism is one mark but not the only one. Sometimes it is simply a moral vacuum that people trip over every day, but then pick themselves up and hurry along as if nothing had happened. And since politics, like nature, abhors a vacuum, the void will always be filled by something; sometimes it is merely utopian fantasy, which was Chamberlain's view. Sometimes it is some other sort of fantasy. Arnold was more in the tradition of the other sort of fantasy.

Arnold did not think the future could yet be predicted with scientific certainty, but he did think that what he called "the social philosophy of tomorrow" would be like nothing we have known before. He does not praise the fascists in Germany or Italy or the communists in Russia. The centralized governments "*are* tyrannical, bureaucratic, cruel, and so on." But centralism in America does not have to follow these examples. Sweden, as Arnold notes, is every bit as centralized as Germany but "is a much pleasanter country to love in than Germany" in large part because the government is not organized by the symbolism of the profit motive.[30] It is the climate of opinion, Arnold writes, that makes the New Deal more akin to Sweden than Germany.

Arnold assumed that as a matter of course pragmatic intellectuals would be able both to develop and control the new symbolization of politics. The symbolism got away from the fascists, but the more pragmatic Swedes got it right; perhaps, we may speculate, because Swedes were not as infatuated by the music of Wagner. In any case, Arnold does not elaborate on why the Swedes got it right and the Germans got it wrong. Americans cannot appropriate the symbolism of the Swedes, but the pragmatic reality behind them and the New Deal is essentially the same. No one was going to adopt the symbolism of Nazi Germany. Conflict over the symbols is inevitable, he says, and it "accompanies the struggle of every new organization to attain a respectable place. It is part of the confusion which accompanies growth."[31] This pragmatic change "represents a transition from a negative to a positive philosophy of federal power."[32]

The concentration of federal power in the new paradigm is, of course, handicapped by the lack of a specific symbolic language. But the reality of such concentration is the reality of the social conflicts out of which a new philosophy emerges. "Therefore, if one wishes to guess the social philosophy of the future, he must first guess which class will come into control of the organizations which make and distribute goods and, second, whether the change will be violent or slow." If we take the second part of his statement first, a slow transition will mean that terms will change their meaning; what we now call "capitalism" will become "socialism" over time whereas in a more violent transition "capitalism" will be immediately replaced by "socialism." The latter is what is happening in Russia. "It is part of the process of change in a rational world."[33] In this process, "There is no difference between the demagogue and the statesman, except on the basis of a judgment as to the desirability of social ends and values which move the one or the other."[34]

The first part of the statement is much more subtle in Arnold's work, but much more revealing than the second part. It needs to be spelled out in full because it anticipates the development of subsequent progressive political science to a remarkable degree. The slower transition from capitalism to socialism reflects Arnold's own preferences. The class that will assume control of the symbols of the new order will be the "planners." Control over these symbols is the work of pragmatic liberals and, by implication, the intellectual classes generally but especially in the academy. It is a hopeful sign, Arnold thinks, "that there is beginning to appear a philosophy about social philosophies." Pragmatic liberalism, of the kind embodied in the New Deal, is what he calls "the social bookkeeping of tomorrow." The traditional quest for social justice will remain a permanent part of our political vocabulary.

Arnold recognizes that in symbolic terms there can be no political attainment of social justice. "Injustice obviously must always exist because without it the conception of justice has no meaning; and without the ideal of justice human activity loses all appearance of dignity." Progress in this sense is both symbolic and practical. The symbolic side of perfection is integral to the new symbolization of state power, and the practical side is to be found in the hearts and minds of the planners who move the masses toward symbolic perfection. Men are coming to realize the necessity for government centralization and with it, and perhaps most important, "that these games can be controlled" much like a sporting event. Political spectacles no less than football games can serve to unite people around particular symbols. The "most useful social philosophy of the future is one which recognizes the functions which dramatic contests of all sorts perform in giving unity and stability in government."[35] As an illustration of his point, Arnold quotes, favorably, *New York Times* Moscow correspondent, Walter Durante, who gave him a word portrait of how Joseph Stalin was building Russia by symbolically creating dramatically new spectacles for public consumption. "When Stalin recently abandoned this technique for a great purge, the morale and prestige of Russia fell. International opinion realized, that Russia, *for some inexplicable reason*, was failing in organizational methods, in spite of the evidence of the internal power which the purge represented" (italics mine).[36]

Arnold had put his finger on perhaps the central feature of progressive politics when he singled out intellectuals as the driving force behind the new political order. "Intellectuals symbolize the dreams of mankind or an ordered world. They help to create the intellectual order out of the tangled folklore of the time. They are the makers of policy and the formulation of principles in situations where the public demands slogans."[37] Progressive intellectuals, in the progressive tradition, and Arnold certainly supports and reinforces that tradition, are assumed to be altruistic. Their manipulation of symbols is not so much Machiavellian as it is a commonsense pragmatism made necessary by the changing functions of government. But in the course of manipulating symbols the New Deal emerges from Arnold's defense as little more than folklore itself. This hardly seems his intention, yet it may be the clear meaning if we accept his premise that there is no substantive reality behind language.

Arnold's approach to language reflects an important part of the progressive tradition. Words, as emerged from Arnold's pen, were not intended to convey either information of knowledge, but rather emotion. Words in this context were not a medium of rational exchange, as Hobbes so famously observed, but instead were autonomous and valuable in their own right for their emotional impact. This reflected the role of the new intellectual class for whom Rousseau is perhaps a better guide than Marx. Words were neither true nor false in any traditional sense; how could words possibly convey any sense of right or wrong, justice or injustice? Words in Arnold's political science do not reveal a political reality so much as they conceal it. And the reality behind Arnold's words is "power"; power concentrated, power unified, and power wielded by a new class of planners such as him.

Arnold on Theory and Practice in the Progressive Tradition

It is appropriate to focus on Arnold and his psychological reductionism because psychological reductionism has become one of the staples of the modern therapeutic culture. Therapists have jumped from being third or fourth responders in any disaster to at least second and often first responders. Psychological reductionism is not the only pathology of progressivism, but it is one of the dominant strains and it is the basis for the emphasis on language as the defining feature of political reality. Properly understood, it helps to knit the labyrinth of progressive ideas together in a single fabric. The thread for that link is language, or, more accurately perhaps, words. So confident was Arnold in the power of words that the adroit use of words became the substance of reality rather than serving as a description of reality. And the words Arnold consciously used to defend progressivism had no fixed meaning in his own presentation of them.

The tradition Arnold represents and articulated retains its hold on the commonplace interpretation of American politics. Writing about the 2012 presidential election, James Ceaser and his colleagues saw the contest and the results is rooted in the ongoing quarrel between the progressives and the founders. He wrote, "For progressives, what is at stake is a vision of society in which justice is defined by egalitarianism, personal 'autonomy' in moral matters, and the values of the (French) enlightenment above all else. To this view, the American founding, with its emphasis on natural rights and limited government, is an anachronism and an obstacle." On the other side of this electoral divide, he observed, "what is at stake is a vision of society in which justice is defined, or at any rate secured, by liberty and many of the things that progressives disdain; decentralized and limited government aiming for the preservation of natural rights (including property rights) under a fixed constitution, a political economy in which effort and enterprise regularly lead to unequal wealth, and a social order undergirded by enduring morals derived from the Judeo–Christian tradition. To this view, concentrated government power itself is the greatest danger—the problem, not the solution."[38] The two sides could not really engage in a genuine quarrel with each other because they could not find a common ground that is the necessary precondition for a genuine argument.

One of the characteristics of the progressive tradition, from Woodrow Wilson through Thurman Arnold and into the twenty-first century, is the celebration of the power of the state. After World War II, the defense of a powerful state in terms Arnold described as "the religion of government" lost much of its appeal, even among some New Dealers. Arnold recognized the problem when, serving in the Justice Department, he applied antitrust laws to unions as well as businesses. But this only served to alienate Arnold from some of the more hardline New Dealers. Alan Brinkley, for example, thought that *The Folklore of Capitalism* did not wear well over time because it was too countercultural.[39] But Brinkley wrote in the immediate aftermath of the Reagan administration when progressive-liberalism seemed to have lost much of its electoral appeal. The idea of natural law had more life in it that most progressives imagined. Natural law returned with something of a vengeance during the presidency of Barack Obama, the very embodiment of the progressive politician. When it returned it did so, as we might expect after a prolonged absence, largely unrecognized by most progressives.

A single example will suggest the continuity and inherent dilemmas of progressive leadership in the American system. Following his election, in 2009 President Obama took the occasion of one his first policy speeches to differentiate himself from his predecessor by conspicuously denying that there was anything of intellectual substance behind the idea of American exceptionalism. He said in an interview, "I believe in American exceptionalism, just as I suspect that Brits believe in British exceptionalism and the Greeks believe in Greek exceptionalism." In other words, everyone is exceptional and, presumably, no one can lay an exclusive claim to exceptionalism. Even with the sarcasm that accompanied his remark, there is a sense in which he had a point. No doubt foreigners grow weary of hearing bombastic accounts of American exceptionalism. But that was not the end of the matter and it does not begin to touch on the subject of any form of American exceptionalism. The problem was exposed in the opening months of his second term in 2013 as the president sought to rally Americans to his foreign policy issues.

When President Obama faced an unpopular policy crisis over a potential American military strike on Syria he couched his appeal to the American people in precisely those terms of American exceptionalism he had earlier rejected; America must act for humanitarian reasons because of who we are. The gap between the two speeches on American foreign policy was widely noted at the time of the second speech, most especially by Russian President Vladimir Putin. In an extraordinary opinion editorial in the *New York Times,* President Putin threw back in President Obama's face precisely the progressive criticism of natural law exceptionalism that President Obama had just embraced.[40] The irony was obvious. It would appear that American natural law is more easily dismissed in the classroom than as a presidential appeal to the American people in time of crisis. One lesson we may draw from this is that natural law is the missing and necessary ingredient in Wilson's idea of the rhetorical presidency. It is the salt of American popular appeal that is omitted at the president's peril. America had defeated the old Soviet Union animated by a communist ideology partly because of a commitment to the natural law of Declaration of Independence.

Was Strauss right? Had the United States been deprived of the fruits of victory by having its adversary impose upon us the yolk of its own ideology? President Putin seems to think so.

The paradox of Arnold in this context, and much of the progressive tradition as well, is that he does have a point when he noted that political symbols in the American regime have often been cynically manipulated for unsavory purposes. He would have had a stronger point if he had not called on intellectuals as a class to resymbolize regime principles along the lines of a religious paradigm; such a call also smacks of a cynical manipulation of symbols and not necessarily for more noble ends. The reasoning behind Arnold's own version of Machiavellian cynicism probably owes as much to Voltaire and Croly as anyone. Is Vladimir Putin the *telos* of progressive political science? What was the link between the New Deal intellectuals, such as Arnold, and the post-Soviet era? The answer is complex, but one thread we can pick up here that helped to link them is a general attitude toward free-market capitalism that required the concentration of political power to overcome market-based economics. The point needs additional comment.

It was a commonplace attitude, with some reason, among New Dealers to think that capitalism had reached a crisis stage and was in the process of being replaced by something else; something else that might be socialism. For many New Dealers, Arnold among them, the lines between fascism and communism were blurred, to say the least. Some New Dealers embraced fascism early in their careers and later communism with scarcely a pause between them.[41] The spirit of the time certainly seemed ripe for the "end of capitalism" thesis and progressives had no immunity to it. Arnold's faith in the pure motives of experts was such that he tended to measure intellectual progress by the absence of debate.[42] And for the progressive mind, there was nothing really to debate beyond squabbles over means; the end was never in doubt. Progressives did not really debate with nonprogressives because debate would mean taking the opposition points of view seriously. The past, whatever else it may have been, was only folklore for the present. References to the founders after the New Deal became increasingly symbolic.

What the original progressives had done in theory, the New Dealers had done in practice; they had made the founders irrelevant. Arnold, among others, was well aware of this point, when he wrote, "The Constitution of the United States that in the early days stood as an unyielding obstacle to practical legislation attempting to relieve human needs and correct social injustices has gone and a different kind of Constitution has taken its place. The New Constitution stands as a vision of radical equality, civil rights, and human freedom."[43] In brief, not only have progressives finally replaced the founders' Constitution but the replacement is morally and political superior to the original. The truth of the progressive assumption was thought to be beyond rational debate.

The model for replacement of the founders' Constitution was to be along the lines of the new political order they saw emerging in the European social-welfare system; if not in every specific, certainly in its broad outlines. And perhaps most important, this new political order was only marginally affected by classical economic calculations. The basic calculation was political in the narrow sense of the term while economic calculation was an add-on. The new political order was to be dominated by the "planners" who were motivated, presumably, by science alone. The ideology of the planners never entered into the role they were to play in this drama. He wrote, "One of the few useful things to come out of the Bolshevik revolution and the Second World War was the growing realization that production is wealth and that money is a form of national bookkeeping necessary for the distribution of that wealth. . . . In Russia, if more schools are needed, the planners ascertain whether there are enough bricks and lumber and steel to built them without interference with the military budget."[44] Arnold did not make this point because he agreed with Stalin, but since all politics was represented by the symbols of national folklore he never saw what grotesque reality was masked by those symbols. When the foundational principles of any regime are treated as nothing more than symbolic folklore, it appears that the very distinction between justice and injustice become hopelessly incoherent.

The Labyrinth of Progressivism

At the outset of the twenty-first century it is not obvious how many intellectuals any longer truly believe in the idea of social and political progress. The course of the twentieth century has not been kind to theories of progress. On the other hand, the enduring strength of the progressive impulse in politics is its always implicit, and often explicit, promise of earthly perfection, typically cast as a just society; a society without factions. Organized by "social justice" in common parlance. At different times this promise of secular perfection has taken different forms, but the promise remains and it is the promise rather than the practice that counts the most in the progressive tradition; it is the source of progressive idealism. But the studied refusal of most progressives to address both the theoretical as well as practical implications of the foundational arguments that make up this promise is one of its blind spots. This blind spot has, in turn, made it difficult to see the tyranny of progressive ideologies such as Marxism or the commonality of both fascist and Marxist ideology in their respective rejection of natural law. The absence of natural law in progressive political science has helped to create a breeding ground for termites in the basement of the liberal edifice. Hearing the Russian President hurl the heart of the progressive argument back at a progressive president in such a mocking tone ought to be a sobering experience, but only if they are listening.

The original progressivism lingers on in the form of the methodologies and broad-based attitudes developed by the early progressives and, wittingly or not, attitudes and methodology shape substance. The only language and social research methodology the heirs of the original progressives know is the language of progressivism. Once it is assumed that all law is a product of human imagination, rooted by its nature in time, place, and circumstance, any notion of law that is not derived from ordinary legislation is simply beyond imagination. The notion that any laws might come ultimately from God had helped to keep power in check. Once it is imagined that all law comes from legislation there is one less check on the raw exercise of power. The language of natural law, the vocabulary of purpose and cosmic moral order, has disappeared down a memory hole and has ceased to exist as a working foundation for progressive moral calculations. The case may be different with regard to theories of progress in the natural or physical sciences, but the political history of the past two hundred plus years has been a series of accumulating horrors, each seemingly more repugnant than the one before. And much of the cause for that horror is a direct consequence of attempts to construct new theories of politics of which the builders consciously think of as progress. But because reality never matches the perfected society of the progressive imagination no political action is ever an end in itself and the idea of progress never seems to apply a break to progressive political actions.

We may speculate that the attitudes of progressivism may be even more fundamental than academic methodologies. Attitudes do not require serious discussion; they are merely character traits. The Manichean division of politics into progressive versus reactionary, the scientists versus the unscientific, warps ordinary political discourse. The symbolic language of progressives, the language of Arnold, has led progressives to think that the term "progressive tyranny" is an oxymoron. The very idea that progressivism may harbor tyrannical attitudes is so inconceivable to most progressives that the prospect is seldom discussed, much less explored. Madison's definition of tyranny in *Federalist* 47 as "The accumulation of all powers legislative, executive, and judiciary in the same hands, whether of one, a few or many, and whether hereditary, self-appointed, or elective, may justly be pronounced the very definition of tyranny" is a definition that has no meaning in progressive political science. This seems to be one of the consequences of thinking about politics in terms of Right versus Left instead of politics as justice versus injustice. The very language of progressivism works against political debate in terms the original founders would have recognized.

Even if we grant that advances in physical sciences have taken place in opposition to classical modes of thinking, which is much disputed, the price paid by transforming that methodology to the human sciences has been high; Rousseau had a point, that there is something in modern science that seems dehumanizing, even if he exaggerated it. The ruptured relationship between the physical and the human sciences that has contributed to so much of modern political horror stands accused as one of the prime reasons for the difficulty progressives have to distinguish good from evil. It is difficult to deny the horrific consequences of this rupture, but it can be ignored. And ignoring the consequences of this rupture is one of the unfortunate hallmarks of the progressive tradition. The American founders stand on the other side of this rupture and it is one of the reasons why a defense of the American founders is so important in the contemporary world. Not because they got everything right; they did not. But because natural law gave them a foundation from which good and evil could be differentiated, insofar as it is humanly possible to make these distinctions. Natural law made it at least possible for them to act politically in a reasonably just and decent manner.

This makes understanding the progressive critique of the founders, most especially the natural law arguments of the Declaration and the constitutional arguments of *The Federalist*, all the more important than merely an intermural squabble among academics. It is tempting to simply identify what the progressives did not like about the founding and then defend everything about it—limited government, fragmented political power, a generally laissez faire approach to economic activity, and a social culture that supports individualism. Madison certainly thought that persons of a religious disposition would regard the founding as reflecting the guidance of Divine Providence. And he may be right. But Madison also noted that because the Almighty has to work with such frail and limited material as human beings not everything comes out the way it should. Neither the natural law foundations of the republic nor the Constitution should be regarded as a closed case. The founders did not regard their work as complete and neither should anyone else.

Some progressive scholars, such as Douglas Kendall and James Ryan, have tried to "reclaim" the Constitution for progressivism under the banner of "living originalism"; arguing that the Constitution is properly read as a radically progressive document after all.[45] But reading the founders' Constitution as a progressive document would require that progressives accept a political science with a foundations in natural law and a form of government organized to prevent the concentration of political power; neither seems a likely course of development within the progressive tradition. While both natural law and the Constitution lack a foundation as tidy as many might like, natural law is the most serious stumbling block to any progressive return to the founders' Constitution. The problem for progressives is more than just symbols or even the legislation of particular policies. It is dealing honestly with the problem of power. Constitutional government meant disciplined government for the founders; limited government with enumerated powers. For the progressives who defined the constitutional government in Wilsonian terms, constitutional government carried no hint of how or where to discipline the exercise of power. How could any notion of unlimited government with general powers ever even imply discipline? And where would the discipline originate? Democracy? What if the many are not always right? Does anyone seriously think that reliance on experts is a viable answer?

In policy terms, much of the progressive agenda has not only been enacted, but has gained majority support; Medicare, Social Security, Civil rights and the like. Civil rights for African Americans, for example, is a noble success story but has never been exclusively associated with progressives until the latter half of the twentieth century. Abortion, gay rights, and some other aspects of late progressivism are more controversial and how these will play out in the future cannot be predicted. Whenever a policy becomes law it also acquires a protective cloak that tend to make criticism less significant and, eventually, pointless—most of the time, at least. Still, if a progressive from the era of Woodrow Wilson and Herbert Croly could see what progressivism has accomplished in policy terms by the twenty-first century they could be excused for thinking progressivism is indeed on the side of History. Nevertheless, History is a fickle muse and to the extent that scientific reasoning is part of the human condition, the progressive tradition has a number of vulnerabilities. Ironically, it may be that these vulnerabilities are at precisely those points where the first progressives thought themselves to be most invincible; science and movement toward some sort of rational perfection. Science by itself is neither moral nor immoral and cannot be the basis of moral action and attempts to build a science of politics on such a foundation is to build a house on sand. Does reality have a sobering effect on politicians? The historical record is not encouraging.

Although most progressives assume that natural law has been banished from political discourse, natural law may turn out to be its most vulnerable point: especially if we take the time to reflect on the implications of Vladimir Putin's challenge. Natural law has, more than once, troubled the conscience of even its critics. The Achilles heel of the progressive science of politics may yet turn out to be found in its vehement rejection of natural law. Natural law is perhaps as much of a prism as a creed. And the prism continues to influence much of academic and public discourse in a way that does not entirely depend on whether progressives or their critics are in a temporary majority of minority within the polity as a whole. We may better understand this if we focus on a few examples.

The rational mindset of a more perfect future has some inherent pitfalls for the progressive tradition that are independent of either optimism or stoic resignation. Progressives never seem to read the cautionary observations of a Michael Oakeshott, for example, on the limits of rationalism.[46] It would surely seem to be one of the most rational interpretations of the human condition to argue that secular perfection does not appear to be part of our future. It further seems to be a reasonable conclusion from this that no coherent science of politics can be built on such an assumption. Yet the question remains, how to account for the persistence of such a science of politics? It is a question with multiple answers; with each answer perhaps only a partial one.

We might begin with the observation that the earlier progressives had a materialistic conception of science that has broken down over the course of the twentieth century. The relationship between the atomic and subatomic world of microbiology and the living bodies of human beings is not understood at all; materialism has become an increasingly vague concept in science.[47] Even if God is the god-of-the gaps,

187

modern science has revealed more gaps than the nineteenth century ever imagined. Gaps seem to multiply like rabbits. Like most progress in scientific explanation, this is a reality that cannot help but affect a science of politics built so explicitly on a materialistic view of science. Darwin's theory of random selection in the evolution of the species, for example, might draw fire from more religiously inclined persons, but as long as science was defined in wholly material terms such objections could be branded as unscientific. Modern scientific consensus is not yet ready to concede that it can be proven scientifically that the universe is purposefully designed, but most agree that it is exquisitely designed to allow for the possibility of life. Unless one is close minded, it is no longer valid to deny on the basis of science that the universe is improbably fine-tuned to create life. The argument that we can dismiss purposeful design as unscientific is dogma, not science. A scientific basis for taking intelligent design seriously, what physicists refer to as "anthropic coincidences," is one of the most significant developments in twentieth century physics.[48] Whether or to what extent progressives may or may not take more than passing notice of this new reality is uncertain.

There is no need to undertake an extended discussion of scientific controversies over "anthropic coincidences" other than to suggest how they affect the scientific foundations of the first progressives. Essentially the anthropic argument is that the fundamental constraints of the universe fall within a very narrow range that is thought to be compatible with life. Critics of this "strong" anthropic principle argue that the principle is philosophic and not scientific because it cannot be scientifically falsified. It is, critics allege, essentially a tautology that says the physical principles necessary for life are necessary because there is life. The outside observer might be led to suppose that scientific support for a purposeful cosmos is good news. But some physicists, such as Stephen Hawking, have taken the anthropic principle to mean that there must be an infinite number of universes, most of which are not fine-tuned to support life. But this seems to be one the order of an updated historical relativism in the form of scientific relativism. The theory of multiple universes is as unscientific as one can imagine, even if supported by string theory or some such. Multiple universes are scientifically unverifiable.

Again, to the outside observer, who is not a physicist, this all looks very much as if secular atheism has conceded that this is a purposeful universe and have turned to a nihilistic attitude to support purposelessness.[49] The critique of a purposeful universe must be seen as the party line and not science. But it does suggest that there is some powerful impulse of passion that drives secular atheism that is unrelated to science. That impulse, whatever it is, is what gives progressive political science its staying power independent of any experience outside of the ideology itself. To the extent this is so, we may be excused for thinking that the reliance of progressives on science and historical research as a foundation for progressivism is a mask for a larger revolt against the cosmic order of things that is somehow prior to foundational arguments. That said, exploring the foundational arguments of progressivism must be assumed as one of the first steps undertaken in any systematic analysis of progressivism.

Needless to say, perhaps, there is nothing in science so far that "proves" the idea of a purposeful creation in scientific terms, but the fact that so many scientists have jumped on the bandwagon of speculation that there are perhaps an infinite number of universes, each operating under different physical principles, is revealing. In effect, supporters of multiple universes have, de facto, conceded that this universe seems to have been designed with a cosmic purpose. And since alternate universes are more properly science fiction than science, and since there is no scientific reason or basis to presume even their existence, much less their properties, alternate universes are perhaps best interpreted as a way to avoid confronting the problem of purpose. At the very least, we may observe that nineteenth century on the matter is decidedly less certain in the twenty-first century. Ironically, this may turn out to be a sort of progress.

The Progressive Science of Politics: In Lieu of Conclusions

In policy terms the very idea of progress accounts for much of the resistance of progressives to fundamental change. Resistance to any changes in the modern welfare state by progressives has created the odd specter of reactionary progressives. The very idea of progress itself creates a distinction between a political Left that promotes progress and a political Right that is opposed to progress. For any serious analysis of twentieth century politics this is a demonstrably false dichotomy, as even Arnold well understood. Fascism and communism, to take two iconic ideologies that are all too typically associated with Right and Left respectively, are twins formed from the same zygote; only the language was different, not the intellectual structure. As long as this image of serious metaphysical difference between the two persists it seems unlikely that progressivism can seriously challenge itself. There is a sense in which Chamberlain was right, at least insofar as how he judged the paradigmatic assumptions of progressivism. But this merely brings us back to where the inquiry began; what are we to make of a science of politics built on the idea of historical progress in an evolutionary sense? Assessing strengths and weaknesses on the assumption of progress is, at best, a tentative business because we really do not know what the future holds and that is the basis by which progressives judge themselves. But it is at least reasonable to begin by questioning the assumption of political progress in the first instance.

"Progress," especially secular progress as a science of politics, is a slippery term. We may reasonably ask if it is possible that there can be progress in the natural sciences without similar progress in the human sciences? This was the question asked by Rousseau in the middle of the eighteenth century and he answered in the negative. One need not be a follower of Rousseau to see his point. As a matter of science, few persons really want to go back to some mythical past. Regardless of the many metaphysical barbarisms commonly committed in the name of science, no one doubts that in some sense we know more about the physical world with every passing day. In practical terms, who would want to be subjected today by even the best doctors of a half-century ago, much less eighteenth or nineteenth century physicians? Yet it is increasingly difficult to associate scientific progress with political or social progress. Individually as well as collectively we continue to face the eternal choices between right and wrong, justice and injustice, good and evil; only the context changes, not the principles.

One of the by-products of the progressive mindset, however, is the unwillingness of progressives to question their own foundations and hence to explore the fundamental questions that have driven a serious science of politics since Plato. Given Dewey's prohibition on asking certain types of questions, this is not entirely surprising. Nor is it surprising that the methodologies spawned by this assumption have taken the paths they have. Intellectuals who have most identified with scientific and historical progress have frequently found refuge in total-itarian ideologies. Some, such as Georg Lukács, allied themselves with Marxist regimes in order to make sure that theirs were the only voices heard; others, such as Heidegger, did much the same thing in alliance with Nazis. Such extreme options were not available to American progressives. The founders' constitution provided legal protection for freedom of speech that has made it difficult to silence nonprogressive ideas altogether. Dewey, however, understood that self-censorship of unwelcome ideas, such as a "politically correct" vocabulary that screens-out words that do not convey the progressive mindset, operates much the same way but with less obvious coercive intrusion from the outside. It more closely resembles the world of Orwell than American regime principles.

Nor is it obvious that a quantitative analysis of public opinion and voting as the efficient causality of modern democracy helps to clarify the classical questions that have sparked classical political science. No doubt we have more information about the mechanics of both public opinion and voting than ever before and the cumulative impact of this information has been striking. But the increase in information has not helped to cement any consensus of what it means. Rather it has, as might have been expected, merely spawned new disagreements on how it ought to be interpreted. More gaps keep springing up the more we know. There is nothing inherently unusual with this and if Kuhn is even close to being correct it is the way normal science works. Still, the new quarrels over what it means are confined almost entirely to the process of government and what we normally consider to be the efficient causality of government. The purpose of government remains as elusive in this science of politics as it was for Croly, Becker, or any of the other theorists of progressivism.

Like Freud, progressives aspired to live a life without illusions and that meant a belief in science as the foundation for such a life. But a science of politics that recognizes no transcendent purpose in politics is not a science at all; it is merely a prescription for tyranny because it does not know how or where to draw lines. Fidelity to "scientific integrity" is a thin reed for a science of politics. There is no reason, scientific or otherwise, to believe that literally everything and anything is politically possible or morally permissible as value relativism invites us to do. Further, the prohibition on asking fundamental questions by methodological design will, at best, produce a truncated science of politics that is concerned only with peripheral issues. If a religious or natural law explanation is a true or reasonable explanation, why should it not be considered and analyzed, subjected to whatever assumptions such an explanation may entail? Precluding such explanations at the outset is, to say the least, not very scientific.

The secularization of political science also led to a scorn for any notion of American exceptionalism that referred to itself as "one nation under God." But the notion of one nation under God is properly understood as a sign of religious humility, not religious hubris. What is the alternative, a nation that is *not* under God? It would appear that, at least in this instance, secularism is characterized by a kind of hubris that is as conspicuous as the hubris progressives assign to either natural law or religion. At least religion has traditionally warned against a false pride. Hume was correct to note that moral postulates cannot be derived from the historical record. But if that is the end of the matter then the study of politics can make little sense. To accept formal causality, certainly as it was understood by the American founders', requires speculation about moral purpose in a cosmic sense. Such speculation was thought to come naturally to men in the classical tradition because men naturally desire to know. The desire to know, however, is not the same thing as knowledge itself. And the adoption of methodologies that effectively prohibit asking certain questions on the grounds that scientific certainty may not be possible reflects a lack of basic curiosity that is deadly when it comes from the ranks of a professional class that expects to rule in the name of reason. Such reason may more closely resemble unreason. And as President Obama has (hopefully) learned, it is not as easy to dismiss natural law from public discourse as progressives have so ardently wished.

What is odd about much of modern political science, which progressivism is a part, is not that people disagree, that has always been characteristic of political argument, but that many of the most influential architects of the progressive science of politics have spent so much time arguing that moral purpose has no place in the scientifically rational study of politics. Yet, in practice, progressive political discourse is saturated with morality. It is an odd morality when compared with classical political science. We are all ignorant of more things than we can possibly have knowledge about, but the progressive tradition is one of self-imposed ignorance; one that attempts to suppress ordinary curiosity, that is most troubling. The study of politics devoid of thinking about purposeful moral calculation, however problematic such calculations must be, reduces the study of politics to little more than a boring and pointless hobby. To the extent that progressivism continues to rely on science as a foundation for the critique of natural law, the critique is progressively unpersuasive, although this alone may have scant influence on progressive intellectuals still under the influence of Dewey.

Disdain for the founding principles of the American regime, for the culture that nourished it and for the culture that was in turn nourished by those principles, is so ingrained in the progressive tradition that for most progressives there is no retreat from that opposition. The first progressives made that disdain explicit; for later progressives, especially, the development of the progressive tradition from its foundations made that disdain more visceral than an object of explicit attack. That is why an exploration of the foundations of progressivism is so crucial for a serious understanding of progressivism. What is often merely an attitude for later progressives was the substance of a serious intellectual assault by the founders of the progressive tradition. By the latter half of the twentieth century it is an assault that has spilled out of the classroom and into the public square. And in a popular form of government we must expect that quarrels in the public square will, sooner rather than later, become matters of dispute within the states, Congress, the executive, and the courts. How the public outside of academia receives and interprets these academic quarrels has generally been a puzzle to progressives. The example of religion and its linkage in public opinion with natural law is a case in point.

The progressive assault on religion in American culture seems largely abstract to most progressives since they generally inhabit a secular enclave in American society. But for those Americans who do not inhabit this enclave, the war on religion is very real and very personal as the culture wars that developed over the last half of the twentieth century can attest. Further, although most academics see the conflict in terms of the influence of religion on politics, the religion at issue in the American regime is not Islam, Judaism, or some other religion, but specifically Christianity and Christianity in America is a variegated tradition. As one scholar put it, "To focus on mere religion in American political development, rather than Christianity, is to eviscerate any historical understanding."[50] Christianity is the lynchpin for American religious history and use of the term "religious" to cover both the diversity of religion and natural law is unhistorical. The progressive assault on natural law is very much of a piece with the assault on religion and threatens to open up an unprecedented rift in American politics.

At the same time, it seems increasingly clear, based, it must be said on almost every quantitative study of voting patterns, that there has been a corresponding migration of religious voters toward partisan voting patterns that support the Republican Party and away from the Democratic Party. The polarization shows up in almost every voting study that touches upon the question. Based on a fair reading of the founders on this score, there is no reason to think this is a healthy development. The surprise, to the extent that any of this is a surprise, is rooted in the progressive claim that the modern state administered by experts will be neutral in its operation. The separation of church and state as an idea and as a reality depends on this distinction. But the progressive state is not neutral with regard the political, cultural, and ethical claims it makes on citizens. The polarization of the American state along sharp religious-secular lines may be politically logical, but it cannot be welcome and its meaning must continue to elude progressive political science.

While most progressives have denied that there is anything necessarily hostile to religion in progressivism, this is an increasingly difficult proposition to defend. The progressive disdain for natural law is the central case in point. What accounts for the political hostility to natural law? The answer seems to be that the American experience with natural law has often equated natural law with Divine law. The problem with this equation for progressives is that neither is subject to human control. Secular progress, on the other hand and certainly as progressives have understood it, is uniquely a product of human control. As such the idea of progress is always vulnerable to radical ideologies that promise more than can be delivered if we retain a science of politics that is tethered to the reality of the human condition. Sometimes that ideology will be Marxism, and sometimes something else, but in either case we should not allow different words to obscure the gnostic view of reality that animates them. The progressive claim of a neutral secular state cannot be accepted at face value because the exercise of power is never neutral.

The reality is that the state is not neutral. Progressive political science is an alternative moral perspective that has increasingly brought it into conflict with religious practices over the course of the twentieth century. Both progressivism and religions claim to represent certain truths about the nature of the human condition. Classical liberalism no doubt contained many of the seeds of modern progressivism, but limited government worked to keep clashes between church and state under control, or at least less noticeable. The growth of the modern social-welfare state, however, has not merely increased the points of friction but has also intensified whatever conflict occurs at those points; all of this at a time when the foundations of progressivism have become increasingly problematic. The concentration of political power in the secular state that recognizes no other source of law than its own will is bound to intensify conflicts between church and state. A science of politics ought to be able, at the very least, to point out how these problems affect regime maintenance and, perhaps, regime survival.

A science of politics is intended to give a reasonably accurate description of how things are. But at some point a science of politics must be prescriptive, at least implicitly, for the behavior of citizens and rulers alike. Classical political science, whatever its limitations, always understood that in certain fundamental ways the future would be much like the present because the nature of the human condition always set limits to what is possible and the reality of good and evil are always the context for political as well as personal decisions. The founders' understanding of constitutional government is one example of this and may serve as a benchmark for the differences between the founders and the progressives. The progressive science of politics, on the other hand, thought of the future as something that was not limited by any such thing as a fixed human condition. Good and evil are the result of bad principles of politics and can therefore be overcome. Hence, there were no fixed principles of politics beyond that provided by science. Such a future may as well aspire to perfection, as Croly thought. And if future perfection in the form of progressive democracy is thought to be inevitable future decreed by evolution, it is easy to believe that any defense of the founders is, at bottom, a threat to democracy itself.

A thoroughly secular theory of politics, such as that of the progressives, will inevitably prescribe that citizens behave in a thoroughly secular manner; laws, customs, and policies will reflect this foundation. Value relativism does not mean that the idea of justice disappears in a secular world view, but what does happen is that justice comes to be understood entirely in secular terms. Value relativism does not mean that any polity will treat all values the same. Neither rulers nor ruled can live their daily lives as if all values are relative. In such a polity justice tends to be whatever the law says it is; if there is no law, there is no injustice and there is no punishment for injustices beyond that of secular authorities. This was the state described by Hobbes in his *Leviathan*. The law will consist of an almost infinite series of those petty regulations Tocqueville warned of that are the secular attempt to recreate the world in its own image. This sort of metaphysical atheism or agnosticism that is at the heart of the secular science of politics has been one of the distinguishing characteristics of twentieth century politics and we can see it reflected at the origins of the American progressive tradition.

Finally, a secularized science of politics, cut off as it is from any notion of transcendent justice, always has a problem identifying either good or evil in other than a utilitarian manner. A good example is the very influential work by John Rawls, *A Theory of Justice* (1971) was a serious to rethink the liberal-progressive tradition from the beginnings in social contract theory. Rawls is widely credited with having constructed the most brilliant defense of modern liberalism, albeit mostly by people who have not read him, and as fundamentally incoherent, mostly by those people who have read him. In either case, what he presents is a defense of an egalitarian ethos in a convoluted state of nature that neither Hobbes, Locke, or Rousseau would recognize; ahistorical history is seldom convincing to those who are not already convinced.[51] Rawls' theory was animated by the idea that equality was the rational end of justice as he defined it. And certainly equality has ever been one of the animating characteristics of democracy. For the game of life to be fair, as Rawls understands it, it must be secular; anyone who claims adherence to transcendent principles of moral behavior, derived from God or natural law, is automatically a threat to a fair society. The foundational requirement for all of this, according to Rawls, is that we draw a "veil of ignorance" around fundamental moral choices. What are we to make of a science of progressive justice that uses a metaphor of ignorance to make it sound plausible? Is a "veil of ignorance" really an advance over natural law in how we understand slavery and its attendant problems?

Society may, of course, choose to promote equality in its many forms if it wants. There is a moral equality that is explicit in natural law. But it will not and cannot be based on scientific knowledge; knowledge is always hierarchical because it is the replacement of opinion with knowledge. If everything is opinion, knowledge is scarcely possible and historicism undermines the possibility of knowledge. The promotion of equality is intellectually soft and easy; the acquisition of knowledge is difficult and hard. Knowledge, including scientific knowledge, is typically won, if at all, only over the objections of equality. The same is true of self-government.

If both good and evil are outside of the scope of a political solution the attempt to treat them as if they are entirely political in nature cannot help but distort politics. Value relativism operates not to make all values relative, but to make it impossible to determine if the laws we enact have a moral foundation outside of our own limited understanding of things. A thoroughgoing secularism always runs the risk of transforming things that are evil into something lawful and therefore acceptable because lawfulness rather than transcendent justice defines the progressive conception of right and wrong. The progressive science of politics at the outset never intended such an outcome, but the logic of its founding has hastened such an outcome. Not because any progressives necessarily desired it, but because the language of progressivism made it difficult to recognize the sort of injustice scientific nihilism could unleash. Ideas do have consequences independent of whoever may be their author. Tyranny that promised progress, such as Marx, did not seem like tyranny but merely "liberals in a hurry."

The deconstruction of political language, as reflected in Arnold, was central to the progressive project. George Orwell, a man of the Left himself, was one of the first to recognize and capture the moral disorientation involved in the new language. Progressives were instinctively correct in their belief that much of political power consists in the power of language. Rhetoric is part of politics, especially democratic politics. Our experience with reality, whatever that may be, is shaped through language that is a symbolic representation of our experiences. Much of political power is the power to determine the symbolic representation of reality through the manipulation of these symbols. But at some point the symbols used must correspond to our experience with reality and not merely our imagination. The confusion of the two is the essence of the gnostic interpretation of reality. And there is a tendency of progressive intellectuals to fall into this trap. The Manichean assumption of the progressive tradition was that of light versus darkness, with progressives always on the side of the light. Progressives were universally convinced that they were entitled by their monopoly on scientific reason to provide the rulers for the new democracy they sought to establish. This makes the quarrel over language also a quarrel over who has the authority to define the nature of the regime; the founders or progressives?

What, precisely, is gained by the progressive science of politics? The easy answer is the illusion of precision, and that element is certainly present in progressive political science. The classical-religious understanding of truth, whatever it may be, was well understood to be something that could only be experienced partly or incompletely at best. There are a number of theories as to why religious sentiment, at least among intellectuals, has declined in the West over the past two or three centuries. But the lack of certainty that is a hallmark of religion, its foundation in faith, has surely been a contributory factor. The modern secular intellectual, it seems, prefers a certain untruth to an uncertain truth. To say that certainty is possible is, implicitly, to say that the source of certainty has been found and someone is in possession of it, usually whatever writer is making the statement. It is a habit of mind that is foreign to classical political science and the political science of *The Federalist*. Such an attitude toward politics is only likely to produce intellectual incoherence. It is always interesting to note how much of the modern debates over scientific knowledge quickly become a debate over what do we know and how do we know it? And when the consensus results in the notion that we really do not know anything it is hard to believe this will be a useful political science either for ordinary citizens or their elected representatives. It looks more like a labyrinth of dead ends that no doubt leads many outside of the academy to the notion that some college professors should never be allowed near a word processor.

Progressive secularism, however, is not merely confined to the classroom where dozing undergraduates miss some of the nuances of anti-foundationalism. The corruption of the progressive intellectual is perhaps nowhere better illustrated than the overwhelming identification of progressives with the Democratic Party since the days of Woodrow Wilson. Why is this a source of corruption? There are any number of practical reasons why any individual might identify with one political party or another or no party; particular interests, interesting candidates, direct rewards of one sort or another, etc. But the near unanimous identification of a certain type of intellectual, the progressive intellectual, with the Democratic Party reveals the inherent tension in progressivism between the intellectual as prophet and the intellectual as herald. To be a prophet presupposes a commitment to the Truth, whatever that might mean, normally defined as speaking truth to power. For academics, it generally means a willingness to let the chips fall where they may as a result of historical–political–economic research. But to be a herald seems to require a partisan identification and the partisan identification undermines the commitment to prophetic truth. Ideology trumps any search for truth. And ideology in the service of concentrated political power does not have a particularly uplifting history in the twentieth century. There is no rational reason to suppose that history will prove to be any kinder to Americans than it has been elsewhere.

Partisan identification has other corrupting influences on progressivism, an influence suggested by Arnold but more fully developed in its implications by later progressives. When language is no longer used to clarify or describe it can become simply a tool of political attack; a function that further undermines the progressive intellectual's commitment to seek truth but is fully consistent with the commitment to serve power. What matters when progressivism is translated into partisan politics is no longer reality but "the cause." It is not merely that the end justifies the means, although that is part of the equation, but if justice has no substantive quality other than as a symbol, it becomes increasingly difficult to distinguish means from ends. Whatever the shortcomings of natural law political science, it was less of a problem in this regard than it is in progressive political science.

In classical political science, the opposite of justice was injustice and the opposite of truth was untruth. But the opposite of progressive is "reactionary," "conservative," "racist," or, if the occasion presents itself, "fascist." Each of these terms can and often does have a substantive meaning, but the promiscuous use of these terms by so many progressives, especially in the media, suggests the terms have lost descriptive meaning altogether. They are words more commonly used, as Orwell observed, to express a particular dislike for someone or something rather than because they have any descriptive meaning. In one sense, they are words that confer an authoritative political power on the users and are intended to deprive their opponents of authoritative power. In the rough-and-tumble of democratic politics this is commonplace for practicing politicians; it is impossible to know if they really believe their own rhetoric. But for intellectuals who live by words and rhetoric and set a great store by them, placing themselves at the service of political power cannot fail to have a corrupting influence as truth is invariably sacrificed to power. Intellectual incoherence is scarcely surprising when serving two masters.

Tocqueville was paraphrased earlier in the Introduction with the remark that God does not need theories because he sees every human heart individually, but we do need theories because we can have no such knowledge. Theories are always, in this sense, a serious recognition of the limits of human knowledge. This is one of the truths of the human condition that cannot be reiterated too often. At the same time, common sense and experience suggests that not all theories are equal. And without accepted foundations that are always, to some extent, theoretical there can be no rational discourse. Debate cannot take place between two parties if one or the other refuses to accept as intellectual binding foundational experience that we all know and experience to be true. Some scholars who have inherited the progressive tradition, such as Richard Rorty and Stanley Fish, have sought some sort of intellectual refuge in the notion, borrowed in part from Nietzsche, that the social construction of reality points in the direction of what they call "anti-foundationalism"; that there is no reality beyond how we construct reality through our symbolic uses of language.

Perhaps in the world of academia it appears to some that the world is only a social construct where imaginative experience trumps common sense experience. It is easy to imagine that power is or can be tamed by an appeal to reason. But outside the ivy-covered walls of faculty clubs, the reality that most people experience is not a social construct; it is too often a place where people shoot at each another and get shot. The notion that all reality is a social construct, a mere matter of symbolism in language, has become a political philosophy imagined largely by people who have never been shot at and never expect to have that sobering experience. Sometimes hard power enters politics with all of the impact of a blitzkrieg attack and the notion that reality is merely a social construct is revealed as not only ridiculous but dangerous as well.

Every science of politics must have the problem of political power at the center of its focus. Any survey of the progressive tradition will soon discover that power is the central concern, but it is disguised in a way not always recognized because the language of progress tends to obscure rather than illuminate this reality. The progressive tradition has rejected both divine and natural law as potential checks on the exercise of power. And it must be admitted that the American founders, especially Madison, while they did not doubt the reality of such checks on power, were almost equally skeptical that either divine or natural law would prove to be a final and wholly effective check on abuses of power. Pursuant to this understanding of human nature, they constructed a political system where power checked power in what Madison referred to as an "auxiliary precaution" to more lofty sources of restraint. But in the progressive science of politics only the laws of science were invoked to shape the use of political power and science required no checks; all other restraints on the exercise of power were categorically rejected. But this vision of political power unleashed in the service of science in turn depended on the notion, more typically asserted than systematically argued, that scientific reason alone could provide the basis for a science of politics.

The application of pure reason as a political science to the human condition has been a dubious notion from the French Revolution through the Russian Revolution and after. And there is no reason to believe that any American experiment with scientific reason as the foundation for a science of politics will fare any better than every other attempt to build a political order on reason alone. The alternative to unbridled reason is not unreason, as progressives have argued, but rather a form of government with a decent respect for human nature that was the foundation of the political science in *The Federalist*. Reason is part of human nature, but it is not the alpha and omega of political reality. Exactly what the future of the progressive tradition in America will turn out to be cannot be known. But insofar as the foundational principles of the American progressive tradition are built on the idea that scientific reasoning is the sole basis for political science, and such is the thrust of the entire progressive tradition, there is no reason to think that the future of progressivism will have the happy ending that has been denied to all other such experiments. Perhaps at that point progressives will rediscover *The Federalist*.

The chief task of any philosophy is to explore the nature of justice and injustice, as well as the sources of good and evil. It becomes a science of politics when it suggests practical policies that will move any particular polity in the general direction of greater justice and away from injustice. When a science of politics can marry theory with practice in this way, it may be described as a sort of "progress." But even this limited progress will work only if a science of politics can truthfully help to make the political world more coherent in moral terms. But truthfulness, in this sense, must be at least partly knowable; this is the heart of natural law and it is the root problem of progressive political science. The foundational assumptions of the progressive paradigm of political science seems intent on making the political world less coherent because it deliberately excludes any questions that might disturb its own self-contained structure; it reflects the dead hand of Dewey for later progressives who have never read him. It has both theoretical and political consequences. In the history of political philosophy since Plato, the progressive prohibition on asking certain questions is an odd development. The classical definition of philosophy, or the etymological origins of the word "philosophy," is "love of knowledge," and not, as progressives would implicitly have it, the "possession of knowledge." On this basis, it would seem that progressivism is premised not merely on the denial of political knowledge in the classical sense but paradoxically assumes that modern science has somehow closed the chasm between the love and the possession of such knowledge.

To note that these are both dubious and contradictory assumptions is simply to point out the obvious.

The first generation of American progressives imagined that a truly scientific science of politics would be the foundation for political progress. Toward this end, they at least had the virtue that most of them took the original American founders seriously and actively attempted to refute the foundations of a natural law political science with all of its assumptions in the Constitution. Subsequent generations of progressives have not been so clear in their assumptions in a large part because they no longer take the founders seriously and see no need to even make a gesture at taking their concerns seriously. Modern progressivism seems to be as much an attitude as a body of knowledge. The founders' science of politics, encapsulated in *The Federalist* for example, is almost as much of an intellectual black hole for most progressives as any cosmic example could be. The practical consequence of avoiding certain questions is a truncated academic scholarship and intellectual shallowness that makes an open and honest debate between the founders and the progressives all but impossible. Arguments over natural law, the size of government, freedom, political equality, and the like are quarrels rooted in our notions about the moral nature of the universe; they are not trivial subjects and avoiding them does not make them go away. Further, treating such problems as beyond the scope of political science merely because they are scientifically unknowable in the modern sense of science is a prescription for moral and political disaster. In politics, such an attitude is indistinguishable from nihilism and moral nihilism, in whatever forms it takes, is unlikely to result in a regime that very many real people will find suitable for human habitation. It will almost certainly not have a happy ending.

Notes

1. John Chamberlain, *Farewell to Reform: Being a History of the Rise, Life and Decay of the Progressive Mind in America* (New York: Liveright Publishers, Inc., 1932), 304–5.
2. See Howard Zinn, *A People's History of the United States* (New York: Harper Collins, 1980). Zinn's work has gone through several subsequent editions without interpretative revision. Evidently Zinn's initial Manichean interpretation is so self-evidently reasonable that no earlier of later scholarship need be considered. It has become the standard progressive interpretation of American history since its introduction.
3. See Amity Shlaes, *The Forgotten Man: A New History of the New Deal* (New York: Harper Collins Publisher, 2007).

4.   Katie Louchheim, ed., *The Making of the New Deal: The Insiders Speak* (Cambridge, MA: Harvard University Press, 1983), 222. On the place of Arnold within the circle of New Dealers in general, see Michael Janeway, *The Fall of the House of Roosevelt: Brokers and Ideas from FDR to LBJ* (New York: Columbia University Press, 2004).

5.   Charles Corwin, untitled book review, *The American Political Science Review* 32, no. 4 (August 1938): 745–46.

6.   Louis Hartz, *The Liberal Tradition in America* (New York: Harcourt, Brace, and World, Inc., 1955), 259–83.

7.   Thurman Arnold, *The Folklore of Capitalism* (New Brunswick, NJ: Transaction Press, 2010/New Haven: Yale University Press, 1937), 115. Hereafter cited as *Folklore.*

8.   Ibid., 12.

9.   See Neil Duxbury, "Some Radicalism about Realism? Thurman Arnold and the Politics of Modern Jurisprudence," *Oxford Journal of Legal Studies* 10 (1990). Douglas Ayer, "In Quest of Efficiency: The Ideological Journey of Thurman Arnold in the Interwar Period," *Stanford Law Review* 23 (1971): 1049–86.

10.   Ibid., 388.

11.   Louchheim, xxi.

12.   Arthur M. Schlesinger, Jr., *The Age of Roosevelt: The Politics of Upheaval* (Boston, MA: Houghton Mifflin Company, 1960), 649. Progressivism as pragmatism was also the thesis of Hartz, *op. cit.*

13.   Howard Zinn, ed., *New Deal Thought* (Indianapolis, IN: The Bobbs Merrill Company, Inc., 1966), 36.

14.   For a more extended discussion of Arnold's status among New Deal historians, see Sidney A. Pearson, Jr., *Introduction to the Transaction Edition,* "Thurman Arnold's Defense of the New Deal: The Folklore of Liberalism," in *Folklore.*

15.   *Folklore,* 3.

16.   Ibid., 391.

17.   Ibid., 3.

18.   Ibid., 34.

19.   Ibid., 36.

20.   Ibid., 184.

21.   Ibid., 389.

22.   Thurman W. Arnold, *The Symbols of Government* (New Haven: Yale University Press, 1935), iv.

23.   Ibid., 5.

24.   Thurman Arnold, *Democracy and Free Enterprise* (Norman, OK: The University of Oklahoma Press, 1942), 17, 25.

25.   *Folklore,* 311.

26.   Ibid., 312.

27.   Ibid., 322.

28.   The contrary argument is well explored in Arthur Herman, *Freedom's Forge: How American Business Produced Victory in World War II* (New York: Random House, 2012).

29.   *Folklore,* 142.

30.   Ibid., 333.

31. Ibid., 135.
32. Ibid., 339.
33. Ibid., 342.
34. Ibid., 380.
35. Ibid., 342–44.
36. Ibid., 345–46. This is not the place to develop a discussion regarding the Moscow purge trials of the 1930s or in Walter Durante's place in deliberately obfuscating their true nature for readers of the *New York Times*. What is interesting here is Arnold's incredulity on the point; a view adopted by numerous progressive intellectuals of the era. See S. J. Taylor, *Stalin's Apologist. Walter Durante: The New York Times Man in Moscow* (New York: Oxford University Press, 1990). The great work exploring the intellectual structure of the purges and why so many intellectuals were attracted to them remains Arthur Koestler, *Darkness at Noon* (New York: The Macmillan Company, 1940).
37. Ibid., 385.
38. James W. Ceaser, Andrew E. Busch, and John J. Pitney, Jr., *After Hope and Change. The 2012 Elections and American Politics* (Lanham, MD: Rowman and Littlefield Publishers, Inc., 2013), 174–75.
39. Alan Brinkley, *The End of Reform: New Deal Liberalism in Recession and War* (New York: Alfred A. Knopf, 1995), and his most insightful collection of essays, *Liberalism and Its Discontents* (Cambridge, MA: Harvard University Press, 1998).
40. Vladimir V. Putin, "A Plea for Caution from Russia," *New York Times*, September 11, 2013.
41. See Jonah Goldberg, *Liberal Fascism: A Secret History of the American Left from Mussolini to the Politics of Meaning* (New York: Doubleday, 2007). I think Goldberg overly stresses the fascist aspects of many of these writers on the Left, but his point is well taken that, apart from linguist symbols, fascism and communism were essentially alike in practice.
42. Christopher Lasch, *The True and Only Heaven: Progress and Its Critics* (New York: W. W. Norton and Company, 1991), 432. Lasch's discussion of the place of Arnold in the context of the progressive tradition is, in my opinion, the best discussion of Arnold to date. On Arnold's faith in the capacity of the "planner" to replace both constitutional and economic relationships between the government and its citizens, see his essay "Why the Full Employment Act of 1946 Became a Dead Letter," in Thurman Arnold, *Fair Fights and Foul: A Dissenting Lawyer's Life* (New York: Harcourt, Brace, and World, 1951), 76–81.
43. Ibid., 68.
44. Ibid., 272.
45. Douglas Kendall and James Ryan, "How Liberals Can Take Back the Court," *The New Republic*, August 6, 2007.
46. Michael Oakeshott, *Rationalism in Politics, and Other Essays* (New York: Basic Books Publishing, Inc., 1962).
47. Arthur S. Eddington, *The Nature of the Physical World: The Gifford Lectures* (New York: The Macmillan Company, 1928).
48. Stephen M. Barr, *Modern Physics and Ancient Faith* (Notre Dame, IN: University of Notre Dame Press, 2003), especially Part IV, 115–64.

49. One of the best guides on this is David Berlinski, *The Devil's Delusion: Atheism and Its Scientific Pretentions* (New York: Crown Publishing Group, 2008).

50. Hugh Heclo, *Christianity and American Democracy* (Cambridge, MA: Harvard University Press, 2007), 4.

51. For a more complete discussion of Rawls, see Brian Barry, *The Liberal Theory of Justice: A Critical Examination of the Principle Doctrines in a Theory of Justice by John Rawls* (Oxford: Clarendon Press, 1973). See also, Alan Bloom, "Justice: John Rawls Versus the Tradition of Political Philosophy," in *Giants and Dwarfs: Essays 1960–1990*, ed. Alan Bloom (New York: Simon and Schuster, 1990), 315–45.

Bibliography

Works and Authors Cited

Adams, Henry. *Communication from Henry Adams, President of the Association.* Annual Report of the American Historical Association for 1894, 17–23.

Adler, Mortimer J., and William Gorman. *The American Testament.* New York: Praeger Publishers, 1975.

Arnold, Thurman W. *The Symbols of Government.* New Haven, CT: Yale University Press, 1935.

———. *The Folklore of Capitalism.* New Brunswick, NJ: Transaction Press, 2010/New Haven, CT: Yale University Press, 1937.

———. *Democracy and Free Enterprise.* Norman, OK: The University of Oklahoma Press, 1942.

———. *Fair Fights and Foul. A Dissenting Lawyer's Life.* New York: Harcourt, Brace, and World, 1951.

Asher, Herbert. *Polling and the Public: What Every Citizen Should Know.* 5th ed. Washington, DC: CQ Press, 2001.

Augustine, Saint. *Confessions.*

Ayer, Douglas. "In Quest of Efficiency: The Ideological Journey of Thurman Arnold in the Interwar Period." *Stanford Law Review* 23 (1971): 1049–86.

Baker, Ray Stannard, and William S. Dodd, eds. *The Public Papers of Woodrow Wilson. College and State.* 2 vols. New York: Harper and Brothers, 1925.

Barr, Stephen M. *Modern Physics and Ancient Faith.* Notre Dame, IN: University of Notre Dame Press, 2003.

Barrow, Clyde W. *More than a Historian. The Political and Economic Thought of Charles A. Beard.* New Brunswick, NJ: Transaction Publishers, 2000.

Barry, Brian. *The Liberal Theory of Justice. A Critical Examination of the Principle Doctrines in a Theory of Justice.* Oxford: Clarendon Press, 1973.

Beard, Charles A. *The Republic. Conversations on Fundamentals.* New York: The Viking Press, 1943.

Becker, Carl. *The History of Political Parties in the Province of New York.* Madison, WI: The University of Wisconsin Press, 1909.

———. *The Heavenly City of the Eighteenth Century Philosophers.* New Haven, CT: Yale University Press, 1932.

———. *Freedom and Responsibility in the American Way of Life.* New York: Alfred A. Knopf, 1946.

———. *The Declaration of Independence. A Study in the History of Political Ideas.* New York: Random House, 1970/1922.

Beeman, Richard. *Plain, Honest Men: The Making of the American Constitution.* New York: Random House, 2009.

Berlinski, David. *The Devil's Delusion. Atheism and Its Scientific Pretentions.* New York: Crown Publishing Group, 2008.

Bloom, Alan. "Justice: John Rawls versus the Tradition of Political Philosophy." In *Giants and Dwarfs: Essays 1960–1990*, edited by Alan Bloom, 315–45. New York: Simon and Schuster, 1990.

Boyd, Julian P. *The Declaration of Independence. The Evolution of the Text as Shown in Facsimiles of Various Drafts by Its Author, Thomas Jefferson.* Princeton, NJ: Princeton University Press, 1945.

Brinkley, Alan. *The End of Reform. New Deal Liberalism in Recession and War.* New York: Alfred A. Knopf, 1995.

———. *Liberalism and Its Discontents.* Cambridge, MA: Harvard University Press, 1998.

Brown, Robert E. *Carl Becker on History and the American Revolution.* East Lansing, MI: The Spartan Press, 1970.

Brownson, Orestes O. *The American Republic. Its Constitution, Tendencies and Destiny.* Clifton, NJ: Augustus M. Kelly Publishers, 1972/New York: P. O'Shea, 1865.

Bryce, James. *The American Commonwealth.* 2 vols. 3rd ed., rev. New York: The Macmillan Company, 1895.

Campbell, Angus, Philip E. Converse, Warren E. Miller, and Donald Stokes. *The American Voter.* New York: John Wiley and Sons, 1960.

Ceaser, James W. *Liberal Democracy and Political Science.* Baltimore: Johns Hopkins University Press, 1990.

———. *Nature and History in American Political Development. A Debate.* Cambridge, MA: Harvard University Press, 2006.

———. *Designing a Polity. America's Constitution in Theory and Practice.* Lanham, MD: Rowman and Littlefield Publishers, Inc., 2011.

Ceaser, James W., Andrew E. Busch, and John Pitney, Jr. *After Hope and Change. The 2012 Election and American Politics.* Lanham, MD: Rowman and Littlefield Publishers, Inc., 2013.

Chamberlain, John. *Farewell to Reform. Being a History of the Rise, Life and Decay of the Progressive Mind in America.* New York: Liveright Publishers, 1932.

Cicero, Marcus Tullius. *De Re Publica.* With an English Translation by Clinton Walker Keyes. Cambridge, MA: Harvard University Press, 1928.

Comte, Auguste. *Auguste Comte and Positivism: The Essential Writings.* Edited by Gertrud Lenzer. New York: Harper Torchbooks, 1975.

Converse, Jean M. *Survey Research in the United States: Roots and Emergence 1890–1960.* Berkley, CA: University of California Press, 1987.

Converse, Philip E. "Information Flow and the Stability of Partisan Attitudes." In *Elections and the Political Order*, edited by Angus Campbell, Philip E. Converse, Warren E. Miller, and Donald Stokes, 136–57. New York: John Wiley and Sons, 1966.

Corwin, Charles. "Untitled Book Review." *The American Political Science Review* 32, no. 4 (August 1938): 745–46.

Cost, Jay. *Spoiled Rotten. How the Politics of Patronage Corrupted the Once Nobel Democratic Party and Now Threatens the American Republic.* New York: Broadside Books, 2012.

Croly, Herbert. *The Promise of American Life.* Edited by Arthur M. Schlesinger, Jr. Cambridge, MA: The Belknap Press of Harvard University Press, 1965/Macmillan, 1909.

———. *Progressive Democracy.* New Brunswick, NJ: Transaction Press, 1998/New York: The Macmillan Company, 1914.

Darwin, Charles. *On the Origin of the Species.* Edited by Jim Endersby. Cambridge: Cambridge University Press, 2009.

Darwin, Francis, ed. *The Life and Letters of Charles Darwin.* 2 vols. New York and London: D. Appleton and Company, n.d.

Eddington, A. S. *The Nature of the Physical World. The Gifford Lectures.* New York: The Macmillan Company, 1928.

D'Elia, Donald J., and Stephen M. Krason, eds. *We Hold These Truths and More. Further Reflections on the American Proposition.* Steubenville, OH: Franciscan University Press, 1993.

Dewey, John. *The Influence of Darwin on Philosophy. And Other Essays in Contemporary Thought.* New York: Henry Holt and Company, 1910.

———. *The Quest for Certainty. A Study in the Relation of Knowledge and Action.* New York: Minton, Balch, and Company, 1929.

———. *A Common Faith.* New Haven, CT: Yale University Press, 1934.

———. *Reconstruction in Philosophy.* Enlarged Edition with a New Forty Page Introduction by the Author. Boston, MA: Beacon Press, 1948/1920.

DeWitt, Benjamin Parke. *Progressive Democracy. A Non-Partisan, Comprehensive Discussion of Current Tendencies in American Politics.* New York: The Macmillan Co., 1915/New Brunswick, NJ: Transaction Publishers, 2012.

Diamond, Martin. "The Dependence of Fact upon Value." In *As Far as Republican Principles Will Admit: Essays by Martin Diamond,* edited by William A. Schambra, 309–18. Washington, DC: AEI Press, 1992.

Dray, William. *Laws and Explanation in History.* Oxford: Oxford University Press, 1957.

Dreisback, Daniel L., Mark D. Hall, and Jeffrey H. Morrison, eds. *The Founders on God and Government.* Lanham, MD: Rowman and Littlefield Publishers, Inc., 2004.

Duxbury, Neil. "Some Radicalism about Realism? Thurman Arnold and the Politics of Modern Jurisprudence." *Oxford Journal of Legal Studies* 10, no. 1 (1990): 11–41.

Eberstadt, Nicholas. *The Tyranny of Numbers. Measurement and Misrule.* Forward by Daniel Patrick Moynahan. Washington, DC: American Enterprise Institute, 1995.

Eden, Robert. *Political Leadership and Nihilism. A Study of Weber and Nietzsche.* Tampa, FL: The University Presses of Florida, 1983.

Eisenach, Eldon J. *The Lost Promise of Progressivism.* Lawrence, KS: University Press of Kansas, 1994.

Engman, Thomas S., and Michael P. Zuckert, eds. *Protestantism and the American Founding.* Notre Dame, IN: University of Notre Dame Press, 2004.

Faulkner, Harold Underwood. *The History of American Life. The Quest for Social Justice 1898–1914.* New York: The Macmillan Company, 1931.

Friedenwald, Herbert. *The Declaration of Independence. An Interpretation and an Analysis.* New York: The Macmillan Company, 1904.

Furet, François. *Interpreting the French Revolution.* Cambridge: Cambridge University Press, 1981.

Gallagher, Gary W. *The Union War.* Cambridge, MA: Harvard University Press, 2011.

Gallup, George, and Saul F. Rae. *The Pulse of Democracy. The Public Opinion Poll and How It Works.* New York: Simon and Schuster, 1940.

Goldberg, Jonah. *Liberal Fascism. A Secret History of the American Left from Mussolini to the Politics of Meaning.* New York: Doubleday, 2008.

Goldwin, Robert A., and William A. Schambra, eds. *How Democratic is the Constitution?* Washington, DC: The American Enterprise Institute, 1980.

Gould, Lewis I. *Four Hats in the Ring. The 1912 Election and the Birth of Modern American Politics.* Lawrence, KS: University Press of Kansas, 2008.

Guelzo, Allen C. *Gettysburg: The Last Invasion.* New York: Alfred A. Knopf, 2013.

Hamilton, Alexander. *The Papers of Alexander Hamilton.* 26 vols. Edited by Harold C. Syrett and Jacob E. Cooke (Associate Editor). New York: Columbia University Press, 1961–1979.

Hamilton, Alexander, James Madison, and John Jay. *The Federalist.* Edited, with Introduction and Notes, by Jacob E. Cooke. Middletown, CT: Wesleyan University Press, 1961.

Hartz, Louis. *The Liberal Tradition in America.* New York: Harcourt, Brace, and World, Inc., 1955.

Hazelton, John W. *The Declaration of Independence. Its History.* New York: Dodd, Mead, and Company, 1906.

Heclo, Hugh. *Christianity and American Democracy.* Cambridge, MA: Harvard University Press, 2007.

Herbst, Jurgen. *The German Historical School in American Scholarship. A Study in the Transfer of Culture.* Ithaca, NY: Cornell University Press, 1965.

Herman, Arthur. *Freedom's Forge. How American Business Produced Victory in World War II.* New York: Random House, 2012.

Himmelfarb, Gertrude. *The Roads to Modernity. The British, French, and American Enlightenments.* New York: Alfred A. Knopf, 2004.

Holmes, David L. *The Faiths of the Founding Fathers.* New York: Oxford University Press, 2006.

Horowitz, Louis. *The Decomposition of Sociology.* New York: Oxford University Press, 1993.

Hutson, James H., ed. *The Founders on Religion. A Book of Quotations.* Princeton, NJ: Princeton University Press, 2005.

Jaffa, Harry V. *Crisis of the House Divided. An Interpretation of the Issues in the Lincoln-Douglas Debates.* Seattle, WA: University of Washington Press, 1959.

Janeway, Michael. *The Fall of the House of Roosevelt. Brokers and Ideas from FDR to LBJ.* New York: Columbia University Press, 2004.

Jefferson, Thomas. *Thomas Jefferson: Writings.* Edited by Merrill D. Peterson. New York: The Library of America, 1984.

de Jouvenal, Bertrand. *Sovereignty. An Inquiry into the Political Good.* Cambridge: Cambridge University Press, 1957.

Kalb, Marvin. *The Nixon Memo. Political Respectability, Russia, and the Press.* Chicago: The University of Chicago Press, 1994.

Kendall, Douglas, and James Ryan. "How Liberals Can Take Back the Court." *The New Republic,* August 6, 2007.

Key, V. O., Jr. *Public Opinion and American Democracy.* New York: Alfred A. Knopf, 1961.

Koestler, Arthur. *Darkness at Noon.* New York: The Macmillan Company, 1940.

Kuhn, Thomas S. *The Structure of Scientific Revolutions.* Chicago: The University of Chicago Press, 1962.

Lasch, Christopher. *The True and Only Heaven. Progress and Its Critics.* New York: W. W. Norton and Company, 1991.

Lazarsfeld, Paul F., Bernard Berelson, and Hazel Gaudet. *The People's Choice. How the Voter Makes Up His Mind in a Presidential Campaign.* New York: Columbia University Press, 1948.

Lefebvre, George. *The Thermidorians and the Directory. Two Phases of the French Revolution.* Translated from the French by Robert Baldick. New York: Random House, 1964.

Link, Arthur S., ed. *The Papers of Woodrow Wilson.* 69 vols. Princeton, NJ: Princeton University Press, 1966–1994.

Lippmann, Walter. *Drift and Mastery. An Attempt to Diagnose the Current Unrest.* New York: Mitchell Kennerley, 1914.

———. *Public Opinion.* New York: The Macmillan Company, 1922.

Locke, John. *Questions Concerning the Law of Nature.* Ithaca, NY: Cornell University Press, 1990.

Louchheim, Katie, ed. *The Making of the New Deal. The Insiders Speak.* Cambridge, MA: Harvard University Press, 1983.

Lowell, A. Lawrence. *Essays on Government.* Boston, MA: Houghton, Mifflin, and Company, 1889.

———. *Public Opinion and Popular Government.* New York: Longman's, Green, and Co., 1913.

Löwith, Karl. *Meaning in History.* Chicago: The University of Chicago Press, 1949.

———. *From Hegel to Nietzsche. The Revolution in Nineteenth Century Thought.* New York: Holt, Rinehart, and Winston, Inc., 1964.

Maier, Pauline. *American Scripture. Making the Declaration of Independence.* New York: Alfred A. Knopf, 1997.

———. *Ratification. The People Debate the Constitution, 1787–1788.* New York: Simon and Schuster, 2011.

Mansfield, Harvey C. "Social Science and the Constitution." In *Confronting the Constitution,* edited by Alan Bloom, 430–31. Washington, DC: AEI Press, 1990.

Marion, David E. "Alexander Hamilton and Woodrow Wilson on the Spirit and Form of a Responsible Republican Government." *The Review of Politics* 42, no. 3 (July 1980): 309–28.

Marx, Karl. *Economic and Philosophic Manuscripts of 1844.* Edited, with an Introduction, by Dirk J. Struick. Translated by Martin Milligan, 142–46. New York: International Publishers, 1964.

Mayhew, David R. *Electoral Realignments. A Critique of an American Genre.* New Haven, CT: Yale University Press, 2002.

McDougall, Walter A. "The Unlikely History of American Exceptionalism." *The American Interest* VIII, no. 4 (March/April 2013): 6–15.

Meacham, Jon. *American Gospel. God, the Founding Fathers, and the Making of a Nation.* New York: Random House, 2006.

Meinecke, Friedrich. *Historism. The Rise of the Historical Outlook.* Translated by J. E. Anderson. London: Routledge and Kegan Paul, 1972.

Merriam, Charles E. *Civic Education in the United States.* New York: Charles Scribner's Sons, 1934.

Milkis, Sidney M. *Theodore Roosevelt, the Rise of the Progressive Party, and the Transformation of American Democracy.* Lawrence, KS: The University Press of Kansas, 2009.

Miller, Warren E., and J. Merrill Shanks. *The New American Voter.* Cambridge, MA: Harvard University Press, 1996.

Mulder, John M. *Woodrow Wilson. The Years of Preparation.* Princeton, NJ: Princeton University Press, 1978.

Murray, S. J. John Courtney. *We Hold These Truths. Catholic Reflections on the American Proposition.* New York: Sheed and Ward, 1960.

Natchez, Peter B. *Images of Voting. Visions of Democracy.* With an Introduction by John C. Blydenburgh, Jr. and Sidney A. Pearson, Jr. New York: Basic Books, Inc., 1985/New Brunswick, NJ: Transaction Publishers, 2012.

Oakeshott, Michael. *Rationalism in Politics, and Other Essays.* New York: Basic Books Publishing, Inc., 1962.

Pestritto, Ronald J. *Woodrow Wilson and the Roots of Modern Liberalism.* Lanham, MD: Rowman and Littlefield Publishers, Inc., 2005.

Peterson, Merrill D. *The Jefferson Image in the American Mind.* New York: Oxford University Press, 1960.

Pocock, J. G. A. *The Machiavellian Moment. Florentine Political Thought and the Atlantic Republican Tradition.* Princeton, NJ: Princeton University Press, 1975.

Popp, Jerome E. *Evolution's First Philosopher. Dewey and the Continuity of Nature.* Albany, NY: State University of New York Press, 2007.

Putin, Vladimir V. "A Plea for Caution from Russia." *New York Times,* September 11, 2013.

Rahe, Paul A. *Republics Ancient and Modern. Classical Republicanism and the American Revolution.* Chapel Hill, NC: The University of North Carolina Press, 1992.

Rawls, John. *A Theory of Justice.* Rev. ed. Cambridge, MA: The Belknap Press of Harvard University Press, 1999.

Ritchie, David G. *Natural Rights. A Criticism of Some Political and Ethical Conceptions.* London: George Allen and Unwin, 1894.

Rogers, Lindsay. *The Pollsters. Public Opinion, Politics, and Democratic Leadership.* New York: Alfred A. Knopf, 1949.

Roosevelt, Theodore. *An Autobiography.* New York: Charles Scribner's Sons, 1915.

Rosenof, Theodore. *Realignment. The Theory That Changed the Way We Think about American Politics.* Lanham, MD: Rowman and Littlefield Publishers, Inc., 2003.

Schambra, William. "Saviors of the Constitution." *National Affairs* 10 (Winter 2012): 91–107.

Schlesinger, Arthur M., Jr. *The Age of Roosevelt. The Crisis of the Old Order.* Boston, MA: Houghton Mifflin and Company, 1957.

Shlaes, Amity. *The Forgotten Man. A New History of the New Deal.* New York: Harper Collins Publisher, 2007.

Storing, Herbert J. *The Complete Anti-Federalist.* 7 vols. Edited, with Commentary and Notes, by Herbert J. Storing. With the Assistance of Murray Dry. Chicago: The University of Chicago Press, 1981.

Story, Joseph. *Commentaries on the Constitution of the United States.* Reprinted, with an Introduction, by Ronald D. Rotunda and John E. Nowak, 639–702. Durham, NC: Carolina Academic Press, 1987/1833.

Stouffer, Samuel A. *Communism, Conformity, and Civil Liberties. A Cross-Section of the Nation Speaks Its Mind.* New York: Doubleday and Company, 1955.

Stove, David. *Darwinian Fairy Tales. Selfish Genes, Errors of Heredity, and Other Fables of Evolution.* Introduction by Roger Kimball. New York: Encounter Books, 1995.

Strauss, Leo. *Natural Right and History.* Chicago: The University of Chicago Press, 1953.

Talmon, J. L. *The Origins of Totalitarian Democracy.* New York: Frederick A. Praeger Publishers, 1960.

Taylor, Charles. *A Secular Age.* Cambridge, MA: The Belknap Press of Harvard University, 2007.

Taylor, Fred M. "The Law of Nature." *Annals of the American Academy of Political and Social Science* 1, no. 4 (1891): 558–59.

Taylor, S. J. *Stalin's Apologist. Walter Durante: The New York Times Man in Moscow.* New York: Oxford University Press, 1990.

de Tocqueville, Alexis. *Democracy in America.* Translated, Edited, and with an Introduction, by Harvey C. Mansfield and Delba Winthrop. Chicago: The University of Chicago Press, 2000.

Trende, Sean. *The Lost Majority. Why the Future of Government is Up for Grabs and Who will Take It.* New York: Palgrave Macmillan, 2012.

Tulis, Jeffrey K. *The Rhetorical Presidency.* Princeton, NJ: Princeton University Press, 1987.

Turner, Frederick Jackson. *The Significance of the Frontier in American History.* Annual Report of the American Historical Association for the Year 1893. Washington, DC: Government Printing Office, 1894.

Voegelin, Eric. *The New Science of Politics.* Chicago: The University of Chicago Press, 1952.

———. *Hitler and the Germans.* Columbia, MO: University of Missouri Press, 1999.

Walling, William. *Progressivism – And After.* New York: The Macmillan Company, 1914.

Weyl, Walter E. *The New Democracy: An Essay on Certain Political and Economic Tendencies in the United States.* New York: Macmillan, 1912/ New Brunswick, NJ: Transaction Press, 1998.

Whittemore, Robert C., ed. *Dewey and His Influence. Essays in Honor of George Estes Barton.* Tulane Studies in Philosophy, Volume XXII. New Orleans, LA: Tulane University, 1973.

Willoughby, Westel Woodbury. *An Examination of the Nature of the State. A Study in Political Philosophy.* New York: Macmillan and Co., 1889.

Wilson, Woodrow. *Congressional Government. A Study in American Politics.* Boston and New York: Houghton, Mifflin and Company, 1885/New Brunswick, NJ: Transaction Publishers, 2002.

———. *Constitutional Government in the United States.* New York: Columbia University Press, 1908/New Brunswick, NJ: Transaction Press, 2002.

———. *Mere Literature and Other Essays.* Boston and New York: Houghton and Mifflin, 1896.

Wolfe, Christopher. "Woodrow Wilson: Interpreting the Constitution." *The Review of Politics* 41, no. 1 (January 1979): 121–42.

Zinn, Howard. *New Deal Thought.* Indianapolis, IN: The Bobbs Merrill Company, Inc., 1966.

———. *A People's History of the United States.* New York: Harper Collins, 1980.

Zuckert, Michael P. *Natural Rights and the New Republicanism.* Princeton, NJ: Princeton University Press, 1994.

———. *The Natural Rights Republic. Studies in the Foundation of the American Political Tradition.* Notre Dame, IN: University of Notre Dame Press, 1996.

Index

For Product Safety Concerns and Information please contact our EU
representative GPSR@taylorandfrancis.com Taylor & Francis Verlag GmbH,
Kaufingerstraße 24, 80331 München, Germany

Batch number: 08158437

Printed by Printforce, the Netherlands